AI and the Legal Profession:
Transforming the Future of Law
Second Edition

EDITED BY FRANCESCA RAMADAN

Commissioning editor
Francesca Ramadan

Managing director
Sian O'Neill

***AI and the Legal Profession: Transforming the Future of Law, Second Edition*
is published by**

Globe Law and Business Ltd
3 Mylor Close
Horsell
Woking
Surrey GU21 4DD
United Kingdom
Tel: +44 20 3745 4770
www.globelawandbusiness.com

AI and the Legal Profession: Transforming the Future of Law, Second Edition

ISBN 978-1-83723-088-4
EPUB ISBN 978-1-83723-089-1
Adobe PDF ISBN 978-1-83723-090-7

Contents

Executive summary

Published in November 2023, the first edition of *AI and the Legal Profession: Transforming the Future of Law* explored the profound impact of artificial intelligence (AI) on the legal industry and the transformative possibilities it offered at the time. However, the capabilities and applications of AI within legal practice are evolving at breakneck speed, and much has changed in the short time since the publication of the first edition. This second edition of *AI and the Legal Profession: Transforming the Future of Law* represents a deeper and more nuanced exploration of the profound impact of AI at both a systemic and individual level. This new frontier for the legal profession brings challenges and opportunities, raising questions that are both critical and existential: will safe, sustainable, and secure AI in law ever be possible? How can human and machine work together in a way that is complementary, rather than combative? Indeed, in what ways can the machine shape what it means to be human and a practitioner of law? The second edition of *AI and the Legal Profession: Transforming the Future of Law* delves into these uncertainties, equipping legal professionals, technologists, and policymakers with the knowledge and insights needed to navigate a rapidly evolving landscape, embrace AI's potential, and harness its power to shape the future of law.

We begin by tackling one of the fundamental challenges presented by AI's usage in law: what role does the human element play? In Chapter 1, Colin Levy, general counsel at Malbek, expands on the critical role of human judgment in AI-augmented legal practice. While AI offers powerful capabilities for document review and analytics, true legal reasoning requires the contextual understanding and ethical navigation that only humans provide. This chapter explores how governance frameworks should be structured around "judgment points" where human oversight is essential, rather than focusing primarily on technical controls. It proposes specific protocols for when AI outputs require human review and criteria for escalation to senior decision-makers. Legal professionals will require new skills to effectively question AI-generated insights; this chapter, therefore, presents case studies where human and AI assessments diverge, offering frameworks for reconciling these differences and introducing a "judgment-centered monitoring" approach. To conclude, new professional standards and ethical guidelines which specifically address human–AI collaboration are proposed, underlining the fact that, as AI capabilities advance, strengthening the human element becomes more crucial, rather than less.

Our journey into the future of AI-augmented legal practice continues with an exploration of both human and machine cognition. In Chapter 2, Dr Valérie M. Saintot acts as our guide to the future of legal reasoning, proposing that, as legal professionals adapt to the rapid evolution of AI, the role of the legal thinker will also need to evolve. Generative AI (genAI) tools, such as large language models (LLMs), offer unprecedented opportunities to improve legal thinking, automate repetitive tasks, and simulate arguments. However, effective use of these tools requires more than adoption; instead, it necessitates a change in the ways in which lawyers think and develop their legal thinking skills, to both contrast with and complement genAI reasoning patterns. Valérie presents an outline of the new skills that legal professionals must learn and develop and the ways in which practitioners can establish an ethical and cognitive framework to keep legal prompting work in check.

The release of OpenAI's ChatGPT in late 2022 triggered the beginning of a global AI race; in 2025, genAI has become increasingly influential in the practice of law, driving notable changes in how legal services are delivered. GenAI tools offer tremendous potential for efficiency and innovation in legal practice; however, it is no secret that these tools bring challenges alongside opportunity, mainly related to accuracy, ethics, and privacy. In Chapter 3, Stephanie Goutos, head of employment law practice innovation, and Natalie Pierce, partner at Gunderson Dettmer, explore the critical responsibility of legal professionals to adopt a careful approach in their utilization of genAI. Designed as a practical guide for law firms and practitioners, this chapter provides actionable strategies for managing organizational risks and ensuring legal compliance. The importance of embracing genAI's transformative power, while still upholding the core principles and values that define the legal industry, is critical.

Continuing our exploration of the challenges AI introduces to legal practice, we turn to the fuel powering the AI engine: data. In Chapter 4, Joanne Brook, solicitor (intellectual property and tech law) at Lionshead Law, considers who owns the engine, who owns the oil that powers it, and what this means for the public whose data was syphoned to service the machine and drive innovation. Having considered these fundamental elements, Joanne turns our attention to the originality of AI's output and considers the definition of creation itself: who owns the words and images AI produces, and could it ever be the machine? What does it mean to create and be creative, and what does this imply for the future of copyright? To envision what might be in store, Joanne explores the historical context of copyright ownership and how this might evolve in the long term. In a post-AI world, in which creativity is "democratized" and data bought, shared, and sold, is the concept of ownership outdated? What does this mean for rewarding creativity? And can regulatory and compliance efforts really balance the rights of the creator with the need for data to fuel the machine?

Our exploration of the ways in which AI can hinder, rather than help, emphasizes the necessity of proactive safeguarding and a thoughtful and strategic approach to implementation. Too often, organizations jump into technology adoption without fully understanding their processes, leading to costly failures and missed opportunities. In Chapter 5, Justin Turman, founder of Automate Office Work, offers an accessible and practical roadmap for law firms and legal departments looking to revolutionize their operations through legal technology. This chapter first explores the critical relationship between process awareness and successful legal technology adoption before guiding the reader through a step-by-step process to understand and overcome the complexities and challenges of technology implementation. Whether you or your organization is considering automation, AI-powered tools, or case management systems, this chapter provides structured guidance to navigate the journey effectively.

Further delving into the practical side of AI utilization and implementation in the legal profession, Chapter 6 sees Mark Gediman, senior research analyst at Alston & Bird, draw from his knowledge management and legal research background to cut through the hype to the current reality of legal technology. His chapter explores the real-world applications and limitations of AI tools in legal research, encompassing discussions of the expectations versus reality of AI's capabilities and the importance of user assumptions. A person's utilization of an AI tool is just as vital as the functionality of the technology itself, which is why this chapter delves into what constitutes proper training and due diligence processes. Seeking existing solutions from external vendors is often the first choice for firms and legal departments looking to augment their practice with AI, which comes with its own challenges. Referencing his recent participation in a panel assessing selected AI tools, Mark breaks down what comprises the perfect AI solution into its disparate components, including accuracy, relevance, and depth of output.

Successful implementation and utilization of AI are not the only hurdles that legal practitioners, firms, and in-house departments must overcome; there are also complex regulatory requirements to understand and adhere to. The rapidly evolving and expanding technological frontier, which often outpaces legislative developments, renders this especially challenging for professionals and organizations seeking to remain compliant and responsible in their use of AI. In Chapter 7, Itsiq Benizri, counsel at WilmerHale, discusses the profound impact of the European Union's Artificial Intelligence Act, a global first in AI regulation. The Act's challenging requirements, significant extraterritorial effects, and substantial fines are comprehensively explored; this chapter's scope then broadens to consider the ways in which the Act will adapt to rapid technological developments and influence AI regulation around the world in the long term.

Indeed, the future of law is littered with complex ethical and regulatory challenges that will shape the reality of legal practice. AI is not a neutral technology; there are inherent ethical considerations faced by developers and legal professionals alike, and legal compliance alone does not equate to ethical practice. In Chapter 8, Harry Borovick, general counsel at Luminance, draws from his experience of the intersection of tech and law to outline the principles of fairness, transparency, and accountability – each of which are necessary for building trustworthy systems within the legal sector. Harry delves into the key challenges for organizations seeking to create their own in-house AI solutions, such as algorithmic opacity, potential biases, data privacy, intellectual property frameworks, and the complexities of liability when AI systems contribute to legal processes.

Every legal organization using either a proprietary or an external vendor's AI tool must prioritize the safety of client data. Client information uploaded to AI platforms may be exposed to third parties or stored insecurely, potentially compromising attorney–client confidentiality. Many AI companies retain input data to improve their systems, meaning that sensitive client information could become part of the AI's training data without proper safeguards. Privacy concerns intensify when considering that different AI providers have varying security standards, such as storing data for extended periods or in countries with weaker privacy laws. Additionally, many AI tools require broad terms of service agreements, which might give external vendors extensive rights to use uploaded data. In Chapter 9, Erick Robinson, partner at Brown Rudnick LLP, offers practical solutions to security concerns, including using local AI implementations that keep data under attorney control, anonymizing client information, implementing verification protocols, and establishing clear governance policies. Additional recommendations include carefully evaluating AI providers' terms of service and creating client consent procedures.

We return to the human side of legal AI with Chapter 10, authored by Rasmus Kirkeby Salling, head of transition, new markets, and Peter Kaas, head of digital legal and compliance at Falck, who explore how in-house legal teams can implement genAI through a Nordic leadership approach. Drawing from their professional experience, the authors examine how legal leaders can capture both non-financial value (improved job satisfaction, talent retention, shift to high-value work) and financial value (cost savings from reduced FTEs, decreased external spending, and revenue opportunities) generated AI utilization through practical measurement approaches, such as the quantification of employee engagement, internal customer satisfaction, and quality of strategic work in tandem with the assessment of traditional financial metrics. Rather than solely recruiting new talent, Rasmus and Peter advocate for the upskilling of existing team members, highlighting the ways in which experienced lawyers can leverage their instructional skills when working with AI and legal leaders can foster experimentation, lead boldly by example, and create safe spaces for teams to adapt to this transformative technology.

While developing existing team members may be preferable, there are instances in which legal firms and departments must source external talent in their pursuit of AI integration. However, the question remains as to how these organizations strategically build teams equipped to manage and leverage AI. In Chapter 11, Matthew Dunne, senior innovation and data science manager at Katten Muchin Rosenman LLP, examines certain assumptions commonly associated with this complicated question. In answering it, Matthew guides readers through several different frameworks from the worlds of business, law, and technology. First, what an AI strategy means for law firms and how it departs from traditional practice will be discussed; this chapter then considers what skills will be necessary to achieve that strategy, as well as how to acquire and evaluate them. In addition to the who, what, how, and why of hiring for this new field, Matthew covers the hidden pitfalls that go beyond choosing the right personnel.

We conclude with a look towards the future of AI and the legal profession. The integration of frontier technology (including genAI) into legal practice stands at a critical inflection point, demanding innovative research approaches that bridge theoretical possibilities with practical applications. In Chapter 12, Dr Megan Ma, executive director, Stanford Legal Innovation through Frontier Technology Lab, proposes a framework for "research prototyping" – a methodology that accelerates understanding of how emerging technologies can transform legal processes while addressing ethical and practical constraints. Unlike traditional legal research that often remains theoretical, or technology implementations that prioritize commercial viability, this approach centers on lightweight, functional prototypes designed specifically to test research hypotheses about the future of human–machine collaboration and technology's impact on legal reasoning and procedural efficiency. By compressing the research implementation cycle, this prototyping paradigm not only accelerates knowledge creation, but also democratizes the evolution of legal technology, ensuring innovations are guided by empirical evidence of their effects on legal institutions, professional roles, and justice outcomes, rather than technological determinism.

About the authors

Itsiq Benizri is a counsel at WilmerHale (Brussels). Itsiq advises clients on all artificial intelligence, data protection, and cybersecurity compliance issues, including global compliance programs and strategies, internal procedures and policies, outsourcing, security measures, breach notifications, cross-border data flows, and interactions with competition law. Itsiq has also been involved in several high-profile judicial and administrative proceedings, both at a national and EU level. His experience covers a broad set of sectors, including social media, IT and cloud computing, communications, banking, energy, chemicals, transport, automotive, gaming, pharma, food and beverage, sports, media, pharmaceuticals, and cosmetics.

Itsiq is qualified as a Certified Information Privacy Professional (CIPP/E) and an Artificial Intelligence Governance Professional (AIGP) by the International Association of Privacy Professionals. Itsiq is also a member of this association. Itsiq holds an LLM in law and artificial intelligence. Itsiq is the author of numerous publications on EU artificial intelligence and data law.

Harry Borovick is general counsel and AI governance officer at Luminance, which provides advanced AI for the processing of legal documents. As well as working at the forefront of the development of AI for legal operations, Harry lectures at King's College London and Queen Mary University of London on applied legal AI and AI ethics. Harry currently sits as an AI advisor to CiArb, has previously contributed to Globe Law and Business' *Legal Operations in the Age of AI and Data* (2024), and most recently published his book *AI and The Law: A Practical Guide to Using AI Safely* (2024).

Joanne Brook is a solicitor who qualified as the internet was launched and has been a legal technologist ever since. She advises innovators across the creative sectors, from software developers to theatre producers, AI and VR developers, and artists who distribute NFTs. She focuses on helping clients achieve commercial solutions to previously unconsidered legal issues that arise from developing and using their technology. She critically protects and licenses their intellectual property rights to ensure business expansion and growth in a fast-paced market. Prior to becoming a legal consultant, she was a partner at both a West End law firm and a boutique City law firm. She describes her view of the digital revolution and use of new technologies as being somewhere between sitting in the jump seat with a super-sonic test pilot and calmly evacuating the plane whilst wearing a parachute and hi-vis, carrying a laptop, and inflating a lifeboat. In the midst of this, she feels privileged to advise passionate, smart, and more creative people than herself daily.

Joanne is an intellectual property professional expert for LexisNexis and an author of intellectual property and data management precedents for various professional publications. She regularly contributes legal insight to the legal press and lectures on technology and new law.

In his role at Katten, **Matthew Dunne** combines several areas under the umbrella of "innovation". This includes data science, management consulting, implementing legal tech software, and creative strategic thinking. He leads Katten's DataLAB, which provides legal data science services, including custom genAI applications for lawyers. Matthew holds an MS in Applied Data Science from the University of Chicago and a JD from Indiana University Maurer School of Law. He is also a licensed attorney.

Mark Gediman is a senior research analyst for Alston & Bird LLP and graduated from the University of California, Riverside. He is the past president of the Southern California Association of Law Libraries (SCALL), as well as a co-founder and co-chair of the PLL–IP Competitive Intelligence Caucus.

Mark writes and presents regularly on competitive intelligence, research, and library management issues for the American Association of Law Libraries (AALL), the California Lawyers Association, the Legal Marketing Association (LMA), the Special Libraries Association (SLA), the Southwestern Association of Law Librarians (SWALL), SCALL, the Northern California Association of Law Libraries (NoCALL), ACI, and HALL. He contributed to *Business Intelligence for Law Firms* (2012), *Innovations in Legal KM* (2017), and *Strategic Intelligence for Law Firms* (2018), and has written articles for *AALL Spectrum*, Practicing Law Management Week, *Paralegal Today*, and *Facts & Findings*, the award-winning journal of the National Association of Legal Assistants (NALA).

Stephanie Goutos is the head of employment law practice innovation for Gunderson Dettmer's Employment & Labor Practice Group, where she leads the group's innovation and knowledge management initiatives. With a background in class action defense, litigation, and employment counselling, Stephanie combines her legal expertise with a strong commitment to leveraging emerging technologies to enhance the delivery of legal services. Her work reflects a passion for improving access to justice and fostering inclusivity within the legal sector.

Stephanie's contributions have earned significant recognition, including being named the sole finalist for Relativity's 2024 Innovation Awards in the "Stellar Women" category, one of the "2024 Young Professionals to Watch" by the International Legal Technology Association (ILTA) in their Distinguished Peer Awards, and as one of vLex Fastcase 50's 2024 Honorees. Most recently, Stephanie was selected as a 2025 Perplexity AI Fellow, further highlighting her leadership in advancing legal technology and innovation.

Peter Kaas is the head of digital legal & compliance at Falck, a global emergency and healthcare service provider headquartered in Copenhagen Denmark. Peter leads a team of commercially oriented lawyers and compliance professionals in the digital, privacy, and AI space. The team includes the Group Data Protection Officer (DPO) function, privacy operations, and legal business partnering to Falck Digital Technology. Peter's team also leads Falck's global AI compliance program, including preparations for the EU AI Act.

Prior to joining Falck, Peter worked in-house in the Nordic IT industry (Atea and NNIT) and in private legal practice in top-tier Danish law firms; he has specialized in IT and tech law for 20 years. Peter is an attorney-at-law, licensed to practice in Denmark. He has a master's in law from the University of Copenhagen, an LLM from the University of Virginia, and holds several data privacy and information security certifications. He is an external associate professor of tech law, IT contract law and data protection at the University of Copenhagen and a frequent speaker on tech law, data privacy and AI.

Rasmus Kirkeby Salling is head of transition, new markets at Falck, a global emergency and healthcare service provider headquartered in Copenhagen, Denmark. Prior to this, Rasmus served as head of commercial legal at Falck, leading an international team of in-house counsels supporting and leading the commercial agenda of Falck's global businesses.

Prior to joining Falck, Rasmus was head of IP legal services with Schneider Electric, a French Fortune 500 Company, and in private legal practice at top-tier Danish law firms; he has specialized in commercial law, M&A, IP, and tech over the last 20 years.

Rasmus is an attorney-at-law, licensed to practice in Denmark (deposited). He has a master's in law from the University of Copenhagen, an Executive MBA from the International Institute for Management Development (IMD), and is a frequent speaker on topics related to in-house leadership and legal tech. Rasmus allocates part of his time to being a leadership mentor for first-time managers and professionals with leadership aspirations.

Colin S. Levy works within the intersection of law and technology and is dedicated to transforming the legal landscape through education and innovation. As general counsel at Malbek, he brings frontline expertise in Contract Lifecycle Management to legal professionals worldwide.

His works include *The Legal Tech Ecosystem* (2023), *Contract Lifecycle Management (CLM) for Dummies* (2024) (co-author), and the *Handbook of Legal Tech* (2023) (editor). Colin's thought leadership extends through columns for *Today's General Counsel*, speaking engagements, and his role as a judge for the American Legal Technology Awards.

Beyond his publications, Colin actively advises start-ups and invests in emerging technologies, consistently advocating for meaningful technological adoption in legal practice. His website, colinslevy.com, chronicles his journey and insights gained from conversations with industry pioneers.

Colin remains committed to empowering legal professionals to embrace technology, proving that when law and innovation converge, the possibilities for positive change are limitless.

Dr Megan Ma is the executive director of the Stanford Legal Innovation Center through Frontier Technology Lab (liftlab). Her research focuses on the use and integration of generative AI in legal applications and the translation of legal knowledge to code, considering their implications in contexts of human–machine collaboration. She also teaches courses in computational law and legal technology at Stanford Law School.

Dr Ma is also currently an advisor to the PearX for AI program; editor-in-chief for the Cambridge Forum on AI, Law, and Governance; the managing editor of the *MIT Computational Law Report*; and a senior research affiliate at Singapore Management University in their Centre for Digital Law. Megan received her PhD in Law at Sciences Po and was a lecturer there, having taught courses in artificial intelligence and legal reasoning, legal semantics, and public health law and policy. She has previously been a Visiting PhD at the University of Cambridge and Harvard Law School, respectively.

Natalie Pierce is a partner at Gunderson Dettmer and chair of the firm's employment and labor practice. Natalie is a trusted advisor to start-ups and venture capital and growth equity firms on all employment-related matters. She also focuses on the future of work, including counseling on transformative technologies, and is a frequent speaker and contributor on the topic. Natalie hosts Gunderson's FutureWork Playbook podcast and was selected as a Fast Case 50 Award Winner, one of the *Daily Journal*'s "Top Artificial Intelligence Lawyers" and "Top Labor and Employment Lawyers," and *San Francisco Business Times'* "Bay Area's Most Influential Women". She was also a member of the American Bar Associtión's Center for Innovation Governing Council, and co-authored "Why law firms must responsibly embrace generative AI", published by the *Berkeley Business Law Journal.* Natalie earned her BA at UC Berkeley with Honors, and her law degree from Columbia University School of Law, where she was a Harlan Fiske Stone Scholar and recipient of the Emil Schlesinger Labor Law Prize at graduation.

Erick Robinson is a partner and co-chair of the Patent Trial and Appeal Board Practice at Brown Rudnick in Houston. He is a leading patent litigator with 25 years' of experience litigating and trying "bet-the-company" patent and trade secret cases. Erick has managed and tried patent cases in the United States and around the world, including Europe and Asia. In addition to his time at top law firms, he also previously served as director of patents for Qualcomm and as senior patent counsel at Red Hat, as well as director of patent litigation at a top Chinese law firm.

Erick is a trusted authority on intellectual property and AI law, having published and been quoted in over 100 articles. Erick is also an established expert in legal finance, as well as AI and its applications, and is a certified mediator.

Valérie M. Saintot, LL.M., Phd, is a multidisciplinary legal expert, educator, and advocate for innovation in business and the public sector. With three decades of experience, spanning EU public and private sectors as well as academia, she teaches leadership, change, legal tech, AI, and organizational performance. Valérie integrates philosophy, ethics, and design thinking into her work. Known for her groundbreaking insights at the intersection of technology, project management, and mindfulness, she inspires leaders to embrace digital transformation and personal growth to impactfully contribute to society using life-centric pathways.

Justin Turman is the founder of Automate Office Work and a passionate advocate for process-driven legal innovation. An American lawyer with a background in computers and linguistics, Justin spent a decade working in-house at a Fortune 500 company, where he transformed legal workflows by streamlining processes and automating his work.

Through LinkedIn, he shares insights via articles, tutorials, podcasts, and videos, helping legal professionals improve efficiency without unnecessary complexity or exorbitant costs. He firmly believes that process improvement should come before technology adoption. By leveraging small, nimble tools integrated into platforms like Office 365, organizations can achieve remarkable results without the risks of large-scale tech failures.

Justin's approach is practical, actionable, and rooted in real-world experience. His mission? To help legal teams harness the power of automation and smart workflows – without getting lost in the hype of new, expensive, and often underutilized technology.

Chapter 1:
Artificial intelligence, authentic practice: the uneasy partnership reshaping legal services

By Colin Levy, general counsel, Malbek

The legal profession – traditionally about as quick to embrace change as a tortoise with gout – now finds itself thrust into the AI era, ready or not. What happens when machines can review 1,000 contracts before a partner finishes their morning latte? That's the question reshaping law firms from Wall Street to Main Street.

This chapter cuts through the AI hype cycle (currently stuck somewhere between "miracle cure" and "existential threat") to examine what these technologies do in legal practice. We explore how AI has evolved from glorified search engines to systems that can find subtle patterns across thousands of documents – while still occasionally outwitted by a creatively-worded indemnification clause.

We'll dissect AI's impact across legal functions: document review that doesn't require midnight pizza deliveries; research tools that find precedents partners didn't know existed; and practice management systems that track billable activities with unnerving precision. For each, we examine where AI genuinely adds value and where firms are simply buying expensive digital paperweights.

The chapter tackles thorny questions about confidentiality (what happens when client secrets meet cloud computing?), professional responsibility (who's accountable when AI drafts a problematic clause?), and implementation strategies (beyond the "buy it and pray" approach that is the default of many firms).

Finally, we look toward the future, considering which legal skills will remain stubbornly human as technology advances. Throughout, we maintain that, while AI won't replace lawyers, it is redrawing the boundaries of what constitutes legal practice – whether tradition-minded partners like it or not.

The intersection of human judgment and AI capabilities

The distinction between pattern recognition and legal reasoning

AI systems excel at pattern recognition: identifying similar contract clauses across thousands of documents; spotting potential privilege issues in discovery materials; or finding relevant precedents from massive case databases. These capabilities deliver significant value for legal professionals, particularly in tasks involving document review and information retrieval.

Pattern recognition, however, differs from legal reasoning. Experienced attorneys reviewing contracts not only identify standard clauses, but also evaluate their implications within specific business contexts; expect potential disputes; and consider how courts in relevant jurisdictions have interpreted similar language. The most advanced AI contract review systems can flag unusual provisions and suggest alternative language, but they cannot independently assess business risk or strategic implications.

This gap becomes even more apparent in complex advisory work. When counseling clients on novel regulatory issues or developing litigation strategy, attorneys draw on contextual knowledge, analogical reasoning, and professional judgment that current AI systems cannot replicate. Understanding this distinction proves essential for appropriately implementing AI tools in both law firms and legal departments.

In-house counsel face particular challenges when balancing AI efficiency with legal judgment. While they must manage high volumes of routine contracts and compliance matters where AI excels, they also serve as strategic business advisors where judgment is paramount. Law firm attorneys similarly navigate this duality, using AI to enhance efficiency in document-intensive matters while applying their judgment to complex advisory work and litigation strategy.

The most effective implementations recognize this complementary relationship. In due diligence work, AI systems rapidly find patterns across thousands of contracts, flagging potential issues for attorney review. This lets legal professionals focus their knowledge on evaluating the significance of those issues, rather than spending hours finding them. The AI handles pattern recognition; the attorney provides judgment and context.

Judgment points in legal work

Critical "judgment points" exist throughout legal workflows, where human evaluation remains essential despite technological advancement. These points typically involve contextual understanding, ethical considerations, or strategic decisions that AI systems cannot adequately address.

In transactional practice, judgment points include:

- Evaluating how contract provisions interact with specific business objectives;
- Assessing risk tolerance for particular clients or matters;
- Determining negotiation priorities based on relationship dynamics; and
- Identifying novel issues without clear precedent.

For litigation, judgment points encompass:

- Evaluating the credibility and persuasiveness of potential arguments;
- Determining case strategy based on court dynamics and opposing counsel;
- Assessing settlement options against litigation risks; and
- Making ethical decisions about evidence presentation.

In regulatory compliance, critical judgment points involve:

- Interpreting ambiguous regulations in novel situations;
- Balancing compliance costs against legal risks;
- Making disclosure decisions where requirements are unclear; and
- Focusing on remediation efforts for identified issues.

Corporate legal departments face additional judgment points related to business integration, such as:

- Aligning legal advice with corporate strategy and risk tolerance;
- Balancing legal risks against business opportunities;
- Assigning resources across competing priorities; and
- Managing relationships with business units and executive leadership.

These judgment points cannot be automated away; they are the core value at legal professionals provide. Rather than threatening this value, AI tools can enhance it by letting attorneys focus more attention on these critical decisions while spending less time on routine information processing.

The evolving nature of legal judgment

Legal judgment has always adapted to technological and social changes. Introduction of computerized legal research in the 1970s changed how attorneys found precedent, but enhanced – rather than reduced – the importance of evaluating its relevance and persuasiveness. Digital communication technologies changed client interaction patterns, but increased the value of clear legal advice amid information overload.

AI represents the next evolution in this trajectory, changing how attorneys locate and process information while potentially enhancing the value of judgment applied to that information. The increased volume and complexity of data available through AI tools demand more sophisticated judgment in evaluating and applying those data.

For example, litigation analytics platforms can find patterns in judicial decisions across thousands of cases, but attorneys must still determine which patterns matter for their specific case and how to adapt their strategy. Contract analysis systems can find unusual provisions across hundreds of agreements, but attorneys must still assess which variations create material risk for the specific transaction.

This evolution requires expanding legal judgment beyond traditional doctrinal analysis to include technology assessment. Attorneys must evaluate when AI tools can provide reliable insights, when those insights require more validation, and when human analysis remains necessary despite technological capabilities. This "meta-judgment" about technology itself will become increasingly important as AI capabilities advance.

The evolving nature of legal judgment applies differently across practice settings. In-house counsel must integrate technological judgment with business judgment, considering how AI capabilities affect legal operations and broader business processes. Law firm attorneys must develop judgment as to when and how to deploy AI tools for different client matters, recognizing that usage varies with client needs, matter complexity, and risk profiles.

Both settings require developing frameworks for exercising judgment in technology-enhanced practice, showing when and how human judgment should supplement or override machine analysis. These frameworks must be principled yet flexible, adapting to both evolving technologies and varying practice contexts.

Governance frameworks centered on human judgment

Designing governance around judgment points

Traditional technology governance frameworks often focus primarily on technical controls: access management, data security, and performance tracking. While these controls remain necessary, they prove insufficient for AI in legal practice. Effective governance must center on judgment points where human oversight becomes essential, making sure these points receive attention despite technological capabilities.

Governance frameworks should map critical judgment points throughout legal workflows, documenting where and how human evaluation must supplement machine analysis. This mapping should consider both obvious judgment points, such as strategic decision-making, and less obvious ones, such as confirming assumptions underlying AI models or identifying novel issues that fall outside established patterns.

For each identified judgment point, the governance framework should specify:

- Required qualifications for human reviewers;
- Information necessary for informed judgment;
- Documentation standards for judgment exercises;
- Escalation paths for complex or novel issues; and
- Feedback mechanisms to improve system performance.

Law firms and legal departments require different governance approaches reflecting their distinct operating models. Law firms typically serve multiple clients across various matter types, requiring governance frameworks that adapt to different client needs and risk profiles. Legal departments serve a single organizational client, but must integrate their governance with broader corporate frameworks for technology and risk management.

Despite these differences, both settings benefit from governance that explicitly distinguishes pattern recognition from judgment tasks. This distinction ensures resources for each function, with technology handling information processing while skilled legal professionals focus on evaluation and decision-making.

Governance frameworks should evolve alongside technology capabilities, regularly reassessing judgment points as AI systems improve. This evolution should be deliberate rather than automatic – when systems show improved capabilities in specific areas, governance can adapt through careful change in human oversight requirements, rather than wholesale delegation to machines.

The most effective governance approaches treat judgment as a resource to be deployed strategically, focusing human attention where it adds the most value while leveraging technology for supporting functions. This approach recognizes that human judgment remains limited and valuable, requiring thoughtful allocation across legal work.

Protocols for human review of AI outputs

Protocols for human review of AI outputs should vary based on task features, system reliability, and risk factors. Low-risk, routine tasks where AI systems have shown high reliability require less intensive review than high-risk or novel applications. These protocols should establish not only when review occurs, but how it should be conducted to ensure meaningful human judgment rather than cursory approval.

For document review applications, effective protocols include:

- Sampling methodologies that ensure review of both normal and edge cases;
- Attention-directing mechanisms that focuses human review on potential issues;
- Comparative review processes that evaluate AI findings against human judgments; and
- Escalation criteria for complex or ambiguous findings.

For research and analytics applications, review protocols should address:

- Validation of underlying data completeness and relevance;
- Evaluation of multiple interpretations of identified patterns;
- Assessment of factual and legal distinctions that may affect applicability; and
- Considerations of counter-arguments and alternative perspectives.

For document generation applications, review standards should include:

- Verification of factual accuracy and contextual appropriateness;
- Assessment of strategic implications beyond technical correctness;
- Evaluation of tone and presentation for client-specific considerations; and
- Confirmation of compliance with professional responsibility obligations.

Legal departments should integrate these protocols with broader business review processes, ensuring legal judgment incorporates business context. For significant matters, this may include multi-disciplinary review involving both legal and business stakeholders, with clear delineation of respective responsibilities.

Law firms should adapt review protocols to client-specific requirements while maintaining consistent standards across their practice. This adaptation may include varying review intensity based on client risk tolerance, industry-specific considerations, or matter features, while ensuring all reviews meet minimum professional standards.

Review protocols should be documented and regularly evaluated, with changes based on observed error patterns and evolving system capabilities. This documentation creates accountability and enables continuous improvement of both AI systems and review processes.

Criteria for escalation to senior decision-makers

Not all judgment points require the same level of seniority or knowledge. Effective governance establishes clear criteria for when issues identified through AI analysis require escalation to senior attorneys or practice leaders, ensuring experience and judgment for complex or high-risk matters.

Escalation criteria should consider:

- *Novelty:* Issues without clear precedent or established handling procedures;
- *Magnitude:* Matters with significant potential impact on clients or the organization;
- *Complexity:* Issues involving multiple legal domains or conflicting considerations;
- *Strategic importance:* Matters affecting client relationships or organizational reputation; and
- *Error patterns:* Recurring issues that suggest systemic problems in AI applications.

Legal departments should align escalation paths with corporate governance structures, ensuring legal issues receive executive attention when necessary. This alignment should define when matters require general counsel review, executive committee consideration, or board oversight, based on established materiality thresholds and risk profiles.

Law firms should establish escalation frameworks that account for both legal knowledge and client relationships, recognizing that complex matters may require both substantive knowledge and client-specific understanding. These frameworks should define clear roles for practice group leaders, relationship partners, and managing partners in addressing issues identified through AI analysis.

Escalation protocols should include documentation requirements that capture decisions and underlying reasoning. This documentation preserves institutional knowledge, supports client communications, and enables quality improvement. It also provides evidence of professional judgment if questions arise later.

The most effective escalation frameworks create a culture of judgment that values raising complex issues, rather than penalizing it. This culture encourages attorneys to identify matters requiring senior attention without fear of negative consequences, recognizing that emerging difficult issues represents good judgment rather than failure.

Judgment-centered monitoring and evaluation

Traditional technology tracking focuses on technical metrics: system performance, usage patterns, and error rates. While these metrics remain important, AI governance requires additional tracking centered on judgment exercises; tracing instances where human reviewers change or override AI recommendations; and analyzing patterns in these interventions.

Judgment-centered tracking should track:

- Override frequency by task type, user role, and matter characteristics;
- Patterns in judgment changes that suggest system limitations;
- Time allocation to judgment tasks across different user groups; and
- Correlation between judgment exercises and matter outcomes.

This tracking provides valuable insights beyond simple error detection, helping organizations understand where and how human judgment adds value in AI-augmented workflows. These insights guide both technology development priorities and professional development needs.

For legal departments, judgment tracking should integrate with broader legal operations metrics, connecting judgment exercises to business outcomes and department performance indicators. This integration helps to show the value of legal judgment to business stakeholders, while finding opportunities for targeted technology improvement.

Law firms should incorporate judgment tracking into their quality management and professional development systems, using insights to improve both AI implementations and attorney capabilities. This approach recognizes that effective human–AI collaboration requires development of both the technological and human parts of the system.

The most sophisticated tracking approaches employ AI tools themselves to analyze judgment patterns, identifying correlations and trends that may not be immediately apparent. This "meta-analysis" helps organizations to understand their judgment exercises at scale, moving beyond anecdotal evidence to systematic understanding of how human and machine intelligence interact.

Tracking results should inform regular governance reviews, with analysis of judgment patterns driving changes to review protocols, escalation criteria, and system configurations. This feedback loop enables continuous improvement of the overall governance framework, adapting to both changing technologies and evolving legal needs.

Developing judgment skills for AI-augmented practice

New skills for questioning AI-generated insights

Effective collaboration with AI tools requires the development of specific skills for questioning and evaluating machine-generated insights. These skills differ from traditional legal analysis, focusing instead on understanding AI capabilities and limitations rather than merely applying legal doctrine.

Key questioning skills include:

- Identifying underlying assumptions in AI analysis and assessing their validity;
- Recognizing when AI outputs reflect statistical correlations rather than causal relationships;
- Detecting potential biases in training data that may affect analysis reliability; and
- Determining when found patterns apply to specific situations versus representing general trends.

For legal departments, development of these skills requires cross-disciplinary training that combines legal knowledge with a basic understanding of data science and machine learning principles. This training should focus on practical application rather than technical depth, enabling attorneys to ask questions without becoming technical experts.

Law firms should incorporate AI questioning skills into their professional development programs, recognizing these capabilities represent an increasingly important part of practice knowledge. These programs should include both formal training and experiential learning opportunities in which attorneys practice evaluating AI outputs in realistic scenarios.

The most effective skill development approaches emphasize active learning rather than passive instruction, with attorneys applying questioning frameworks to actual AI outputs and receiving feedback on their evaluations. This practical application helps to develop intuition about when to trust AI insights and when to investigate further.

These skills must extend beyond technical understanding to include ethical questioning, enabling the identification of potential issues related to bias, fairness, and transparency in AI systems. This ethical dimension proves important in legal applications where decisions affect rights, obligations, and access to justice.

Organizations should develop questioning frameworks that guide attorneys through systematic evaluation of AI outputs, providing structure for assessment without constraining professional judgment. These frameworks should be specific enough to provide practical guidance, while remaining flexible enough to adapt to different practice areas and AI applications.

Reconciling divergent human and AI assessments

When human and AI assessments diverge, legal professionals need structured approaches for reconciliation that neither automatically defer to machines nor reflexively override them. These approaches should recognize that disagreements may reflect limitations in either human or machine analysis, requiring careful evaluation rather than simple hierarchy.

Effective reconciliation frameworks include:

- Examining the information basis for each assessment, identifying differences in underlying data;
- Evaluating the reasoning process used by both human and machine, looking for logical gaps or unwarranted assumptions;
- Considering whether the disagreement reflects a new situation outside the AI system's training experience; and
- Assessing whether human assessment incorporates contextual factors inaccessible to the AI system.

Legal departments should incorporate reconciliation processes into their matter management workflows, establishing clear protocols for addressing disagreements between in-house attorneys and AI systems. These protocols should include documentation requirements and escalation paths for persistent disagreements, ensuring resolution without unnecessary delay.

Law firms should develop client-specific reconciliation approaches that reflect both firm knowledge and client preferences. These approaches may include validation through multiple analytical methods, consultation with subject matter experts, or application of client-specific risk tolerance frameworks.

Organizations should maintain records of significant divergences and their resolutions, creating a knowledge base that informs both system improvements and attorney development. This documentation enables identification of patterns in divergences that may show either system limitations or training needs.

The reconciliation process should remain focused on reaching the best outcome, rather than determining whether human or machine was "correct". Often, the best resolution incorporates elements from both assessments, synthesizing different analytical strengths into a more comprehensive understanding.

Hypothetical case studies of human–AI judgment alignment

The following case studies illustrate how judgment alignment works in practice across different legal contexts.

Corporate transaction due diligence

An AI contract analysis system reviews 5,000 customer agreements during acquisition due diligence, flagging 50 contracts with unusual termination provisions as high risk. The reviewing attorney notes that these contracts follow a pattern common in the target company's industry; they seem problematic by general standards, but function as normal practice in this specific sector. The attorney reclassifies these contracts as medium risk based on industry context that the AI system couldn't incorporate.

Simultaneously, the attorney identifies three contracts that the system classified as low risk, with subtle language creating significant post-closing obligations. These contracts used terminology specific to the target's business that the AI system didn't recognize as creating material obligations. This complementary analysis shows how human judgment related to industry context and business implications can supplement AI pattern recognition.

Litigation strategy analysis

An analytics platform analyzing a judge's past rulings on summary judgment motions identifies a strong statistical correlation between motion denial and public policy arguments. The litigation team first plans to avoid such arguments based on this analysis.

During review, a senior attorney recognizes that the correlation reflects case type, rather than judicial preference – the judge primarily heard cases in areas where public policy considerations are specifically relevant to summary judgment standards. For the current case, which involves different legal standards, the correlation provides limited guidance. The team recalibrates its strategy based on this contextual understanding, showing how human judgment can identify limitations in statistical correlations.

Regulatory compliance implementation

An AI compliance system analyzing a new financial regulation identifies 15 operational processes requiring change. The legal department implements changes for 12 processes in areas where the AI analysis aligns with their interpretation.

For three processes, the legal team determines that the AI system interpreted regulatory requirements more broadly than necessary, based on the department's knowledge of regulatory intent and enforcement priorities. They document their reasoning for narrower implementation and establish tracking to follow regulatory developments. This approach shows balanced judgment: accepting AI analysis where appropriate, while applying human judgment about regulatory context where necessary.

In-house counsel resource allocation

An analytics system recommends distributing incoming legal requests across the department based on historical handling patterns. The general counsel notes that, while the recommendation optimizes for efficiency, it fails to account for professional development needs and succession planning considerations.

The department adopts a modified allocation that incorporates both efficiency metrics and development goals, assigning matters to attorneys who would benefit from the experience, despite not being the most efficient handlers. This example illustrates how human judgment must balance multiple goals beyond the optimization criteria available to AI systems.

Contract negotiation position analysis

An AI negotiation support system analyzes thousands of past negotiations to recommend positions for a major procurement contract. The law firm team reviews these recommendations against the client's current strategic priorities, which have shifted since most of the historical data were generated.

The team adjusts several recommendations to align with the client's current emphasis on supply chain resilience over cost minimization. This change shows how human judgment incorporates current business context that may not be fully reflected in historical data.

These case studies illustrate how effective judgment alignment involves neither automatic deference to AI nor reflexive override, but thoughtful evaluation of the strengths and limitations of each analytical approach.

Judgment-centered monitoring methods

Traditional AI tracking focuses on technical performance metrics, like accuracy rates and processing efficiency. Judgment-centered tracking expands this approach to track how human judgment interacts with AI analysis, providing deeper insight into the effectiveness of human–AI collaboration.

Effective judgment-centered tracking includes:

- Tracking judgment intervention frequency and patterns by task type, user role, and matter characteristics;
- Analyzing the basis for judgment interventions to identify common rationales;
- Evaluating the impact of judgment interventions on matter outcomes; and
- Finding opportunities for system improvement and attorney development, based on intervention patterns.

For legal departments, judgment tracking should connect to business outcomes, tracking how human–AI collaboration affects resolution time, business satisfaction, and risk management effectiveness. This connection demonstrates the value of legal judgment, while finding specific improvement opportunities.

Law firms should implement tracking that respects client confidentiality while gathering enough data for meaningful analysis. This approach may include anonymized tracking of intervention patterns across matter types, helping to identify areas where AI systems require enhancement or attorneys need more guidance.

Organizations should regularly review tracking results with both technical and legal teams, fostering collaborative improvement rather than creating defensive dynamics. These reviews should focus on systemic patterns rather than individual decisions, promoting learning rather than criticism.

The most sophisticated tracking approaches use qualitative and quantitative methods, combining statistical analysis of intervention patterns with deeper examination of selected cases. This mixed-method approach provides both broad trends and detailed understanding of judgment processes.

Tracking results should directly inform both system refinement and professional development, creating a continuous improvement cycle that enhances both technological and human capabilities. This feedback loop makes sure judgment-centered governance remains adaptive rather than static, evolving alongside both technological capabilities and organizational needs.

Professional standards for human–AI collaboration

Evolving ethical guidelines for augmented practice

Professional responsibility in legal practice has always evolved alongside technology, but AI presents novel challenges to traditional ethical frameworks. The duty of competence, traditionally focused on legal knowledge, increasingly encompasses an understanding of AI's capabilities and limitations. Attorneys need not become technical experts, but must comprehend sufficiently to make informed decisions about AI implementation and oversight.

This technical competence requirement extends beyond merely operating AI systems to understanding their underlying methodologies and potential biases. Attorneys using predictive analytics for litigation strategy must understand how the system generates predictions, what data sources it relies on, and what limitations might affect accuracy for particular types of cases or jurisdictions.

The oversight responsibility for automated systems presents another evolving duty. When attorneys delegate tasks to junior colleagues, they understand their supervision obligations. When similar tasks shift to AI systems, supervision becomes less straightforward. Professional standards must define what level of review is required for AI-generated work product and how attorneys should verify the accuracy and completeness of AI analysis.

The duty of candor takes on new dimensions in AI-enhanced practice. Attorneys must be truthful about the capabilities and limitations of the technology they employ, avoiding exaggerated claims about AI "reviewing" documents or providing "legal advice". This candor applies in client communications, court submissions, and regulatory contexts. When AI tools contribute significantly to work product, transparency about their role may be required as a matter of professional honesty.

Perhaps most fundamentally, attorneys must navigate potential tensions between efficiency and professional values. AI tools often promise significant time and cost savings, but these benefits cannot come at the expense of quality, judgment, or ultimate professional responsibility. Finding this balance requires thoughtful consideration of how technology affects both the mechanics of legal work and its professional character.

These evolving obligations apply differently across practice contexts. In high-volume, routine matters where AI has proven highly reliable, less extensive human oversight may be appropriate. In novel, complex, or high-stakes matters, more comprehensive review and validation become essential. Effective standards should provide nuanced guidance, rather than one-size-fits-all requirements.

Client communication about human–AI collaboration

Client communication about AI usage has become an increasingly important part of attorney–client relationships. The nature and extent of disclosure should be tailored to the specific context, considering factors including client sophistication, the centrality of AI to the representation, and matter sensitivity.

For sophisticated clients with their own AI governance frameworks, detailed technical disclosures may be appropriate. For other clients, functional explanations focusing on benefits and limitations may be more suitable. The key principle remains the client's up-to-date and comprehensive understanding of how services are delivered and what role technology plays in that delivery.

In some contexts, explicit client consent may be required before the use of certain AI tools, particularly those that process highly sensitive information or send that information outside the firm's direct control. This consent should be informed by clear explanations of how the technology works, what information will be processed, and what safeguards are in place to protect confidentiality.

Setting realistic expectations represents another important element of client communication. Clients increasingly hear about AI capabilities through media coverage, vendor marketing, and general business literature. These sources often create inflated expectations about what legal AI can actually deliver. Attorneys must realistically assess what AI tools can and cannot do in the specific matter context, managing expectations while still conveying the genuine benefits the technology offers.

Trust-building in an AI-enhanced environment requires transparency about how technology contributes to legal services. Rather than presenting AI as mysterious or magical, attorneys should explain its role in straightforward terms, emphasizing how it complements – rather than replaces – professional judgment. This transparency demonstrates both technical competence and professional honesty, strengthening – rather than undermining – client confidence.

The human element remains essential in client relationships, despite AI sophistication. Technology may handle document review or research tasks, but clients still seek the judgment, wisdom, and personal connection that skilled attorneys provide. Understanding which parts of legal service are most valued by clients – often the strategic guidance, judgment, and counseling functions – helps attorneys to maintain these elements while leveraging technology for tasks.

Documentation standards for human–AI decision-making processes

As AI systems take on larger roles in legal work, documentation of decision-making processes becomes essential for accountability, quality assurance, and knowledge preservation. Comprehensive documentation standards should address which parts of AI usage require documentation, what information should be recorded, and how this documentation should be maintained.

Key documentation elements include:

- AI systems used for specific legal tasks, including version information and configuration details;
- Information sources provided to AI systems as analysis inputs;
- Human review processes applied to AI outputs, including reviewer identity and qualifications;
- Significant changes or overrides of AI recommendations, with rationales; and
- Final decisions and their bases, outlining the respective contributions of human and machine analysis.

Legal departments should integrate this documentation with their matter management systems, creating consistent records across different matter types and AI applications. This integration supports both immediate accountability needs and longer-term knowledge management goals.

Law firms should develop documentation approaches that satisfy professional responsibility obligations while respecting client confidentiality and reducing administrative burden. These approaches should focus on substantive parts of decision-making rather than technical details, emphasizing the legal reasoning behind significant decisions.

Documentation standards should explicitly define how AI-related information is communicated to clients, courts, and regulatory bodies. When AI systems contribute significantly to work product or decisions, appropriate disclosure may be required as a matter of candor and transparency. The form and extent of this disclosure should be tailored to the specific context and recipient needs.

The most effective documentation approaches are integrated into workflow rather than added as separate processes, capturing decision information at the point of creation rather than retrospectively. This integration improves documentation quality while reducing administrative burden, increasing the likelihood of consistent implementation.

The heightened importance of the human element as AI Advances

As AI capabilities advance, the importance of distinctly human elements in legal practice increases, rather than goes down. Technical capabilities for pattern recognition, information retrieval, and basic analysis continue to improve, but the need for judgment, creativity, empathy, and ethical reasoning remains constant or even grows. This reality requires deliberate attention to preserve and develop these human elements alongside technological advancement.

Key human elements requiring heightened attention include:

- Contextual understanding that incorporates business, social, and political factors beyond legal doctrine;
- Empathy and relationship-building that foster client trust and effective communication;
- Creative problem-solving that generates novel solutions to complex challenges;
- Ethical navigation through ambiguous situations requiring value judgments; and
- Strategic thinking that connects legal analysis to broader client objectives.

Legal departments should explicitly value these human elements in performance evaluation and career development, recognizing that technical efficiency alone provides an insufficient measure of attorney effectiveness. This valuation should include dedicated development programs focused on judgment, creativity, and other distinctly human capabilities.

Law firms should emphasize human elements in both talent development and client communications, positioning these capabilities as core value propositions, rather than mere supplements to technical efficiency. This emphasis helps to differentiate the firm's services in an environment where technical capabilities become increasingly standardized.

Education must evolve to develop both technical understanding and distinctly human capabilities, recognizing that future legal professionals need both to be effective. This evolution requires expanding beyond traditional doctrinal focus to include judgment development, creative problem-solving, and ethical reasoning as core – rather than peripheral – elements.

The legal profession should articulate a vision of human–AI collaboration that enhances, rather than reduces, the profession's core values and role in society. This vision should explain how technology can handle routine information processing while creating more space for the judgment, creativity, and wisdom that represent the profession's highest contributions.

Conclusion: A balanced vision for human–AI legal practice

Reframing the relationship between technology and judgment

The discourse around legal technology often presents a false dichotomy between human judgment and technological efficiency, suggesting an inevitable tradeoff between these values. A more productive framing recognizes their complementary relationship, with technology handling information-processing tasks while creating more space for human judgment, rather than replacing it.

This reframed relationship focuses on augmentation rather than automation: using technology to enhance human capabilities as opposed to substituting them. In this model, AI tools expand the scope and depth of information for judgment without displacing the judgment itself. Attorneys access more comprehensive information, find patterns across larger document sets, and receive analytical insights that guide their decisions without predetermining them.

For legal departments, this reframing supports a vision in which technology handles routine information tasks, letting attorneys focus their attention on strategic counseling, complex problem-solving, and proactive risk management. Rather than reducing in-house counsel to technology supervisors, this approach elevates their role as business advisors and strategic partners.

For law firms, the augmentation model supports a value proposition centered on judgment quality rather than process efficiency alone. While efficiency remains important, firms can emphasize how technology enables their attorneys to develop deeper insights, conduct more thorough analysis, and deliver more thoughtful guidance than possible through human effort alone.

This reframed relationship requires rejecting both uncritical technology enthusiasm and reflexive resistance. It acknowledges the genuine value AI brings to legal practice while maintaining clarity about its limitations. Rather than asking whether machines will replace lawyers, it focuses on how the practice of law evolves when routine information tasks no longer dominate attorneys' time and attention.

The balanced vision recognizes that legal judgment itself evolves alongside technology, incorporating new capabilities while preserving its essential character. Just as the introduction of computerized legal research changed how attorneys find precedent, but not the fundamental nature of precedential reasoning, AI tools change how attorneys process information without changing the core nature of legal judgment.

Future directions for research and development

Advancing the balanced vision requires research and development focused specifically on human–AI collaboration, rather than pursuing either pure automation or maintaining the status quo. This research should examine how different collaborative models affect both efficiency and judgment quality, identifying approaches that enhance both dimensions rather than trading one for another.

Key research directions include:

- Cognitive science research on how attorneys process information and make decisions in technology-enhanced environments;
- Comparative studies of different human review protocols and their effects on error detection and judgment quality;
- Longitudinal analysis of how attorney skills and judgment develop in AI-augmented practice environments; and

- Technical research on interfaces and workflows specifically designed to support legal judgment, rather than merely processing efficiency.

Legal departments should participate in this research through partnerships with technology providers, academic institutions, and industry groups. Through contribution of their practical experience and organizational context, they ensure research addresses real-world needs and produces implementable solutions.

Law firms should similarly engage with research communities, both as participants in studies and as funding partners for applied research. This engagement helps to advance the knowledge base while providing early insights into emerging capabilities and best practices.

Professional organizations should coordinate research efforts across the profession, identifying common priorities and distributing findings. This coordination helps to prevent fragmentation and duplication while ensuring research benefits the broader profession, rather than only individual organizations.

Research and development should explicitly address both technological and human elements, recognizing that effective augmentation requires advancing both parts of the system, rather than focusing exclusively on either. This balanced approach makes sure that human capabilities develop alongside technological capabilities, maintaining effective partnership, rather than creating capability gaps.

A call to action for judgment-centered practice

Moving from idea to implementation requires deliberate action by legal organizations, technology providers, and individual practitioners. These actions should be guided by a clear vision of judgment-centered practice that leverages technology while preserving and enhancing distinctly human contributions.

Legal departments should:

- Develop explicit governance frameworks focused on judgment points, ensuring human involvement despite technological capabilities;
- Implement professional development programs that build both technical understanding and judgment capabilities;
- Design workflows that integrate AI capabilities while preserving space for strategic thinking and contextual understanding; and

- Measure both efficiency gains and judgment quality, recognizing that both contribute to organizational value.

Law firms should:

- Articulate value propositions centered on judgment quality enhanced by technological capabilities, rather than efficiency alone;
- Invest in attorney development programs that build judgment skills alongside technical understanding;
- Develop client communication approaches that clearly explain the complementary roles of human judgment and technology; and
- Create feedback mechanisms that track both process metrics and judgment quality to drive continuous improvement.

Technology providers should:

- Design tools specifically to support judgment rather than merely automate tasks, with interfaces that reveal relevant information without predetermining conclusions;
- Develop capabilities for explaining system outputs that help attorneys to understand underlying patterns and limitations;
- Create flexible workflows that accommodate different judgment models, rather than imposing rigid processes; and
- Build tracking capabilities that track judgment intervention patterns to support continuous improvement.

Individual practitioners should:

- Develop both technical literacy and enhanced judgment capabilities, recognizing that future practice requires both;
- Engage actively in defining how technology integrates with their practice, rather than passively accepting imposed solutions;
- Maintain focus on the distinctive value they provide through judgment, creativity, empathy, and ethical reasoning; and
- Contribute to evolving professional standards that address technology usage while preserving core professional values.

The legal profession must champion a vision where technology serves as a catalyst for justice, not merely as a tool for efficiency. By articulating how technological advances can amplify – rather than replace – the human elements that give law its moral force, we create a framework in which digital tools strengthen – rather than diminish – the profession's core values. The irreplaceable nature of human judgment, empathy, and ethical reasoning must remain at the center of this vision, even as AI and automation reshape procedural aspects of legal work.

By embracing this balanced approach, we can forge a future where technology and human judgment exist not as competing forces, but as powerful allies, in service of justice. The result will be a legal profession that harnesses digital innovation to become simultaneously more efficient and more profoundly human – one that better fulfills its essential social contract, while meeting the complex challenges of our rapidly evolving world.

Chapter 2:
The law, genAI, and us: a journey into the future of legal thinking

By Dr Valérie M. Saintot

As legal professionals begin to integrate generative AI (genAI) tools into their daily workflows, a deeper transformation is unfolding. For the sake of clarity, we define legal professionals as people working in legal ecosystems, irrespective of their place on the ladder or their seniority, and including those who may not possess a law degree, as is more often the case nowadays than in past decades.

The legal revolution underway has the potential to go well beyond efficiency gains and enter the realm of thought itself. This is what we are set to explore in the present chapter. We will use our own experience, background, knowledge, and understanding to share some reflections that have emerged out of three years of very regular use of genAI. Here, we compile a collection of perspectives regarding legal prompt engineering and how it challenges traditional notions of human thinking.

While genAI does not think as humans do, it is reshaping how humans think, especially within legal ecosystems. This chapter represents an attempt to pause and reflect about what genAI can do and how to think about legal prompt engineering. Originally, this chapter was intended to be a synthesis of our legal prompt engineering practice. However, not only has our mastery evolved, but – even more extraordinarily – so has the capacity of large language models (LLMs). Had we adhered to this original intention, the only real message shared would have been: "Keep practicing, keep practicing, keep practicing." This is the only way to really appreciate and tap into the power of genAI for legal professionals. Fail fast; journal your practice; develop your own first-hand experience; and, sooner or later, you will deeply understand genAI's immense potential and its risks.

Instead of pursuing our original goal, we evolved our value proposition by offering the reader a set of insights and questions to provoke greater thinking and reflection. Our focus is on how we believe genAI appears to change the way humans think. The core question to explore and discuss in this chapter is this: what happens to legal thinking when humans no longer write, but instead prompt, and machines do not think, but convincingly simulate?

Legal professionals are undergoing a subtle but profound transformation. Traditionally, lawyers were authors of legal texts: legislation, legal advice, court submission, contract, commentary, doctrinal analysis, and so on. Now, with tools like ChatGPT, Harvey, and Copilot – to name a few – we are shifting toward a new role: prompt designers.

Legal professionals now input commands, refine queries, and select from machine-generated drafts what they author. We enter an epistemic dialogue, a two-way cognitive process between them and the machine that evolves in what we call the "prompting cycle". How can this evolution be qualified: is it mere complementary technology, or are we witnessing a deeper cognitive shift?

If we use genAI to draft legal output while not taking the context into account, the result may be coherent, even persuasive. However, genAI does not consider courtroom dynamics, the jurisdictional preferences a human may have observed, or the strategic value of what is left unsaid. If you have ever asked genAI to summarize a court ruling, you will have had the chance to witness how it limits its rendering to the written words, not to the 3D human reality in and around the case.

In the present chapter, we propose a series of perspectives that embody our provisional understanding. We use a well-established taxonomy (the Bloom taxonomy) to make the act of human thinking more concrete and comprehensible. Three items will be explored: the ways in which AI changes how we think; a proposal to train and reclaim the legal mind; and, finally, a checklist to remain accountable when prompting for legal purposes.

How genAI is changing our thinking

The imperfect yet explicit glossary of terms outlined in Table 1 is intended to establish a common understanding to aid the reader when proceeding with the ideas and terminology explored in the present chapter, particularly those that are less obvious, like fluency illusion, epistemic dialogue, or black box normativity. To ground this reflection, Table 1 introduces a glossary of core terms emerging from our genAI practice.[1]

Table 1: Glossary of key terms and concepts

Term	Characteristics	GenAI reasoning levels
Prompting	The act of formulating an input or query for a genAI system to generate a response	Central to interacting with genAI; affects the quality and relevance of output
Legal prompting	The use of prompts specifically tailored to legal tasks (e.g., drafting, argument analysis)	Blends legal expertise with prompt engineering
Prompted cognition	Human thinking shaped by the process of crafting and interpreting AI-generated outputs.	A hybrid form of cognition emerging from human–AI interaction
GenAI reasoning	Text generation by AI based on statistical associations, not understanding or reasoning	Lacks intentionality, context awareness, or ethical consideration
Human legal thinking	Context-aware reasoning involving interpretation, precedent analysis, and ethical judgment	Emerges from experience, culture, and legal education
Fluency illusion	Mistaking coherent AI output for meaningful or reasoned understanding	A risk when AI output sounds plausible but lacks depth or nuance
Epistemic dialog	A reflective, two-way cognitive process between human and machine in the prompting cycle	Promotes critical thinking and self-awareness in legal practice
Black box normativity	Reliance on AI outputs whose internal logic is opaque or inaccessible	Undermines transparency and accountability in legal decisions

We will now delve into a comparison of legal thinking and genAI reasoning: the illusion of thought; how we can define thinking; and a new genre: prompted cognition.

The illusion of thought: what genAI is (and isn't) doing

GenAI systems like GPT-4 do not think; they do not reason, interpret, or understand. Instead, they predict the most likely next word or phrase based on massive datasets. This creates an "illusion" of intelligence. It leads to some form of legal fluency, without legal thinking underpinning the output.

This is what philosopher John Searle called the Chinese room argument: a machine can appear to understand language while merely manipulating symbols, giving the illusion of understanding. Similarly, genAI can draft a convincing motion to dismiss without grasping the stakes, the forum, or the client's interests. We risk mistaking fluency for judgment, especially in law, where nuance and sensitivity when considering the ethical dimensions of the context matter.

Legal thinking traditionally involves interpretative judgment, the weighing of a corpus of existing legal knowledge and ethical considerations. Legal thinking is situated, context-sensitive, and fundamentally human. In contrast, genAI operates via statistical pattern matching across massive datasets. It generates text not by understanding, but by predicting what words are likely to come next. For example, when prompted with, "Is a given non-competition clause enforceable in Germany?", genAI might accurately respond that such clauses are generally unenforceable under German law. However, it cannot ask the critical follow-up questions a lawyer would: who is asking? In what context? Are there trade secret implications?

As legal professionals, we must resist the temptation to perceive fluency as comparable to thinking. GenAI mimics the surface of legal thinking, but lacks intentionality, accountability, or normative commitment. Still, the apparent fluency it displays challenges us to articulate what we mean by thinking in the first place.

Bloom's taxonomy: a way to define thinking

Since its inception in 1956, Bloom's taxonomy has served as a foundational model for classifying levels of human thinking and learning and has been influential in education and corporate training. Its six-tiered levels span from remembering to creating. However, with the rise of genAI and the complex domain of legal thinking, revisiting appears meaningful. We have extended it to propose two adaptations: legal thinking and genAI reasoning. We do not claim any academic validity, but see this exercise as a way to self-prompt our thinking.

The two complementary taxonomies we propose are displayed in Table 2 below and draw on the logic of Bloom's foundational model.

Table 2: Extended Bloom's taxonomy

#	Bloom level (generic)	Legal thinking levels	GenAI reasoning levels
1	Remember	Recall	Retrieve
2	Understand	Interpret	Parse
3	Apply	Apply	Synthetize
4	Analyze	Distinguish	Reframe
5	Evaluate	Argue	Calibrate
6	Create	Construct	Generate

Traditionally, Bloom taxonomy focused on human learning, where memory, logic, and creativity are sequentially developed. Yet, genAI does not "learn" like humans; it synthesizes, extrapolates, and adapts based on training data and prompts. In turn, legal thinking is deeply tied to an existing body of knowledge, interpretation, and formal argumentation. Legal thinking often requires simultaneous multi-level thinking (in Bloom's taxonomy logic). With Table 3 on the next page, we have tried to make explicit how Bloom's taxonomy could be described in terms of action supported at each of its six levels, creating a scaffolding that mirrors three different cognitive landscapes: Bloom's thinking, legal thinking, and genAI reasoning.

Our goal is to deconstruct the complexity we are facing. Before having a dialogue with a machine, we might not have really thought too much about the act of (legal) thinking. To clarify and nurture our added value in the human–machine paradigm we have been engaged in, beyond our own agency and choice, we need to work on embracing the complexity it represents, to articulate the entire conversation. We see more risks in denying the crisis than embracing it, including its potential to set humans free from many of their cognitive blind spots, such as biases and limiting mental models.

Table 3: Comparative cognitive taxonomies, building on Bloom's

#	Bloom's levels	Bloom's thinking	Legal thinking	GenAI reasoning
1	Remember	Recall facts and basic concepts	Recall laws, facts, precedents	Retrieve training data patterns
2	Understand	Explain ideas or concepts	Interpret legal norms and language	Parse prompts and user intent
3	Apply	Use knowledge in new situations	Apply legal rules to factual scenarios	Synthesize inputs into structured outputs
4	Analyze	Draw connections; dissect logic	Distinguish precedents; assess legal logic	Reframe content across formats or styles
5	Evaluate	Justify decisions; critique claims	Argue and evaluate competing legal positions	Calibrate for accuracy, coherence, bias
6	Create	Design new products or solutions	Construct legal theories, proposals, rulings	Generate contextually adaptive content

A proposal to reclaim and train the legal mind

We return to the core question: is prompting a form of thinking? The answer is complex. It involves intention, reflection, and creativity. Equally, it includes outsourcing, dependency, and automation. The legal mind must evolve in the genAI era. Lawyers need to master the art of asking powerful questions, not just searching for superficial answers. Prompting is not the end of legal thinking – one could say it is its next frontier. Perhaps the future lawyer is no longer the best drafter, but the best thinker-about-thinking: someone who knows that judgment cannot be prompted, only exercised.

Reclaiming the legal mind

Legal professionals – and, even more explicitly, lawyers – have long prided themselves on their capacity for thought through argument, deep interpretation, and normative judgment. These intellectual aptitudes are embedded in the very fabric of legal education and professional identity. What happens when a machine, which does not think in any human sense, begins to perform tasks that we have historically associated with legal thinking?

Interacting with genAI changes us. When we prompt effectively, we become more reflective, hypothesis-driven, and systemic in our approach. This is "prompted cognition" – a cognitive mode emerging from the act of regularly and sustainably engaging with genAI. Prompting requires metacognition: how should I frame this question? What do I expect as an answer? How do I validate it? We become the curator of questions, not just the seeker of answers.

Consider asking genAI a GDPR liability question. A small change in prompt framing yields vastly different outputs. By prompting not just once or twice, but several times – both in a row and again sometime later – we are taught precision and helped to realize how fragile and evolutive machine-generated thought can be. The rather significant change in possible answers and in machine reasoning is a huge differentiator from human thinking.

Legal prompting is both art (intuitive and unique) and science (systematic and repeatable), and is meant to craft inputs to query genAI and generate legal analysis, argument, or drafting. It is more than a technical skill; it is a new mode of cognitive engagement, where human thought meets machine pattern recognition. This encounter does not merely support legal work; it alters the process of legal thinking itself. The question is no longer whether genAI will change law, but how it is changing legal professionals, individually and collectively.

Law is not merely a body of rules; it is a linguistic system that structures thinking. Legal professionals use language not just to express ideas, but to shape reality by the choices they make when constructing and interpreting contracts, judgments, statutes, and various argumentations. When prompting genAI, we are engaging with a system that treats language statistically, not semantically.

Prompting becomes an act of translation between human legal intentionality and machine linguistic patterning. This interaction reframes language as both a bridge and a boundary between two forms of cognition: one conscious and ethical, and the other unconscious and statistical. For instance, a lawyer drafting a contract clause can now ask genAI to generate three different variations. The final decision may still rest with the lawyer, but the source of initial thought, like the language, structure and tone, comes from the machine.

Bloom's taxonomy has guided generations of educators in scaffolding learning objectives, from demanding memorization to creative synthesis. Yet, as genAI reshapes how machines reason and legal systems grow increasingly combined with automated tools, we face a challenge: how do we educate ourselves and grow new skills to optimally partner with the machine?

In Table 4, we propose a way to look at upskilling from the perspective of what we could deliver when teaming up with the machine. The way to interpret this table is by asking oneself if we know what the proposed output is and if one can produce it or not. In the instance of a negative answer, one can get a sense for where learning could be meaningful.

Legal thinking stresses rigorous interpretation, structured logic, knowledge analysis, and argument construction; genAI reasoning emphasizes fluidity, multimodal synthesis, and iterative calibration with human input. Both diverge from Bloom's taxonomy in that they often deal with incompleteness. GenAI infers missing context, while legal thinking often fills analytical gaps or is called to solve conflicting norms, which require a real sensitivity to the context that may never have previously been articulated in words.

In practice, as legal educators, we need to rethink cognitive goals for AI literacy. Rather than treating AI tools as passive data processors, we must teach users how to prompt, critique, and collaborate with these systems effectively. Legal education should include practical guidance on how to interact with genAI, perform legal research, tap the potential of predictive tools, and find clear ways to teach a deep understanding of AI's "cognitive limits". This represents a balancing act between tapping genAI's concrete added value and avoiding over-reliance on it. Teaching the ethical use of genAI and the art of sound argumentation outside and within the human–machine relationship is becoming ever more crucial and urgent.

Even AI developers and AI ethicists can benefit from using the adapted Bloom taxonomy proposed in this chapter, drawing on such new cognitive frameworks to develop appreciation of the fact that the programmed system is not sentient, but is a layered reasoning engine. This avoids too much humanizing of the machine while enabling structured improvement and evaluation of every new generation of LLM.

Table 4: Comparing thinking and reasoning outputs

#	Thinking	Legal output	GenAI use case	Legal + genAI
1	Computational	Legal problems viewed as code (if/then logic)	Prompt engineering, rule modelling	Logic trees, decision automation
2	Visual	Legal diagrams, flows, timelines	AI-generated mind maps, case visualizations	Pattern recognition and communication
3	Collaborative	Team-based legal drafting and negotiation	Human-AI pair programming for contracts	Prompt libraries, versioned co-creation
4	Metacognitive	Monitoring one's reasoning process	Prompt reflection and iterative querying	Prompt journals to trace skill evolution
5	Critical	Scrutinizing precedent, bias, logic	Legal thinking tests on AI output	Error-spotting, counterargument generation
6	Creative	New legal arguments, policy design	Divergent idea generation	Prompt storms for novel interpretations
7	Systems	Seeing broader regulatory/ social contexts	AI-assisted regulatory mapping	Scenario building, impact forecasting
8	Strategic	Litigation strategy, compliance planning	Scenario simulation, decision trees	Risk matrix prompting, policy generation
9	Reflective	Ethical and procedural self-review	Prompt-testing journals	Debrief AI outputs after use

(Re)training the legal mind

This chapter introduces a strategic roadmap designed to help legal professionals enhance both their individual legal thinking and their collaboration with genAI tools. By integrating foundational cognitive frameworks with practical prompting strategies and critical reflection, legal professionals can move from passive users to confident, ethical co-creators (human–genAI) of legal output. We propose a seven-step process to cultivate human–genAI combined agency that is flexible enough to be adapted to your context and the legal topics of direct relevance to you.

Step 1: Reground in the craft of recalling and interpreting law

Legal professionals must start by strengthening their command of relevant foundational legal knowledge. This includes revisiting key case law, statutory frameworks, and doctrinal interpretations. Practicing the ability to restate these concepts in accessible language helps in both client communication and better engineering of any prompts using genAI tools. Legal professionals should spend time comparing AI-generated summaries of legal concepts with their own, to assess clarity and accuracy.

Exercise 1: Summarize the risk taxonomy of the EU AI Act.

Key actions:

1. Access the EU AI Act in Eur-Lex. Summarize the risk taxonomy in plain language.
2. Upload a PDF of the EU AI Act into a genAI tool and ask for a summary of the risks.

Step 2: Develop the double lens of parallel legal and AI reasoning

Legal professionals need to learn to think in dual modes: legal thinking and computational prompting. This involves understanding how AI models process context, as well as evaluating the legal soundness of their output.

Exercise 2: Highlight and explain the important parts of a case generated by genAI.

Key actions:

1. Prompt AI with case references and ask for summaries.
2. Annotate the output, applying legal thinking.

Step 3: Structure before prompting and think like a legal architect
Effective prompting begins with structure. Lawyers can improve AI results by using clear roles, formats, and constraints in their prompts. If you have a template and it does not contain any protected data and confidential information, you can also upload it to guide the genAI tool used.

Exercise 3: Act as an EU privacy officer. Analyze the following DPIA draft and flag any GDPR Article 35 issues in a tabular format.
Key actions:
1. Break problems into promptable chunks.
2. Use structured prompt formats: Role + Task + Format + Constraints.
3. Create modular prompts based on legal templates.

Step 4: Interrogate, don't automate, to build your "argument muscles"
Rather than relying on AI-generated answers, lawyers must interrogate them. What assumptions does the AI make? Are the analogies use-appropriate? Legal thinking thrives on rigorous testing, and genAI can serve as a devil's advocate to grow argumentation skills.

Exercise 4: Ask AI to simulate rebuttals to your position or judicial questions a judge might ask.
Key actions:
1. Challenge AI with counterarguments.
2. Evaluate legal logic and citation relevance.
3. Use legal thinking tools, like deductive logic or thinking by analogy, to challenge the output.

Step 5: Calibrate with a human compass of ethics, bias, and judgment
Legal professionals must remain grounded in ethical frameworks when using AI tools. This includes preserving confidentiality, avoiding over-reliance, and reflecting on the biases inherent in both model training and output. AI should support, not replace, legal judgment.

Exercise 5: Outline the ethical risks of AI (confidentiality, competence, fairness) in immigration legal advice.
Key actions:
1. Check for bias, hallucinations, and jurisdictional accuracy.
2. Reflect on the ethics of using genAI in practice.
3. Rehearse scenarios where legal ethics intersect with AI tools.

Step 6: Co-create legal intelligence and advance from consumer to collaborator

Lawyers can elevate their role by using genAI not as a static tool, but as a creative partner. By iteratively drafting, refining, and validating legal documents, they develop workflows that combine human expertise and machine efficiency. Internal prompt libraries and collaborative review cycles enhance quality and consistency.

Exercise 6: Draft a clause, adjust jurisdiction, and simulate objections.

Key actions:

1. Use AI to draft and iteratively improve legal documents.
2. Build a prompt library for your team or firm.
3. Train junior staff in responsible AI-aided legal writing.

Step 7: Reflect, iterate, elevate in a never-ending process

The learning loop must remain open. Legal professionals should reflect on what worked, what failed, and how their understanding of legal thinking is evolving through AI interaction. Journals, checklists, and sharing with peers encourage continuous improvement and professional growth.

Exercise 7: Reflect on the following: what did the AI miss? What legal dimension was overlooked?

Key actions:

1. Keep a prompt/reflection journal.
2. Set learning goals for genAI and legal thinking.
3. Share prompt strategies and insights with peers.

The integration of genAI into legal practice does not mark the end of legal thinking but, rather, its transformation. Legal professionals who engage with these tools critically and creatively will not only improve efficiency, but also expand the boundaries of legal interpretation, advocacy, and client service. Every team needs to invest in designing their own roadmap. Time is of essence when understanding and utilizing genAI, so it is highly advisable to make the time investment in upskilling valuable and impactful. Tailoring training units helps to achieve engagement and impact when back at one's desk.

A genAI prompting accountability checklist

What happens when lawyers lean too heavily on genAI? If the AI produces a flawed clause, a biased summary, or a shallow legal opinion, one can legitimately ask: who is responsible? The machine cannot be sued; the prompt engineer is most likely invisible.

This chapter has shown how much legal authorship is being redefined. In hybrid workflows, accountability blurs. Lawyers must remain critical custodians of meaning, not passive editors of machine text. This is not hypothetical: courts in Colombia and jurisdictions in China have begun accepting AI-generated decisions or advice. The law must now wrestle with questions of epistemic authority and human oversight.

As is often the case in the author's work, an inventory of questions is often more valuable than any overpromising simplified acronyms. We, therefore, asked GPT-4o to propose a list of questions related to genAI usage in legal practice and adjusted these to reflect our own understanding and experience. By engaging with these questions, we believe that you will be better able to assess your own readiness and responsibility when using genAI for legal thinking, drafting, or research. Check each item thoughtfully and reflect before integrating AI-generated content into any professional legal context.

1. **Legal accuracy and jurisdictional relevance**
    - Is the AI-generated content legally accurate and up to date?
    - Are all legal citations real, relevant, and jurisdiction-specific?
    - Have I verified that the AI's legal interpretation is consistent with applicable law?
    - Is there evidence of hallucinated or fictitious legal content?

2. **Context and prompt quality**
    - Did I clearly define the legal issue, jurisdiction, and context in the prompt?
    - Have I tested different prompt versions to reduce ambiguity?
    - Does the AI's output reflect a legally appropriate understanding of the facts?

3. **Ethical and professional responsibility**
    - Does my use of genAI align with the bar association I am accountable to?

- Have I adequately protected confidential client information when using public AI tools?
- Have I disclosed AI assistance to the client or court where ethically necessary?
- Could this use of AI be construed as unauthorized practice of law?

4. **Procedural and practical integrity**
   - Would I submit this output as-is to a court or regulatory body?
   - Have I reviewed, edited, and fact-checked the output myself?
   - Have I identified any misleading, vague, or inaccurate content?
   - Would opposing counsel or a judge challenge this AI-generated content?

5. **Risk and accountability**
   - Am I prepared to take professional responsibility for the AI-generated content?
   - Have I documented my use of AI and the review process?
   - What legal or reputational risks would arise from relying on this output?
   - Do I know who would be accountable in case of errors?

6. **Client interest and communication**
   - Does the output serve the client's best legal and strategic interests?
   - Have I used the AI to supplement – not replace – my legal judgment?
   - Have I communicated the nature and limits of AI involvement to the client?

7. **AI tool awareness**
   - Do I know what AI system was used and what data it was trained on?
   - Is the AI tool appropriate for legal work or fine-tuned for legal domains?
   - Does the system indicate uncertainty?

The more the machine makes us methodically doubt, the more we become ethically coherent both in relation to the machine and in its absence. We truly believe that a constructive approach to the human–machine relation allows open-minded legal professionals to reach to new and higher levels of consciousness, thanks to the reflexive impact that prompt engineering can have on human thinking.

Conclusion

As we reach the end of this chapter, one thing remains clear: we are only at the beginning of understanding what genAI means for legal thinking. What began for many as a tool to save time or automate routine tasks is quickly revealing itself to be something far more consequential. GenAI is becoming a catalyst for rethinking the very processes through which legal professionals observe, analyze, decide, and act.

Legal prompt engineering is not just a technical skill; it is a new cognitive practice. It invites legal professionals to engage in a continuous dialogue and prompts human legal professionals to revisit and re-own their own thinking habits. When prompting, we are not merely instructing a system, but we also shape and are being shaped by the possibilities of legal imagination, inference, and judgment that emerge from this interplay.

We have argued that genAI challenges legal professionals to transition from being the sole authors of legal texts to becoming co-designers of legal reasoning pathways. This shift comes with responsibility. The risks of oversimplification, hallucination, or misplaced trust in machine-generated outputs are real. Equally, there are many opportunities, such as making the law more accessible, identifying patterns invisible to the human eye alone, and rediscovering the ethical core of legal reasoning in a new light.

This chapter has offered three entry points – cognitive, pedagogical, and ethical – to exploration and navigation of emerging legal prompting landscapes. Together, these form an invitation: not to fear this transformation, but to meet it with curiosity, with critical rigor, and with the humility to learn and unlearn. We urge readers to treat this chapter not as a conclusion, but as a checkpoint and an invitation to pause, reflect, and decide what kind of legal professional you want to become in this new terrain.

It is tempting to frame the use of genAI in law as a technical issue, something that can be resolved with the right toolkits or the most efficient prompts libraries. However, our exploration suggests otherwise: the real shift lies in how we think about thinking, how we relate to knowledge production, and how we define what counts as legal authorship. These are not marginal concerns; they go to the heart of what it means to practice law, reason legally, and uphold the values we associate with justice.

We are convinced that the most meaningful engagement with genAI will not be driven by efficiency alone, but by intentionality. By cultivating deliberate practices of prompting, reflecting, revising, and interrogating, legal professionals can begin to reclaim agency in this new epistemic environment. Prompting, when done well, becomes a way of thinking in motion, some iterative and recursive. It blends human intuition with machine capability.

Ultimately, the future of legal thinking does not lie in either resisting the machine nor surrendering to it, but in forging a reflective practice which recognizes the power of technology while reaffirming the centrality of human judgment, responsibility, and care – one prompt at a time.

Further reading

The abundance of articles and books on legal prompt engineering is huge. It is, therefore, best to find the publications that are closest to your legal tradition and jurisdiction. Here, only key works that helped the author shape their way thinking over the years are cited.

Levi, E.H., *An Introduction to Legal Reasoning, Chicago* (IL): University of Chicago Press; 1949

Bloom, B.S. (ed.), *Taxonomy of Educational Objectives: The Classification of Educational Goals. Handbook I: Cognitive Domain*, New York (NY): David McKay Company; 1956

Habermas, J., *Between Facts and Norms: Contributions to a Discourse Theory of Law and Democracy*, Cambridge (MA): MIT Press; 1992

Sunstein, C.R., *Legal Reasoning and Political Conflict*, Oxford: Oxford University Press; 1996

Anderson, L.W. and Krathwohl, D.R. (eds.), *A Taxonomy for Learning, Teaching, and Assessing: A Revision of Bloom's Taxonomy of Educational Objectives*, New York (NY): Longman; 2001

Mollick, E., *Co-Intelligence: Living and Working with AI*, New York (NY): Crown Publishing Group; 2023

References

1 Several tables of this chapter have been partly co-created using GPT-4.0; any flaws thereof contained remain the responsibility of the author.

Chapter 3: Challenges and ethical considerations in the age of generative AI

By Natalie Pierce, partner and chair of the Employment & Labor Group, and Stephanie Goutos, head of employment law practice innovation, Gunderson Dettmer

"AI won't replace lawyers, but lawyers who use AI will replace lawyers who don't."[1, 2]

The release of OpenAI's ChatGPT[3] in late 2022 triggered the beginning of a global race to harness artificial intelligence's (AI) potential and transform society.[4] In 2025, generative AI (genAI) has become increasingly influential in the practice of law, driving notable changes in how legal services are delivered. Microsoft's vice chairman Brad Smith has previously compared the emergence of genAI to the invention of the internet – a comparison that feels even more apt today.[5]

GenAI tools offer tremendous potential for efficiency and innovation in legal practice, but they also introduce complex ethical and operational challenges. For instance, genAI-generated content can inadvertently perpetuate human biases or produce inaccurate and misleading outputs – commonly referred to as AI "hallucinations". These issues can have critical implications for client confidentiality, professional ethics, and legal compliance.[6]

This chapter explores the critical responsibility of legal professionals to approach genAI carefully, recognizing its potential to reshape the practice of law while still adhering to important ethical and professional obligations. Designed as a practical guide for law firms and practitioners, it provides actionable strategies for managing organizational risks and ensuring legal compliance. We emphasize the importance of embracing genAI's transformative power while still upholding the core principles and values that define the legal industry.

Introduction to ethical challenges

The rapid evolution of genAI presents both significant opportunities and complex challenges for the legal profession. This section examines how traditional ethical frameworks, particularly those established by the American Bar Association's (ABA) Model Rules of Professional Conduct, apply to and evolve in response to emerging technological advancements.[7]

Evolution of ethical standards for technology in law

Chief Justice Burger's remark from 50 years ago still rings true: "The advocate must know how to use the tools of his trade."[8]

While genAI's technological capabilities may be new, the ethical issues raised are not. When incorporating technology in the practice of law, lawyers still have the same duties to adhere to their professional and ethical obligations, including the duties of supervision, independent judgment, and competence, regardless of the tools they employ.[9]

The ABA's Model Rules, which serve as ethical guidelines for attorneys, were adopted long before the advent of AI. However, these rules were intentionally designed to evolve and be adaptable to modern times.[10] Model Rule 1.1 states: "A lawyer shall provide competent representation to a client. Competent representation requires the legal knowledge, skill, thoroughness and preparation reasonably necessary for the representation."[11] In the context of using genAI tools, lawyers must understand the technology they use and exercise informed professional judgment when incorporating it into their practice.[12]

Recognizing the growing impact of technology on legal practice, the ABA took proactive steps in 2009 by convening its Commission on Ethics 20/20 to study the ethical and regulatory implications of technological advancements. The Commission's final report offered several key insights:[13]

- Technology has fundamentally transformed legal practice in ways that were unimaginable just a decade earlier. It affects nearly every aspect of legal work, including the storing of confidential information; client communication; discovery processes; research; and the marketing of legal services. Even more fundamentally, technology has transformed the delivery of legal services by changing where and how those services are delivered (e.g., in an office, over the internet, or through virtual law offices), which is having a related impact on the cost of, and the public's access to, these services.[14]
- Lawyers must possess a baseline understanding of technology to meet their clients' expectations for competent and cost-effective representation. For example, tasks such as electronic discovery may require

specialized knowledge about how digital information is stored and retrieved. Therefore, another development associated with technology is that lawyers are increasingly disaggregating work by retaining other lawyers and non-lawyers outside the firm (i.e., outsourcing) to perform critical tasks. Technology also permits the integration of these otherwise disaggregated work streams, encouraging clients and lawyers to outsource elements of a representation.[15]

- Given these developments, the Commission concluded that updates to the Model Rules were necessary to ensure lawyers could ethically serve clients in an increasingly complex and tech-driven marketplace. Because of the bewildering pace of technological change, the Commission believed it was important to make explicit that a lawyer's duty of competence, which requires the lawyer to stay abreast of changes in the law and its practice, including an obligation to understand the benefits and risks of new technology.[16]

Subsequently, in 2012, Comment 8 to Model Rule 1.1[17] was revised to explicitly state: "A lawyer should keep abreast of changes in the law and its practice, including the benefits and risks associated with relevant technology."[18] This revision clarified that lawyers have an affirmative obligation to stay informed about relevant technologies in order to provide competent representation.[19] The language was deliberately left vague to account for future technologies that did not exist at the time of drafting.[20] Legal scholars have noted the addition of just these nine words – "including the benefits and risks associated with relevant technology" – to the Model Rules has significantly expanded the practical scope of what today's ethical lawyer must understand and confront.[21]

The critical role of technological competence in the practice of law

In recognition of this increasingly expansive obligation, at least 40 state bar organizations have adopted similar guidance regarding a lawyer's duty of technological competence.[22] The widespread adoption of this comment has been declared by Bob Ambrogi, a well-respected legal technology and innovation expert, as one of the most significant recent developments in the field of legal technology.[23] These guidelines reflect the growing recognition that lawyers must understand and effectively utilize technology to meet their professional responsibilities.

To support this evolving standard, the ABA recommended that bar associates provide continuing legal education resources on technology. Some states have gone even further, requiring educational programs on legal technology as part of their licensing requirements.[24] In recognition of the importance of technological proficiency for future attorneys, the ABA has also strongly encouraged law schools to incorporate legal technology into their curricula, deeming it an "essential" area of study. To lead by example, the ABA established its Center for Innovation and, more recently, an AI Task Force to address emerging challenges and opportunities in legal technology.[25] Despite these advancements, lawyers should never assume that results generated by genAI tools are inherently accurate or reliable. It is imperative for attorneys to critically evaluate genAI outputs and understand their ethical responsibilities when using these tools. By exercising informed judgment and maintaining technological competence, lawyers can leverage genAI effectively while upholding their professional obligations.[26]

Challenges and professional obligations when using genAI

When using genAI, lawyers must exercise reasonable care in analyzing the output and must be held accountable.[27] The duty of competence regarding new technology is well-established in the legal industry. For example, in 2007, the *Yale Journal of Law & Technology* published an article entitled "Surfin' safari – why competent lawyers should research on the web," arguing that lawyers have a new obligation to use online research platforms, rather than solely relying on books.[28] The author argued that the ethical duties of competence and diligence require lawyers to conduct legal research when representing a client, including the use of the internet.[29] The article further opined that not using technology to perform legal research may constitute a lack of diligence, because online tools provide lawyers with the most up-to-date picture of the law, as opposed to books, which cannot be updated in real time.[30] This highlights the broader obligation for lawyers to stay informed about relevant technologies to competently represent their clients.

Indeed, several courts have penalized attorneys for neglecting essential duties in connection with electronic legal research. For instance, failing to Shepardize case law – a critical process for verifying its subsequent treatment – has led to sanctions in several cases. As technology continues to evolve, lawyers are increasingly required to monitor, analyze, and effectively use new tools. The proper use of technology is no longer optional; it is fundamental to competent client representation. This obligation has been evident in areas such as electronic discovery, where courts have held attorneys accountable for technological incompetence.[31]

Lawyers cannot shift blame onto technology – or their lack of proficiency with it – for failures in representation.[32] In one notable case, a court rejected an attorney's professed technological incompetence as a "valid excuse" and recommended sanctions under the Model Rules of Professional Conduct.[33] The court stated:

> *"Deliberate ignorance of technology is inexcusable ... If a lawyer cannot master the technology suitable for that lawyer's practice, the lawyer should either hire tech-savvy lawyers tasked with responsibility to keep current, or hire an outside technology consultant who understands the practice of law and associated ethical constraints."*[34]

Other courts have echoed this principle, issuing sanctions in similar circumstances where attorneys failed to remain "sufficiently technologically competent".[35] Additionally, existing professional rules already require lawyers who use ChatGPT, Claude, or analogous genAI tools to implement a range of safeguards to stay within their professional boundaries.[36]

Beyond competence, genAI introduces additional ethical concerns under Model Rules 1.4, 1.6, 5.1, and 5.3.[37] These Rules collectively emphasize the importance of effective communication between attorneys and their clients, confidentiality of information, and the duty of supervision to ensure support staff and other team members are complying with the rules of professional conduct.[38] For instance, the duty of supervision states that lawyers should not automatically assume information produced by others (e.g., paralegals, junior lawyers, or technology) is accurate.[39] The same standard of supervision and review applies to work produced by genAI. In 2012, the title of Model Rule 5.3 was updated to explicitly include any "non-lawyer assistance", opening the door for all types of assistance, whether human or otherwise.[40] This revision clarifies that lawyers must supervise and review the outputs of genAI tools with the same diligence applied to human-generated work.[41]

Moreover, ABA professional guidelines caution against both overreliance on and underutilization of AI technologies.[42] While excessive dependence on AI can lead to ethical lapses, failing to leverage AI effectively may pose an even "greater danger" by depriving clients of the benefits these tools offer in terms of efficiency and accuracy.[43] Lawyers must strike a careful balance: embracing genAI's potential while rigorously supervising its outputs to ensure compliance with ethical obligations.

More recently, lawyers have faced sanctions for submitting pleadings that cited nonexistent cases, some of which were apparently generated by AI.[44] Addressing this issue, the US District Court for the District of Wyoming emphasized that "[a]s attorneys transition to the world of AI, the duty to check their sources and make a reasonable inquiry into existing law remains unchanged". [45] The court further clarified: "[a]t its core, when attorneys sign a legal document, they certify that they have "read the document, [have] conducted a reasonable inquiry into the facts and the law and [are] satisfied that the document is well grounded in both, and [are] acting without any improper motive. A failure to comply with such obligations may result in a sanction."[46] The integration of genAI into legal practice demands not only technical competence, but also vigilance in upholding these ethical obligations. By critically evaluating genAI outputs and ensuring adherence to the Model Rules, lawyers can responsibly leverage this transformative technology while maintaining their professional integrity.

Beyond technological competence, lawyers also have a duty to combat bias in their practice – an obligation that becomes particularly significant when using genAI tools, which are known to generate biased outputs.[47] AI algorithms often inherit biases from historical data used during training, which can lead to inequitable outcomes if left unchecked. Regular audits, updates to training data, and collaboration with diverse development teams are essential steps to mitigate these risks. The ABA has acknowledged the risks of bias in AI, noting that it "potentially implicates professional ethics".[48] In 2019, the ABA passed Resolution 112, urging legal practitioners to proactively address the ethical and legal ramifications of AI use. Resolution 112 highlights three critical areas of focus:

- Addressing bias, explainability, and transparency in automated decisions made by AI;
- Promoting ethical and beneficial uses of AI; and
- Establishing appropriate controls and oversight over AI systems and vendors.

The Resolution also makes clear that lawyers need to be aware of how AI can be properly used in the practice of law, allowing lawyers to provide more efficient and effective services to their clients.[49]

Similarly, ABA Resolution 604, unanimously adopted at the ABA's 2023 Midyear Meeting, directs organizations that design, develop, deploy and use AI, including lawyers and firms, to follow specific guidelines addressing accountability, transparency, and traceability.[50] These developments provide a valuable roadmap for the responsible use of AI in the practice of law. To navigate the challenges associated with genAI and to minimize the risks, the legal industry is actively developing strategies such as the formation of specialized AI taskforces, AI governance policies, and comprehensive training. Institutions from academia (like MIT) to law firms are actively contributing to this evolving AI governance. The ABA's recent creation of a Task Force on Law and Artificial Intelligence, focusing on AI-related biases, client confidentiality, and access to justice, is a notable example.[51]

In tandem with these important initiatives, technological safeguards are also being implemented to mitigate risks, such as the unauthorized sharing of confidential or otherwise sensitive information.[52] For instance, OpenAI's policy modifications, which now include the ability to disable the user's chat history in ChatGPT and the introduction of an enterprise-focused model with enhanced security features, act as tangible safeguards against unintended data usage or disclosure.[53] This expands the ability for lawyers to leverage genAI while protecting client confidence.

In parallel, a number of third-party vendors are developing solutions to allow legal professionals to have secure access to enterprise-level genAI models, while still protecting confidential information.[54] These and future advancements help to safeguard privileged attorney–client communications and other confidential data. In 2023, we predicted that many law firms and organizations would adopt custom genAI tools and prohibit inputting confidential information into public genAI tools to mitigate confidentiality risks.[55] This prediction has proven accurate to date, with a clear trend towards proprietary or enterprise genAI solutions, accompanied by strict policies against using public tools for sensitive information.[56] We fully expect this trend toward secure and responsible genAI adoption to continue as firms increasingly recognize its strategic importance in safeguarding client trust and confidentiality.

Failing to leverage genAI responsibly may create serious risks

The responsible integration of genAI is not just a strategic advantage. Widespread adoption of genAI is increasingly inevitable, and failure to proactively adopt this shift may create serious legal and organizational risks.[57] It would be naïve to assume that employees are not already using genAI tools, such as ChatGPT, to support their work.[58] In 2023, studies suggested that as many as 50 percent of employees were using genAI tools at work, with a staggering 70 percent of those not disclosing it to their employers.[59] More recently, a February 2025 report revealed that non-corporate accounts make up 74 percent of ChatGPT use and 74 percent of Gemini/Bard use at work, with 27.4 percent of data inputted into AI tools considered "sensitive".[60] This behavior puts organizations lacking proper oversight measures at serious risk. The risks associated with an organization's reluctance to proactively manage the responsible use of genAI extend beyond what can be fully enumerated here. However, these may include:

- *Unauthorized disclosure of confidential, sensitive business information, or other intellectual property.* The increasing prevalence of shadow IT – employees using unapproved technological solutions to enhance efficiency – has become a significant concern. As noted above, research suggests that large numbers of employees have submitted sensitive or confidential company information into genAI tools, such as ChatGPT. Cyberhaven Labs reported that the "average company leaks confidential material to ChatGPT hundreds of times per week".[61] Cyberhaven analyzed ChatGPT usage for 1.6 million workers across various industries and found thousands of attempts to paste corporate data directly into it. Following an incident at Amazon where genAI output mimicked internal company data, Amazon instituted stringent measures to prevent the unauthorized sharing of internal code with genAI tools.[62] Other organizations have issued similar mandates to reduce the risk of information being shared with genAI tools and their training databases. Companies are facing increasing pressure to establish comprehensive AI governance frameworks.
- *Potential liability for violations of privacy, data protection, and other laws.* Employers may face liability for negligent or intentional acts committed by their employees within the scope of their job duties, particularly when such actions infringe on privacy, data protection, or other legal obligations. This includes scenarios where employers fail to address the misuse of genAI by employees, potentially leading to breaches of privacy or data protection statutes.
- *Inadequate digital safeguards.* Organizations should not fall into the trap of assuming that merely prohibiting genAI technologies ensures their secure use or non-use by employees. This oversight can lead to employees unintentionally sharing confidential or sensitive company information. In 2024, Cisco found that some of the top concerns cited by organizations were that the use of genAI could potentially harm their legal and intellectual property rights (69 percent); that the risk of sensitive information could be shared publicly or with competitors

(68 percent); and the possibility of receiving incorrect information from genAI tools (68 percent).[63] Despite these risks, a significant number of genAI users still input sensitive data, with 62 percent admitting to entering details about internal processes; 48 percent inputting non-public company information; and 45 percent entering employee names or details, underscoring the urgent need for enhanced digital safeguards and risk management strategies in the era of genAI.[64]

- *Reputational risk from data breaches.* The importance of safeguarding client confidentiality cannot be overstated. Clients are (rightly) demanding that organizations protect their confidential information, or they will take their business elsewhere.[65] A data leak has serious consequences, even this occurred unintentionally. The ramifications of a data breach extend far beyond mere operational disruptions, posing a significant threat to a company's reputation. Such incidents, regardless of intent, undermine customer trust and loyalty. Harvey Jang, vice president, deputy general counsel and chief privacy officer at Cisco, articulates the crux of the matter well: "[p]rivacy has become inextricably tied to customer trust and loyalty."[66] This statement highlights the need for companies to ensure adoption of stringent data protection protocols. As genAI technologies become more widespread, the potential for accidental data exposure increases, particularly if employees are not adequately trained. Moreover, even if law firms do not experience a data breach, the reality is clients will increasingly be expecting their lawyers to leverage technology efficiently to better meet their evolving needs.
- *Talent attraction and retention.* The next generation of legal professionals have grown up with technology as an integral part of their lives and expect its adoption in their professional environment. Law firms that ban or significantly restrict genAI or similar technologies will be less attractive to lawyers who place a great value on efficiency and are interested in the significant benefits that AI can provide them. We expect this trend will continue as the use of genAI becomes increasingly common. Daniel Tobey, chair of DLA Piper's AI practice, has succinctly summarized this challenge: "This is an arms race, and you don't want to be the last law firm with these tools ... It's very easy to become a dinosaur these days."[67]
- *Competitive disadvantage.* Law firms that do not embrace genAI will inevitably lag behind other law firms that do so responsibly. John

Villasenor, a professor of electrical engineering, law, public policy, and management at UCLA, proposes this compelling argument: "Law firms that effectively leverage emerging AI technologies will be able to offer services at lower cost, higher efficiency, and with higher odds of favorable outcomes in litigation. Law firms that fail to capitalize on the power of AI will be unable to remain cost competitive, losing clients and undermining their ability to attract and retain talent."[68] His insights highlight the stark reality: organizations that fail to embrace this new technology will fall significantly behind those that do so responsibly. Future requests for proposals (RFPs) are likely to increasingly scrutinize how law firms engage with and leverage new technology, such as AI, to enhance their delivery of legal services. Furthermore, by eliminating genAI from their organization, firms are missing a critical opportunity to monitor, audit, and govern employees' use of the technology. They are also ignoring an important training opportunity to teach their employees how to properly leverage these new tools.[69] This oversight not only diminishes a firm's internal capabilities, but also places it at a tangible disadvantage compared to forward-thinking competitors who recognize and seize the value of training their employees on genAI technologies.

Best practices for lawyers to manage risks relating to genAI

As technology continues to evolve, lawyers must evolve with it. While ChatGPT and other similar genAI technologies are currently new tools, lawyers must always have a foundational understanding of relevant technology, including its limitations and risks, to effectively provide competent legal services.[70] Management of AI-related risks is currently one of the top challenges for businesses.[71]

Lawyers can proactively address these challenges by developing and implementing a set of best practices to encourage the responsible use of genAI. To guide legal professionals in this effort, we have developed an initial top ten list of recommended best practices for leveraging genAI effectively and legal professionals to responsibly in the practice of law.[72]

Prioritize cybersecurity and safety

The 2024 IBM Institute for Business Value report highlights an astounding statistic: 96 percent of executives say that "adopting generative AI makes a security breach likely in their organization within the next three years".[73] In light of this, it is imperative for organizations to take proactive measures to mitigate potential negative impacts from the use of AI technologies, to ensure it is being leveraged in a responsible and compliant manner. Such measures should encompass practices such as implementing systemic audits, using bias detection tools, and continuous monitoring and assessment of the company's technology use. At a minimum, employees should be strictly prohibited from entering private or sensitive information into public AI platforms and be properly trained on the secure use of these tools.[74] Moreover, beyond the establishment of robust security protocols, it is crucial to provide comprehensive education to all stakeholders regarding the advantages, limitations, and possible risks associated with genAI, including the threats posed by social engineering and other sophisticated cyberattacks.[75]

Establish cross-functional teams for continuous collaboration

Assemble a team of cross-functional stakeholders to carefully evaluate the risks and benefits of integrating new technologies into your organization and to continuously monitor it. Ensure team members are from varied backgrounds and span multiple levels of experience, to ensure wide-ranging and diverse perspectives are represented. This is particularly important for effective risk mitigation.[76] Legal professionals specializing in different areas – such as intellectual property, data privacy, and employment law – can provide insights into various aspects of legal risk that might not be apparent to practitioners working in isolation. This comprehensive view allows for the early identification of potential challenges and the development of effective strategies to mitigate these risks before they materialize.[77]

Implement training and education

One of the most critical aspects of successfully integrating genAI into an organization is comprehensive employee education and training. Beyond general awareness, organizations should establish comprehensive training programs and develop educational materials to ensure employees use genAI appropriately and in accordance with their respective policies. This may include measures such as hands-on workshops, online learning platforms, or working with specialized consultants who can tailor programs to the organization's specific needs. At a minimum, employee training should cover the practical applications of AI, and professional and ethical responsibilities. Employee training is also a great opportunity to communicate the company policy on AI to set clear expectations for appropriate use.[78]

Cultivate a responsible AI culture

Senior leadership should actively promote a culture of responsible AI use throughout the organization. It's important to strike a balance that encourages employees to explore and utilize AI technologies, while still maintaining legal compliance. This initiative must originate from the top, with senior leaders committed to open dialogue, critical inquiries, and constructive feedback. Any approach should not only permit but encourage employees to voice questions and concerns without fear of stifling innovation or subjecting them to any negative scrutiny.

Develop confidentiality and privacy policies

Companies should develop comprehensive policies and practices that prioritize the protection of sensitive business information, particularly when engaging with third-party tools. Ensure these policies are flexible and living documents, as AI technology advances rapidly and guidance documentation will need to be able to evolve in line with this. Organizations should include practical items, such as an incident response plan in the event any data are compromised.[79] In addition to formulating these policies, it is equally important to effectively communicate them to all employees. Ensuring that every member of the organization understands the policies, their importance, and their role in maintaining confidentiality is vital for creating a secure information environment. Regular training sessions, updates, and reminders can help keep these policies a priority and reinforce the organization's commitment to protecting client data. Firms should also explore the potential benefits of enterprise solutions, which typically offer a more secure framework for handling sensitive information compared to public or third-party options. These solutions can provide an added layer of security and control, minimizing organizational risk.[80] For additional guidance on crafting and implanting these policies, organizations can look to resources such as the MIT Task Force on Responsible Use of Generative AI for Law. Their published principles and guidelines offer valuable insights regarding the duty of confidentiality, as well as other ethical obligations, in the use of AI applications.[81]

Legal compliance and ethics policies

Work with counsel to establish clear written policies regarding the use of genAI to ensure legal compliance. Some companies have already done so, and have publicly shared their policies and/or guidelines.[82] Several organizations have also developed AI risk management frameworks to assist organizations in proper AI risk management.[83] This is a rapidly evolving field, so it is critical to stay abreast of new laws and developments and continue to update policies accordingly.

Understand the risks, impacts, and limitations

Understand the risks, potential impacts, and technical limitations. This information should be considered when reviewing any output. Users should also understand the genAI provider's terms of service, which should include information regarding how the data collected will be used, including whether they may be included in training for future AI models.[84]

Trust, but always verify

Never rely solely on the information in the genAI output without performing independent verification and due diligence to confirm its accuracy and completeness. In fact, legal professionals have an existing ethical obligation to do so. Attorneys should be aware of the common risks, such as biases or hallucinations, and how those risks may affect the genAI output. Institutions like MIT provide guiding principles and frameworks aimed at reducing the risks associated with AI applications and maintaining human oversight.[85]

Ensure transparency and traceability

Prioritize transparency and traceability. The ABA has urged organizations that design, develop, deploy, or use AI products and services to ensure the transparency and traceability of the products, services, systems, and capabilities. Transparency means ensuring firms understand and can monitor their respective AI systems. Traceability refers to the ability to track and understand the development and deployment of their AI technologies. Leaders should know how AI is being used within their organizations. Similarly, they should be transparent in their use of genAI, such as including disclaimers on blog posts or presentations that were prepared with the assistance of AI, to provide proper attribution.[86]

Appoint an AI leader

Appoint a dedicated individual within the organization as the primary overseer of genAI utilization to manage genAI policies and practices and act as the point of contact for genAI-related questions or challenges. This will help to ensure a unified approach to the management of genAI, as well as provide employees with a clear route to report risks, address challenges, and contribute to the continuous improvement across the organization.

Conclusion

The integration of genAI into legal practice represents both a transformative opportunity and a significant responsibility. As we have explored throughout this chapter, the legal profession stands at a pivotal moment where embracing technological innovation is no longer merely advantageous – it has become an ethical imperative.

Legal professionals who thoughtfully adopt genAI while maintaining rigorous ethical standards will be positioned to deliver superior legal advice and client service, achieve greater efficiency, and maintain their competitive edge. Conversely, those who resist this technological evolution will find themselves at a disadvantage, unable to meet evolving client expectations and professional obligations.

The path forward requires a balanced approach: leveraging genAI's transformative capabilities while implementing robust governance frameworks, appropriate safeguards, and comprehensive training. By following the best practices outlined in this chapter, legal professionals can minimize risks related to confidentiality, accuracy, and bias, while maximizing the benefits that genAI offers. The question is no longer whether legal professionals should embrace genAI, but how to do so responsibly.

References

1 Pierce, N. and Goutos, S., "Why lawyers must responsibly embrace generative AI", *Berkeley Business Law Journal*, 2024, volume 21, issue 2. http://dx.doi.org/10.2139/ssrn.4477704.

2 This chapter was originally researched and drafted in early 2023, with substantive updates incorporated through fall 2024. Due to the exceptionally rapid evolution of artificial intelligence, some details and examples provided herein may inevitably become outdated. Nonetheless, the fundamental concepts and analytical frameworks presented continue to offer valuable guidance and remain applicable as the legal and technological landscapes evolve. Readers should regularly consult current, reputable sources to supplement their understanding and stay informed of ongoing developments.

3 ChatGPT ("GPT" stands for "generative pre-trained transformer") is an AI chatbot developed by OpenAI. It is optimized for dialogue through reinforcement learning with human feedback (RLHF), a technique that refines its responses based on human input and preferences. Users interact with it by submitting various prompts to receive responses. For a detailed timeline of ChatGPT's enhancements and

capabilities, visit OpenAI's blog: https://openai.com/blog. Following ChatGPT's release, numerous companies have launched their own AI solutions, including Google, Anthropic, Meta, and Microsoft.

4 See: Hao, K., "What is ChatGPT? What to know about the AI chatbot", *Wall Street Journal*, 16 May 2023. See: https://www.wsj.com/articles/chatgpt-ai-chatbot-app-explained11675865177?mod=Searchresults_pos1&page=1.

5 Pierce, N. and Goutos, S., "Why lawyers must responsibly embrace generative AI", *Berkeley Business Law Journal*, 2024, volume 21, issue 2. http://dx.doi.org/10.2139/ssrn.4477704.

6 *Ibid.*

7 American Bar Association, "Model Rules of Professional Conduct", 2025. See: www.americanbar.org/groups/professional_responsibility/publications/model_rules_of_professional_conduct/model_rules_of_professional_conduct_table_of_contents/. Additionally, see: Pierce, N. and Goutos, S., "Why lawyers must responsibly embrace generative AI", *Berkeley Business Law Journal*, 2024, volume 21, issue 2. http://dx.doi.org/10.2139/ssrn.4477704.

8 Suarez, C.A., "Disruptive legal tech, COVID-19, and resilience in the profession", *South Carolina Law Review*, 2020, volume 72, issue 2, PP. 417–418. https://scholarcommons.sc.edu/sclr/vol72/iss2/6, citing Burger, W.E., "The special skills of advocacy: are specialized training and certification of advocates essential to our system of justice?", Fordham Law Review, 1973, volume 42, issue 2, pp. 227–242. http://ir.lawnet.fordham.edu/flr/vol42/iss2/1 (internal quotation marks omitted).

9 As an example, see: *Wadsworth v. Walmart Inc.* (2025), United States District Court, D. Wyoming, case no. 2:23-CV-118-KHR (highlighting that, notwithstanding technological advancements, attorneys retain an ongoing ethical obligation to verify sources and conduct reasonable inquiries into current law.)

10 Pierce, N. and Goutos, S., "Why lawyers must responsibly embrace generative AI", *Berkeley Business Law Journal*, 2024, volume 21, issue 2. http://dx.doi.org/10.2139/ssrn.4477704.

11 American Bar Association, "Model Rules of Professional Conduct", 2025. See: www.americanbar.org/groups/professional_responsibility/publications/model_rules_of_professional_conduct/model_rules_of_professional_conduct_table_of_contents/.

12 Merken, S., "New York lawyers sanctioned for using fake ChatGPT cases in legal brief", Reuters, 22 June 2023. See: www.reuters.com/legal/new-york-lawyers-sanctioned-using-fake-chatgpt-cases-legal-brief-2023-06-22/. District Judge P. Kevin Castel ordered lawyers Steven Schwartz, Peter LoDuca and their law firm Levidow, Levidow & Oberman to pay a $5,000 fine for submitting a legal brief that included six fictitious case citations generated by an AI chatbot.

13 Johnson, L.D., "Navigating technology competence in transactional practice", *Villanova Law Review*, 2020, volume 65, issue 1, pp. 159–189. https://digitalcommons.law.villanova.edu/vlr/vol65/iss1/3?utm_source=digitalcommons.law.villanova.edu%2Fvlr%2Fvol65%2Fiss1%2F3&utm_medium=PDF&utm_

campaign=PDFCoverPages (noting the process for amending the Model Rules included a comment period, public hearings, and other methods for obtaining feedback on the proposed resolutions from diverse segments of the bench, bar, and academy). Additionally, see: American Bar Association, "ABA Commission on Ethics 20/20: Introduction and Overview", 2012. See: https://perma.cc/M3MZ-YRJN.

14 American Bar Association, "ABA Commission on Ethics 20/20: Introduction and Overview", 2012. See: https://perma.cc/M3MZ-YRJN.

15 *Ibid.*

16 *Ibid.*

17 Maute, J.L., "Facing 21st century realities", *Mississippi College Law Review*, 2014, volume 32, issue 2. https://dc.law.mc.edu/lawreview/vol32/iss2/8: "Deliberate ignorance of technology is inexcusable ... If a lawyer cannot master the technology suitable for that lawyer's practice, the lawyer should either hire tech-savvy lawyers tasked with responsibility to keep current, or hire an outside technology consultant who understands the practice of law and associated ethical constraints."

18 American Bar Association, *The ABA Model Rules of Professional Conduct*, Chicago [IL]: American Bar Association, Center for Professional Responsibility Model Rules; 1983 and American Bar Association, "ABA Commission on Ethics 20/20: Introduction and Overview", 2012. See: https://perma.cc/M3MZ-YRJN (stating: "The Commission believes that it is important to make explicit that a lawyer's duty of competence, which requires the lawyer to stay abreast of changes in the law and its practice, includes understanding relevant technology's benefits and risks. Comment [6] of Model Rule 1.1 (Competence) implicitly encompasses that obligation, but it is important to make this duty explicit because technology is such an integral – and yet at times invisible – aspect of contemporary law practice. The phrase "including the benefits and risks associated with relevant technology" would offer greater clarity regarding this duty and emphasize the growing importance of technology to modern law practice.").

19 American Bar Association, "ABA Commission on Ethics 20/20: Introduction and Overview", 2012. See: https://perma.cc/M3MZ-YRJN. Additionally, see: Yamane, N., "Artificial intelligence in the legal field and the indispensable human element legal ethics demands", *Georgetown Journal of Legal Ethics*, 2020, volume 33, issue 877, pp. 884–885. https://www.law.georgetown.edu/legal-ethics-journal/wp-content/uploads/sites/24/2020/09/GT-GJLE200038.pdf ("Reading the Model Rules in modern times indicates that, in order for lawyers to provide competent legal representation to clients, they must have a basic understanding of how the AI programs they use operate and not automatically accept the results the AI program produces as true.") and American Bar Association, "ABA Resolutions: Resolution 112", 2025. See: https://www.americanbar.org/groups/judicial/resources/resolutions/ (stating that, under Rule 1.1, "lawyers also must have a basic understanding of how AI tools operate").

20 The Chief Reporter of the Commission wisely recognized "the specific skills lawyers will need in the decades ahead are difficult to imagine" and further concluded the

duty of technological competence is "far broader than simply protecting client information or cyber security". See: Baker, J.J., "Beyond the information age: the duty of tech competence in the algorithmic society", *South Carolina Law Review*, 2018, volume 69, issue 3, pp. 557–577. https://ssrn.com/abstract=3097250.

21 Dryer, R.L., "Litigation, tech. & ethics: teaching old dogs new tricks or legal Luddites are no longer welcome in Utah", *Utah Bar Journal*, 2015, volume 28, issue 3, pp. 1–9. https://law-journals-books.vlex.com/vid/vol-28-vol-28-937359727 (stating: "Our clients are increasingly technologically competent, and the newly adopted comment requires us to be likewise", recognizing today's lawyers must become "... conversant with a new lexicon – filtering, deduplication, machine learning, predictive coding, metadata, and seed sets – and adept at utilizing the related technologies or associating with someone who does").

22 Many states follow the ABA's approach, with some adopting Rule 1.1 verbatim. Other states provide additional guidance or requirements. For instance, in 2015, the State Bar of California issued an influential opinion stating that a lawyer is "not competent to handle complex cases involving ESI without sufficient understanding of the technical skills, knowledge, and aptitude required to conduct e-discovery" (California State Bar, "Standing Committee on Professional Responsibility and Conduct: Opinion 2015-193", 30 June 2015. See: https://www.google.com/url?sa=t&source=web&rct=j&opi=89978449&url=https://www.calbar.ca.gov/Portals/0/documents/ethics/Opinions/CAL%25202015-193%2520%255B11-0004%255D%2520(06-30-15)%2520-%2520FINAL.pdf&ved=2ahUKEwicq_rWmP2MAxXz8wIHHQyCIUgQFnoECBkQAQ&usg=AOvVaw2qyCTXg2NV3AFmfue_FSm0). Additionally, see: Redgrave, B.M. and Zolner, E.B., "Litigation, Technology, and Ethics: The Importance of Technological Competence", Redgrave LLP, 5 January 2022. See: www.redgravellp.com/litigation-technology-and-ethics-importance-technological-competence.

23 Johnson, L.D., "Navigating technology competence in transactional practice", *Villanova Law Review*, 2020, volume 65, issue 1, pp. 159–189. https://digitalcommons.law.villanova.edu/vlr/vol65/iss1/3?utm_source=digitalcommons.law.villanova.edu%2Fvlr%2Fvol65%2Fiss1%2F3&utm_medium=PDF&utm_campaign=PDFCoverPages and Ambrogi, B., "The Decade in Legal Tech: The 10 Most Significant Developments", LawSites, 2 June 2023. See: www.lawnext.com/2020/01/the-decade-in-legal-tech-the-10-most-significant-developments.html.

24 Commission on The Future of Legal Services, "Report on the Future of Legal Services in the U.S.", American Bar Association, 2016. See: www.srln.org/system/files/attachments/2016 percent20ABA percent20Future percent20of percent20Legal percent20Services percent20-Report-Web.pdf (noting "the Florida Bar Board of Governors, for example, has approved a mandatory technology-based continuing legal education requirement") and Cyphert, A., "A human being wrote this law review article: GPT-3 and the practice of law", *UC Davis Law Review*, 2021, volume 55, issue 1. See: https://ssrn.com/abstract=3973961

(noting West Virginia adopted the new Comment 8 to Model Rule 1.1 and further changed the language from "a lawyer should keep abreast" to "a lawyer must keep abreast" of changes to the practice of law, which includes the benefits and risks associated with relevant technology (authors' emphasis)).

25 *Ibid.*

26 Pierce, N. and Goutos, S., "Why lawyers must responsibly embrace generative AI", *Berkeley Business Law Journal*, 2024, volume 21, issue 2. http://dx.doi.org/10.2139/ssrn.4477704.

27 Marathe, I., "Judges, attorneys react to federal court generative AI order: too hot, too cold, or just right?", *Legaltech News*, 1 June 2023. See: https://www.law.com/legaltechnews/2023/06/01/judges-attorneys-react-to-federal-court-generative-ai-order-too-hot-too-cold-or-just-right/ (citing the now infamous example of a New York attorney who filed a legal brief that included cases fabricated by ChatGPT and was ultimately sanctioned by the court).

28 Margolis, E., "Surfin' safari – why competent lawyers should research on the web", *Yale Journal of Law & Technology*, 2007, volume 10. See: https://ssrn.com/abstract=1017022 ("There is little doubt that the internet has become a major tool in a legal researcher's arsenal in the last two decades ... it can safely be said that research via the internet is a standard technique used by a majority of lawyers in a majority of jurisdictions throughout the country.").

29 *Ibid* ("... [i]t would be extremely difficult, if not impossible, to provide today's judges with what they need ... without using the internet as part of the research process. A lawyer who fails to research on the web will not find all of the relevant sources and will likely fall below the standard of competence by any measure.").

30 *Ibid.*

31 *Ibid* (citing, for example, "... [c]ounsel is admonished that diligent research, which includes Shepardizing cases, is a professional responsibility" and "[i]t is really inexcusable for any lawyer to fail ... to Shepardize all cited cases".) Additionally, see: Redgrave, B.M. and Zolner, E.B., "Litigation, Technology, and Ethics: The Importance of Technological Competence", Redgrave LLP, 5 January 2022. See: www.redgravellp.com/litigation-technology-and-ethics-importance-technological-competence (highlighting trends in recent case law demonstrating that courts are willing to impose severe sanctions for deficiencies in technological competence).

32 See, for example: Harvard Law School Center on The Legal Profession, "Ethical Prompts: professionalism, ethics, and ChatGPT", *The Practice*, 2023, March/April. See: https://clp.law.harvard.edu/knowledge-hub/magazine/issues/generative-ai-in-the-legalprofession/ethical-prompts/ (noting that lawyers must adapt and properly use new technology tools, which are not a substitute for critical legal thinking and need to be integrated in conjunction with human oversight) and Formal Opinion 483 (17 October 2018) (American Bar Association, "ABA Formal Ethics Opinions Archive by Issue Dates", 2025. See: https://www.americanbar.org/groups/professional_responsibility/publications/ethics_opinions/aba_formal_ethics_opinions_index_by_issue_dates/), which describes counsel's duty to monitor for and respond to data breaches..

33 *James v. Nat'l Fin.* LLC, 2014 Del Ch. Lexis 254 *36 (Del. Ch., Dec. 5, 2014).

34 *Ibid.*

35 *Disciplinary Couns. v. Valenti*, 165 Ohio St. 3d 49, 51, 21 April 2021 (finding that the Supreme Court of Ohio agreed with the Board of Professional Conduct's conclusion that counsel was not "sufficiently technologically competent" in her representation and imposing a 6-month suspension on her license to practice law; this suspension was stayed on the condition that she partake in technology training, among other requirements).

36 For example, the lawyer's duty of competence extends to understanding the technology used, including its limitations and potential for biased outputs. In tandem with this, the duty to supervise non-lawyer assistance, such as technology-generated content, requires lawyers to not automatically accept such content as reliable. Instead, they should engage in a careful review process to ensure accuracy and reliability before sharing with others, including clients and courts. Lawyers must also be vigilant about the potential for biased language in these tools. See: Pierce, N. and Goutos, S., "Why lawyers must responsibly embrace generative AI", *Berkeley Business Law Journal*, 2024, volume 21, issue 2. http://dx.doi.org/10.2139/ssrn.4477704.

37 American Bar Association, *The ABA Model Rules of Professional Conduct*, Chicago [IL]: American Bar Association, Center for Professional Responsibility Model Rules; 1983 (Model Rules 5.1 and 5.3 impose certain supervision requirements on lawyers to ensure subordinates and third parties are in compliance with ethical rules).

38 Henry, L., "The Intersection of AI and the Model Rules of Professional Conduct", JD Supra, 5 February 2019. See: https://www.jdsupra.com/legalnews/the-intersection-of-artificial-87577/.

39 Pierce, N. and Goutos, S., "Why lawyers must responsibly embrace generative AI", *Berkeley Business Law Journal*, 2024, volume 21, issue 2. http://dx.doi.org/10.2139/ssrn.4477704.

40 Yamane, N., "Artificial intelligence in the legal field and the indispensable human element legal ethics demands", *Georgetown Journal of Legal Ethics*, 2020, volume 33, issue 877, pp. 884–885. https://www.law.georgetown.edu/legal-ethics-journal/wp-content/uploads/sites/24/2020/09/GT-GJLE200038.pdf (concluding that, under Rule 5.3, AI could be considered a "non-lawyer" that is being delegated work by the lawyer, trigging the lawyer's duty to ensure that the work product produced by the AI program is competent). Additionally, see: American Bar Association House of Delegates, "Resolution 112: Adopted August 12–13, 2019", American Bar Association, 12–13 August 2019. See: https://www.americanbar.org/content/dam/aba/directories/policy/annual-2019/112-annual-2019.pdf (directly stating that lawyers must oversee the AI tools used in legal services in order to meet their ethical standards).

41 Pierce, N. and Goutos, S., "Why lawyers must responsibly embrace generative AI", *Berkeley Business Law Journal*, 2024, volume 21, issue 2. http://dx.doi.org/10.2139/ssrn.4477704.

42 American Bar Association House of Delegates, "Resolution 112: Adopted August 12–13, 2019", American Bar Association, 12–13 August 2019. See: https://www.americanbar.org/content/dam/aba/directories/policy/annual-2019/112-annual-2019.pdf (stating that it is easy to see why "the greater danger might very well be the underutilization of, rather than overreliance upon, artificial intelligence".).

43 *Ibid.*

44 Cassens Weiss, D., "No. 42 law firm by head count sanctioned over fake case citations generated by AI", *ABAJournal*, 10 February 2025. See: https://www.abajournal.com/news/article/no-42-law-firm-by-headcount-could-face-sanctions-over-fake-case-citations-generated-by-chatgpt

45 *Wadsworth v. Walmart Inc.* (2025), United States District Court, D. Wyoming, case no. 2:23-CV-118-KHR.

46 *Ibid.*

47 American Bar Association House of Delegates, "Resolution 112: Adopted August 12–13, 2019", American Bar Association, 12–13 August 2019. See: https://www.americanbar.org/content/dam/aba/directories/policy/annual-2019/112-annual-2019.pdf (stating that it is easy to see why "the greater danger might very well be the underutilization of, rather than overreliance upon, artificial intelligence.").

48 *Ibid* (recognizing the adoption of Model Rule 8.4(g), as well as the requirement that lawyers consider how bias in the use of AI "could create risks for clients").

49 *Ibid* ("The end result is that lawyers using AI are better counselors for their clients. In the next few years, the use of AI by lawyers will be no different than the use of email by lawyers – an indispensable part of the practice of law.").

50 Reeves, J., "ABA Adopts Guidelines for AI Usage", Lawyers Mutual, 9 May 2023. See: https://www.lawyersmutualnc.com/blog/aba-adopts-guidelines-for-ai-usage (emphasizing that AI systems should remain under human control and oversight; individuals should be held accountable for the consequences of use of AI products and services; and developers should ensure the transparency and traceability of their AI products and services).

51 Pierce, N. and Goutos, S., "Why lawyers must responsibly embrace generative AI", *Berkeley Business Law Journal*, 2024, volume 21, issue 2. http://dx.doi.org/10.2139/ssrn.4477704.

52 See, for example: Eliot, L.B., "Is generative ai such as ChatGPT going to undermine the famed attorney-client privilege, frets AI law and AI ethics", *Forbes*, 30 March 2023. See: https://www.forbes.com/sites/lanceeliot/2023/03/30/is-generative-ai-such-as-chatgpt-going-to-undermine-the-famed-attorney-client-privilege-frets-ai-law-and-ai-ethics/; Deloitte AI Institute, "proactive risk management in Generative AI", Deloitte, 2023. See: https://www2.deloitte.com/content/dam/Deloitte/us/Documents/deloitte-analytics/us-ai-institute-responsible-use-of-generative-ai.pdf; and National Institute of Standards and Technology, "AI Risk Management Framework (AI RMF 1.0)", January 2023. See: https://nvlpubs.nist.gov/nistpubs/ai/NIST.AI.100-1.pdf.

53 See: Nelson, S.D., Simek, J.W., and Maschke, M.C., "Lawyers breathe a sigh of relief: they can turn off chat history for ChatGPT", *Above The Law*, 2 May 2023. See: https://abovethelaw.com/2023/05/lawyers-breathe-a-sigh-of-relief-they-can-turn-off-chat-history-for-chatgpt/; OpenAI, "New ways to manage your data in ChatGPT", 25 April 2023. See: https://openai.com/blog/new-ways-to-manage-your-data-in-chatgpt; and Open AI, "Introducing ChatGPT Enterprise", 28 August 2023. See: https://openai.com/blog/introducing-chatgpt-enterprise (announcing the launch of ChatGPT Enterprise, which offers enterprise-grade security and privacy, unlimited higher-speed GPT-4 access, longer context windows for processing longer inputs, advanced data analysis capabilities, customization options, and more).

54 See, for example, Microsoft's Azure OpenAI Service: https://azure.microsoft.com/en-us/products/ai-services/openai-service.

55 Pierce, N. and Goutos, S., "Why lawyers must responsibly embrace generative AI", *Berkeley Business Law Journal*, 2024, volume 21, issue 2. http://dx.doi.org/10.2139/ssrn.4477704.

56 Wolfe, O. and Salcedo, E., "With AI use, lawyers need to ponder confidentiality stipulations", *Bloomberg Law*, 1 July 2024. See: https://news.bloomberglaw.com/us-law-week/with-ai-use-lawyers-need-to-ponder-confidentiality-stipulations.

57 Pierce, N. and Goutos, S., "Why lawyers must responsibly embrace generative AI", *Berkeley Business Law Journal*, 2024, volume 21, issue 2. http://dx.doi.org/10.2139/ssrn.4477704.

58 Nelson, S.D., "Why Shadow AI is a Problem for Law Firms", ALPS Insurance, 22 November 2023. See: https://www.alpsinsurance.com/blog/why-shadow-ai-is-a-problem-for-law-firms#:~:text=often percent20unknown percent20to percent20a percent20law,the percent20use percent20of percent20Shadow percent20AI.

59 Pierce, N. and Goutos, S., "Why lawyers must responsibly embrace generative AI", *Berkeley Business Law Journal*, 2024, volume 21, issue 2. http://dx.doi.org/10.2139/ssrn.4477704.

60 Arad, D., "Shadow AI Is Here, And It's Hungry for Your Company Data", Workvivo, 27 February 2025. See: https://www.workvivo.com/blog/shadow-ai-is-here/ (citing Coles, C., "Shadow AI: how employees are leading the charge in AI adoption and putting company data at risk", Cyberhaven, 21 May 2024. See: https://www.cyberhaven.com/blog/shadow-ai-how-employees-are-leading-the-charge-in-ai-adoption-and-putting-company-data-at-risk).

61 Cameron, C., "11 percent of data employees paste into ChatGPT is confidential", Cyberhaven, 28 February 2023. See: https://www.cyberhaven.com/blog/4-2-of-workers-have-pasted-company-data-into-chatgpt (reporting that 11 percent of the data employees paste into ChatGPT is confidential in nature and that the average company leaks confidential material to ChatGPT "hundreds of times per week").

62 Hurler, K., "Amazon warns employees to beware of ChatGPT", Gizmodo, 26 January 2023. See: https://gizmodo.com/amazon-chatgpt-ai-software-job-coding-1850034383.

63 Cisco, "Privacy as an Enabler of Customer Trust: Cisco 2024 Privacy Benchmark Study", 2024. See: https://www.cisco.com/c/dam/en_us/about/doing_business/trust-center/docs/cisco-privacy-benchmarkstudy-2024.pdf?CCID=cc000160&DTID=odicdc000016&OID=rptsc032067 (noting that genAI puts AI in the hands of many more users and describing the impacts of this).

64 *Ibid* ("[m]ost organizations have become aware of these risks, with many working to put in place controls that would limit their exposure").

65 Lieberman, M., "Mind the trust gap: how companies can retain customers after a security breach", Forbes, 8 December 2017. See: https://www.forbes.com/sites/forbestechcouncil/2017/12/08/mind-the-trust-gap-how-companies-can-retain-customers-after-a-security-breach/ (noting that only 25 percent of consumers believe companies handle their personal information responsibly and "87 percent will take their business to a competitor if they don't trust a company to handle their data responsibly").

66 Cisco, "Privacy as an Enabler of Customer Trust: Cisco 2024 Privacy Benchmark Study", 2024. See: https://www.cisco.com/c/dam/en_us/about/doing_business/trust-center/docs/cisco-privacy-benchmarkstudy-2024.pdf?CCID=cc000160&DTID=odicdc000016&OID=rptsc032067

67 Merken, S., "Legal AI race draws more investors as law firms line up", Reuters, 26 April 2023. See: https://www.reuters.com/legal/legal-ai-race-draws-more-investors-law-firms-line-up-2023-04-26/.

68 American Bar Association's Center for Innovation's Innovation Trends Report Committee, "Midterm Innovation Trends Report 2023", American Bar Association, 2023. See: https://www.americanbar.org/content/dam/aba/administrative/center-for-innovation/aba-cfi-innovation-trends-report2023.pdf (noting that clients are demanding more efficient and cost-effective legal work, which is a key driver behind lawyers more readily embracing technology).

69 Hiter, S, "Risks of Generative AI: 6 Risk Management Tips", *eWeek*, 15 August 2023. See: https://www.eweek.com/artificial-intelligence/generative-ai-risks/ (noting that it is important to train all employees on the organization's AI policy as a foundation, and then further explain how it applies in practice to respective roles, departments, and use cases. Employees who work with sensitive data and applications should receive "more detailed and frequent training").

70 *Ibid* ('[w]hile technology continues to evolve, one thing remains the same – checking and verifying the source").

71 Wharry, M., "Public's unease with AI is creating another hurdle for adoption", *New York Law Journal*, 2023, volume 270, issue 59. See: https://www.gunder.com/a/web/qvteL4Z1Xkum13ZJTzJ334/8VBEvz/public_s-unease-with-ai-is-creating-another-hurdle-for.pdf.

72 The following compilation of best practices is not intended to serve as an exhaustive or universal directive. Rather, it functions as an initial framework for law firms to begin to strategize about their respective genAI practices. We recognize that this

field is characterized by rapid technological developments and shifting legal landscapes. Therefore, while we made every effort to provide accurate and up-to-date information at the time of publication, we anticipate the parameters for best practices will continue to evolve over time in response to new advancements and legal precedents. Further, the utility of these initial best practices is not uniform across all market segments. Variances in jurisdictional regulations, client expectations, and firm specialties necessitate a customized application of these respective guidelines. For additional examples and use cases, see: Pierce, N. and Goutos, S., "Why lawyers must responsibly embrace generative AI", *Berkeley Business Law Journal*, 2024, volume 21, issue 2. http://dx.doi.org/10.2139/ssrn.4477704.

73 IBM Institute for Business Value, "Generative AI amplifies risk – and resilience", 2025. See: https://www.ibm.com/thought-leadership/institute-business-value/en-us/report/ceo-generative-ai/cybersecurity.

74 Pierce, N. and Goutos, S., "Why lawyers must responsibly embrace generative AI", *Berkeley Business Law Journal*, 2024, volume 21, issue 2. http://dx.doi.org/10.2139/ssrn.4477704.

75 IBM Security, "Cost of a Data Breach Report 2023", IBM, 2023. See: https://d110erj175o600.cloudfront.net/wp-content/uploads/2023/07/25111651/Cost-of-a-Data-Breach-Report-2023.pdf.

76 Pierce, N. and Goutos, S., "Why lawyers must responsibly embrace generative AI", *Berkeley Business Law Journal*, 2024, volume 21, issue 2. http://dx.doi.org/10.2139/ssrn.4477704.

77 IBM, "AI Alliance Launches as an International Community of Leading Technology Developers, Researchers, and Adopters Collaborating Together to Advance Open, Safe, Responsible AI", 5 December 2023. See: https://newsroom.ibm.com/AI-Alliance-Launches-as-an-International-Community-of-Leading-Technology-Developers,-Researchers,-and-Adopters-Collaborating-Together-to-Advance-Open,-Safe,-Responsible-AI (describing the launch of an AI Alliance and the numerous benefits it will provide).

78 Bonime-Blanc, B., Essenmacher, E., Anzele, M., et al, "AI Governance Playbook: A Sustainable Framework for Empowering Leadership in the Age of Exponential Technology", Athena Alliance, 2024. https://athenaalliance.com/ai-governance-playbook/ (which recommends that organizations should adopt a learner's mindset by engaging in foundational and continuous AI education).

79 Lemos, R., "Employees are feeding sensitive biz data to ChatGPT, raising security fears", *Dark Reading*, 7 March 2023. See: https://www.darkreading.com/cyber-risk/employees-feeding-sensitive-business-data-chatgpt-raising-security-fears (… "[i]n one case, an executive cut and pasted the firm's 2023 strategy document into ChatGPT and asked it to create a PowerPoint deck. In another case, a doctor input his patient's name and their medical condition and asked ChatGPT to craft a letter to the patient's insurance company.").

80 Felz, D., Nauwelaerts, W., Greaves, P., and Fox, J., "ChatGPT & Generative AI: Everything You Need to Know, Part 2", Law.com, 1 March 2024. See:

https://www.lawjournalnewsletters.com/2023/05/01/chatgpt-generative-ai-everything-you-needto-know-part-2/ ("[a]s an example, Microsoft has announced it is offering an 'Azure OpenAI Service' that grants enterprise customers access to OpenAI's suite of generative AI tools (ChatGPT, Codex, and DALL-E) within an Azure environment. Enterprise solutions are more likely to memorialize confidentiality, privacy, security, and IP terms responsive to needs of enterprise customers in an enterprise-level agreement.").

81 Greenwood, D., "Task force on responsible use of generative AI for law", *MIT Computational Law Report*, 28 February 2023. See: https://law.mit.edu/pub/generative-ai-responsible-use-for-law/release/9.

82 *Ibid* (noting that Microsoft published a "Code of Conduct" for its Azure OpenAI Service). Additionally, see: Ironclad, "Generative Artificial Intelligence Policy", 24 April 2023). See: https://explore.ironcladhq.com/rs/528-QBH-821/images/Generative-Artificial-Intelligence-Policy.pdf.

83 National Institute of Standards and Technology, "AI Risk Management Framework (AI RMF 1.0)", January 2023. See: https://nvlpubs.nist.gov/nistpubs/ai/NIST.AI.100-1.pdf.

84 Pierce, N. and Goutos, S., "Why lawyers must responsibly embrace generative AI", *Berkeley Business Law Journal*, 2024, volume 21, issue 2. http://dx.doi.org/10.2139/ssrn.4477704.

85 Greenwood, D., "Task force on responsible use of generative AI for law", *MIT Computational Law Report*, 28 February 2023. See: https://law.mit.edu/pub/generative-ai-responsible-use-for-law/release/9 and Chiruvolu, C., "Security and Best Practices for Lawyers Using Generative Artificial Intelligence and Large Language Models", American Bar Association, 26 February 2024. See: https://www.americanbar.org/groups/gpsolo/resources/ereport/2024-february/security-best-practices-lawyers-using-generative-artificial-intelligence-large-language-models/.

86 Pierce, N. and Goutos, S., "Why lawyers must responsibly embrace generative AI", *Berkeley Business Law Journal*, 2024, volume 21, issue 2. http://dx.doi.org/10.2139/ssrn.4477704.

Chapter 4:
The data drain: navigating copyright challenges in the era of AI

By Joanne Brook, consultant solicitor (intellectual property and technology law), Lionshead Law

AI training data: who owns the engine, and who owns the oil?

In 2016, Professor Gary King of Harvard University suggested that: "Big Data is not about the data"[1] – how prescient this was. He observed that data are largely free-to-use byproducts of the digital economy; whilst the scale of Big Data is exponential, the key component is, according to Professor King, the new applications that use it. Enter AI, with the promise of human-like intelligence and its infinitely superior problem-solving capabilities. The notion of the thinking machine and its genesis is addressed in Chapter 1 of this book; in this chapter, we are primarily concerned with the ownership of input and output data. Big data was a necessary step for the development of AI, because AI needs to be trained and to learn; to do that, it needs to be fed data, lots of data, constantly.

All the data on business and personal websites, news services, public information sites, academic and scholarly databases, maps, patent records, search engines, and innumerable other sources have been added to the data scrapings and the project to digitize our world so that everything is searchable. As Jimmy Wales' vision to create "a world in which every single person on the planet is given free access to the sum of all human knowledge" is realized,[2] our world has been overtaken by programs that collate the "sum of all human knowledge" for us when we ask (and – sometimes – even when we don't). The vast repositories of human interaction and artistic expression that we created with self-congratulatory glee and uploaded to the frontend have been scraped from the program backend, like cleaning plates with a sluice tap at the back of a burger joint. That wash-down data form vast data lakes; the detritus of our combined online activity is fossilized in these data lakes and become the fuel to power the AI engine.

The largest and most pervasive AI programs that allow users to 'create' and 'discover' output in the form of text, video, images, and code are almost all proprietary. Whilst free open-source software exists to build AI enabled tools ("AI code generators") or answer questions and produce output material for smaller projects, their capabilities are more limited, as you would expect from a service that is free to use. Despite the hype, it costs a vast amount of money to create new tech and keep it running. In December 2015, when OpenAI was formed, it was launched on a funding pledge of $1bn. Almost 10 years on, several funding rounds later and with operating losses of almost $5bn, OpenAI announced a further funding bump of $40bn on a $300bn ($300,000,000,000) post-money valuation in March 2025. Last year, CEO of the smaller AI giant Anthropic predicted in an interview with *Time*[3] that developing the next generation of AI it will release will be $1bn. The vast expense of creating and maintaining AI comes with a huge financial and environmental cost,[4] triggering an AI arms race that is the antithesis of Moore's law,[5] in which processing power and costs double every nine months.[6]

All of the images and the language output of every key stroke across each social media platform and the internet at large for the last 15 years have been scraped to train AI programs by tech companies, whose terms told users that the company, as the provider of the service, owned all the content they uploaded. Those businesses encouraged users to scroll straight to the bottom of the page and to click "Accept" if they wanted to use the service – no negotiation, no middle ground, no opting out from transfer of rights. Having put their algorithmic arms around the information uploaded, these companies did not say what they would do with it. Most users thought that using the internet and associated services were free, but the currency was our personal information and the fuel was data.

The all-powerful AI that gives us an instantaneous answer is the combined knowledge from billions bytes of data, crunched by software in relational matrices, sorted into patterns and predictions, and doled out to us as creative content in response to a prompt. These AI technologies were trained, refined, honed, and oiled with that data that we users handed over to the AI businesses and their progenitors – for free. We paid to create the services that we now use (mostly without realizing we were doing so) by giving up our data input and output in a constant feedback loop to feed the AI engine. The engine of AI is owned by the vastly rich companies who built the programs, and (by giving them our data), so is the oil that feeds it.

Claiming back copyright

The process of training AI has doubtlessly compromised the rights of the owners of the works used to train it.

Within the first year of OpenAI launching, lawsuits were issued against it for copyright infringement by comedians and authors for use of their jokes and books in training data (dubbed "systematic [copyright] theft on a mass scale" in the claim).[7] A widely publicized claim by the *New York Times* followed with a suit issued against OpenAI for "unlawful use" of copyrighted news articles, investigations, opinion pieces, reviews, guides, and more[8] to create AI products. At the same time, StabilityAI was sued by Getty Images for use of "millions" of images from its collection, along with metadata and captions, "to build a competing business".[9] The oil-producers began to fight back and reclaim their copyright in the works they had originally made available online for free or for payment. These cases quickly brought to the fore that, whilst data may have been assigned to platform owners and made available on the web, the use they were put to was not permissioned; furthermore, even if it was, the consent was not open and informed. Some AI companies know where their training data originate, and others do not. It is also apparent that, historically, many AI companies have given little regard for the rights of original owners and have kept few records of their training sources.

In 2023, *The Washington Post* and researchers from the Allen Institute for AI analyzed where AI training data originate,[10] which was found to be almost every online entry point. They began with Google's C4 dataset of 15 million websites, used to train some of the largest AI models. Business websites were the largest category of source information: original work, research findings, ideas, confidential information, and paid creative content fell under this category, meaning that work that is proprietary and could be confidential (which might even be protected by intellectual property rights) is being used to train AI programs to create output. Content located behind a paywall is as likely to be scraped as free data; whilst social media platforms like Facebook and X prohibit data-scraping by third parties, this is not to say that they do not scrape data from users on their own platforms to train their own AI. These research findings make interesting reading, particularly when we realize that almost every one of the owners of data used for training will not have given specific and informed consent for this activity. The scale is staggering, and the potential for claims is vast.

The UK Information Commissioner's Office has expressed its belief that "legitimate interests [are] the sole basis for training generative AI models using web-scraped personal data based on current practices".[11] Meta adopted the stance that its utilization of users' data was legitimate, claiming that the only legitimate way to train AI is on data, and the desire for and use of AI makes the training work lawful. This approach saw the EU and Irish data protection authorities raise concerns and ultimately led to the European Data Protection Board giving an opinion on the use of personal data for the development and deployment of AI models,[12] outlining its view in regard to "whether and how legitimate interest can be used as a legal basis for developing or using AI models". US courts have dismissed responses by AI businesses that their technology is similar to the video recording devices of the past, in that they merely provide the means to facilitate copying but do not encourage or undertake it. In *Andersen v. Stability AI Ltd.*, the court noted that the AI "is built to a significant extent on copyrighted works and [that] the way the product operates necessarily invokes copies or protected elements of those works".[13] More recently, in *Thomson Reuters v. Ross Intelligence*,[14] the court also found that data scraping did not fall under the "fair use" copyright exception either, determining that proprietary materials cannot be used as training data without permission.

If this is the stance judges consistently take, copyright infringement claims copyright infringement claims will have a sunrise period, and the cost and complexity of settling historic infringements will impact the speed of AI development. For this reason, AI businesses have already fought back, making strategic alliances with owners of large datasets, back-dating permissions, and establishing business terms of use that proclaim their processing of data is "legitimate" (i.e., falling within Article 6.1(f) of GDPR as having a legitimate interest for processing which is necessary and balanced against the data subjects' rights), effectively stating that – if you use the service – you must give up your data to train the tech.

The other side of the coin is the risk to users of adopting output from AI that is not as original as they believe, or which is a straight copy from the dataset used to train it. This creates a risk of copyright claims for downstream users who need to have sufficient warranties and an indemnity to rely on in the event of a claim. Currently, AI platforms warrant *their* technology does not infringe third-party intellectual property rights, but – understandably – do not warrant that the output is non-infringing. In practice, I have seen an increase in queries about where the data used to train models come from, as the issue of past infringement has gained prominence.

It used to be asked only in occasional email exchanges between chief technology officers, but now the standard tickbox confirming "Is your training data permissioned?" demonstrates that the question has moved from one of technical interest to inherency, where one click reduces a piece of complex software to a yes/no proposition, in which "Yes" means it can be used and "No" means the risk of claim is too great and cannot be justified.

The courts are – as is so often the case – playing catch-up with the technology they are asked to make determinations about, but judges appear less challenged in identifying how the different elements of copyright ownership are infringed by the different use cases and practical applications of generative AI. Wider legal questions will emerge as to whether:

- Both intent and knowledge can apply to data output created in a black box environment; a work created by AI is a derivative work;[15]
- The work created has "identicality" with the original copyright work (in the US);
- The original work been transformed by the AI program to the extent that the characteristics of originality have been abstracted altogether by the data scrape;
- The doctrine of fair use in copyright can be extended so that data scraping falls within criticism, review or quotation; and
- Scraping datasets can be deemed legitimate under data protection legislation.

In each case, it seems the facts will lead the determination, and judges will make their decisions within the constraints of current statute, as past case law might not be a helpful guide to future decisions. How the above questions are answered will change, and cases raising them will take years to wend from first instance to final appeal; settlements are likely to be reached on a confidential basis and licenses to use will be granted, to ensure AI marches on.

Meanwhile, governments will step in to consult – as the UK government is doing[16] – propose,[17] and ultimately legislate, and guiderails will be installed, and tech companies will bend them into shape. For a while, the oil that lubricates the AI machine will feel a bit stickier, but the mechanism will eventually have been reset and will stabilize, with compromises having been made by all in the name of progress.

AI copyright for a bicentennial brain

I use Isaac Asimov's *The Bicentennial Man* as a moniker for AI programs in the following sections of this chapter. It is an interesting short story (with an unusually lackluster film adaptation), which provides a parable for AI and copyright. Asimov's Bicentennial Man is a robot dubbed Andrew; over time, "he" learns to feel human emotion by working, loving, and eventually ageing and dying. Andrew fights for the right to be recognized as human. Interestingly, Asimov chooses creativity as one of the first expressions of Andrew's sentience when the robot decides to make a wooden necklace and to give it as a gift. More artisan work follows; Asimov takes it as a given that the robot will not be permitted to keep the money made from sales of his creative output, because the question of whether Andrew has "created" it is unclear. What also follows is – inevitably – legal proceedings, and the very human characteristic of cheating the system to make things feel fair.

In December 2024, the UK government opened a consultation to secure views on how to protect the creative sector and the need for income from copyright works whilst giving AI firms clarity on how they can legally access training data. Other action plans[18] and a Private Member's Bill[19] have followed. These largely seek to regularize the historic infringement and protect against future use of existing copyright, but they do touch on the wider point of AI output as a creative work and flagging to users that those works are machine-made and not human-created.

The question for us to consider now is whether we allow AI to benefit from its creativity. The ability to be creative has always been considered a human characteristic; from making shell beads to computer programming, the ability to use tools to create those items is considered a defining feature of what sets us apart from our primate cousins. Do we personify AI programs, essentially granting them human-like "status" because they can "create" original works? Do we accept that they have passed the Turing Test and, unlike Asimov's Bicentennial Man, thereby grant AI the right to be recognized as a creator and make money on the back of the "sum of all human knowledge"?[20] It seems that we are moving towards the answer being "Yes".

The UK's Copyright Designs and Patents Act 1988 (CDPA) provides that "computer-generated" works are protected by copyright: "Computer-generated, in relation to a work, means that the work is generated by computer in circumstances such that *there is no human author of the work*" (emphasis added).[21] This seems a simple enough concept to understand – after all, we recognize copyright in photographs, films, and music, which all are captured and recorded using tools that record the works and fulfil the obligation of permanency under CDPA. In the case of "computer-generated" works, the "author" is imputed as the human "by whom the arrangements necessary for the creation of the work are undertaken" under section 9(3) of the CDPA.[22] Assertion of the involvement of a human in the creative process is necessary, because the CDPA remains human-centered; the term of protection of copyright under the legislation is meaningless without the "life of the author", and the moral rights in chapter four of the CDPA[23] are disapplied to computer programs and to any computer-generated work by section 81(2) of the Act.[24] EU law previously only recognized a "natural person"[25] as an author, or a group of them where the work is a database;[26] whilst EU law standardized what is a "work" and "originality", authorship is determined at a national level, which, for AI copyright works, presents an obstacle.[27]

Authorship generally involves a natural person/human being applying creative decision-making to produce the output. The Brompton bicycle decision[28] confirms that the "personality" of the author is an intrinsic part of the creative process and a necessary facet of a copyrighted work. The author of a work must be aware of the creative path and have authorial intention, even if the precise outcome or mechanism of creation is not known at the point of creation. Many artists talk of revealing images from a canvas or the influence of a creative muse, which suggests that they do not always envisage the creative path, making this element a peculiarly difficult test for humans. Conversely, this is a requirement which AI, in which prompts can produce a particular output, can easily achieve. The US courts agree that human authorship is required, which has been confirmed by the US Court of Appeal as recently as March 2025 when determining that Stephen Thaler's AI system DABUS could not claim copyright protection for two novel products it apparently conceived of, as copyright applies only to works created by humans. China has taken a different view, with its courts determining that copyright exists in images created by AI, as they fulfil the criteria of "creativity".[29] Chinese courts have taken a protectionist step and deemed that copyrighted works can be created by AI programs.[30] As DeepSeek muscles in on ChatGPT and other AI programs, US courts will almost certainly follow suit.

Does AI need an "Asenion Law"?

In *The Bicentennial Man*, Asimov assumes that the robot who creates cannot be an author of a work and cannot benefit financially from its sale; the law does not permit it. The family that owns Andrew (the "technology") can reap the profits from their machine, but the robot itself cannot, because it is not human and only humans can have bank accounts into which money can be paid.

We are not reviewing robot-made goods or services here, but AI that "creates" can be likened to the Bicentennial Man imagined by Asimov. In that case, a relevant question to ask is whether we allow AI to benefit financially from its creativity and allow computer-generated works truly created by "the machine" and not solely rendered by it in line with instructions inputted by a human. In doing so, do we in fact personify AI programs, essentially granting them status akin to a human's? Again, this is beyond the scope of this chapter, but let us borrow from Asimov again and consider his Three Laws of Robotics.

The first Law of Robotics[31] is: "A robot may not injure a human being or, through inaction, allow a human to come to harm." Robots programmed so that they cannot break the Laws of Robotics are called Asenion robots.[32] If we interpret "harm" in its broadest sense and extend it beyond the physical to financial harm and damage to human wellbeing and income, does the first Law of Robotics thereby prohibit use of AI to "harm" the rights of humans who are artists, authors, musicians, and creators? Those rights that must be protected from "harm" include copyright; the right to be recognized as the creator of a work; to determine who cannot and cannot use a work and how; the right to object to derogatory use of their work; the right to generate income from their intellectual endeavors; and the right to not have their finances hurt by use of their work by others, alone or in combination with hundreds of thousands of megabytes of other training data. Asimov's Zeroth Law of Robotics states that robots must not harm humanity (not just a single human) – do we now need a foundational Zeroth Law to protect creators against the universality of AI? Should AI itself contain an Asenion safeguard to prevent it from copying the works of others? That programming should be possible to achieve, making it inherent to AI.

Information wants to be shared

When we look at the historical context of copyright, it emerges from a different type of unhappy threesome Henry VIII found himself in. It was a triangle of mistrust between the Sovereign, who wanted to control what was said about him; a Guild, who had the technology to print information and the legal right to censor material; and writers and consumers, who protested against the suppression of information by the Sovereign and the Guild.

During the Reformation and the subsequent turbulence as each Tudor heir took the throne, works critical of the monarchy and their prevailing religion were subject to censure and destruction. As the volume of works grew and books coming into England from other territories burgeoned, the role of censorship and enforcement was passed from the Crown (who had authorized printing and taken the revenue from it) to the Worshipful Company of Stationers, usually known as the Stationers' Guild. Legislation granted the Stationer's Guild the right to authorize how many printing presses could be established, who could undertake printing, what was printed, and what content was removed from a work if it was printed. Licensed printers would register a book, thereby retaining the right to reprint it in perpetuity (the copying right) and retain the profits from its sale, paying only a small fee back to the author for the original work. The owners of the printing presses controlled who could use that technology, what was printed from the original work submitted, and how many copies were produced, retaining the profits from sales. This caused increasing conflict between authors and an expanding group of literate and politicized readers with an interest in new ideas and concepts generated by a changing world. This was the "golden age", and ideas wanted to be free of the constraints of previous century's strictures.

By 1710, the rights of an author to control who printed their work and what appeared in their work was granted in "An Act for the Encouragement of Learning, by Vesting the Copies of Printed Books in the Authors or Purchasers of Copies, during the Times therein mentioned", more usually known as the Statute of Anne. It took nearly 200 years, but control of information and the right of an author to benefit from their work moved from the monarch to the technologists to the creator. Copyright has remained the primary protection for originators of creative output since the Statute of Anne, and licensing of works is the main method to ensure mass distribution of them. The Statute of Anne was the first of its kind, and its concepts have been replicated, finessed, and reproduced since.

Stewart Brand, best known as the co-founder and editor of the *Whole Earth Catalog*, once said (presciently, so it seems): "On the one hand, information wants to be expensive, because it's so valuable. The right information in the right place just changes your life. On the other hand, information wants to be free, because the cost of getting it out is getting lower and lower all the time. So, you have these two fighting against each other."[33] Are we now seeing Brand's dichotomy being played out, and are we capable of finally resolving this conflict?

Information has inherent use and, therefore, it should be valued ("valuable" in the context Brand refers to). If we value information for its uses, it *should* be "expensive". It is not, however, a commodity that is in short supply (it is estimated that, at the end of 2024, there were 44 zettabytes[34] of data on the internet); because we still largely "value" goods based on scarcity in the post-industrial world, we have liberated information *gratis* ("freeing" it in both senses of the word) in our excitement to place information on the internet and share it worldwide. Doing so has democratized access to it; however, by doing so, we have also debased truth, worth, and possibly merit in exchange for content and ignored the creators in favor of unlimited publication and mass instantaneous reproduction.

When the owners of the technology behind Facebook, Instagram, YouTube, TikTok, X, and the plethora of platforms across social engagement, business, research, and academia wrote their terms of use to ensure that every item placed on their system belonged to them, the rights in those works were sacrificed on the altar of "sharing" and syphoned into the data sump. The members of the "Technologists' Guild" own the printing press that is the platforms we use and the content via the terms they have us accept; they control how work is disseminated, as well as determining (through the self-regulation that governments have been so keen to bestow upon them) what is seen and what is censored.[35] The Technologists' Guild decides what is valuable and what is free, and it has determined that all content was available, gratis, and liberated at the moment they used it to train AI.

But is it art?

Media artist Refik Anadol presented an exhibition (titled "Unsupervised") at New York's Museum of Modern Art that was created using generative AI, with the entirety of the museum's art library as its training data. The AI program visualized output artworks, as if dreaming about everything it had "learnt". The result was an installation which projected perpetually changing images – running the gamut of every school of art and style – onto a screen. We accept that, with every interaction with an original work, the viewer/reader/performer has a visceral reaction, but the subjective question of "Is it art?" remains perennial.

Copyright protection makes no judgment and applies no subjectivity of merit, but intellectual endeavor is required for a work to be protected. Would "Unsupervised" not be protected as art because it is "only" rendered by a program that draws on hundreds of years of expression and thousands of hours of learning? Is it not art because it is "only" rendered by a computer taught by a highly skilled program and the most definitive of tutors? Is the issue actually that AI provides the mechanism to democratize creation of works using new tools and devalue human creativity? Or is it that – based on all of the unspecified learning and data input – we cannot verify whether AI work is truly original, making our judgment of what art is (and, therefore, what should be protected) far more difficult?

In *The Bicentennial Man*, the robot creates and chooses to be creative because it perceives creativity as a human trait. AI that is prompted to create artistic output is surely akin to this, selecting inputs and generating a considered output. The argument of ease of generation undermining creativity harks back to the "sweat of the brow" test. Highlighting the fact that AI has been trained on non-permissioned historic works increasingly seems like shouting into the void. The human-like trait of determining a question and seeking an answer is not obviated simply because the tool to ascertain those answers is now a super-powerful computer program.

Meanwhile, creators protest the use of their work in datasets that enable copies, reproductions, derivative works, and hybrid offspring to be spawned from their endeavors without payment or permission, having unwittingly or unwillingly given over control of its use and value when they passed it to the Technologists' Guild. We may yet "Delete all IP",[36] as Jack Dorsey has called for – albeit unknowingly – because of the power of the Guild and its outrage at being asked to account to creators "who don't want their life's work pillaged for profit".[37] How do we realign these competing interests and recognize that data want to be shared and information needs to be valued? Does the new legislation enacted and proposed achieve a rebalancing of value? Probably not. Instead, it paves the way for us to recognize and protect works created by AI in the future, providing revenue for the Technologists' Guild.

Same old new law

Computer-generated works are already protected under English law. It would seem obvious to extend the definition of copyrighted works to "AI originals" under the neighboring rights heading, treating them as databases. Those rights see database compilers/creators receiving financial reward for their efforts, but AI users generally do not invest in the AI model or its creation[38] (where this does happen, it should be straightforward to evidence), which makes sui generis protection less appropriate as a classification for copyright in AI-created works.

The first to regulate AI was the EU, with the Artificial Intelligence Act (AIA).[39] This requires developers who use AI to clearly label output as AI-generated (which addresses "credit" of a work). The EU AIA also requires GenAI developers to implement a policy to respect the EU Copyright Directive, but stops short of saying how they achieve this. A law requiring a policy to comply with another law undermines the effectiveness of both statutes, but the intention is sound: to prevent future mass infringement, as has happened in the past. By this measure and with such policies, the source of training data will have to be identified and use of their works permissioned. Achieving consent retrospectively will almost certainly have to be done via direct licensing, which settles past infringement claims, or through new (or existing) collection societies, where authors can make a claim for payment for use, probably on a one-off basis. This, ironically, will almost certainly use AI to identify all use of works in datasets! Under the AIA, the EU AI Office oversees EU AIA compliance, and AI Pact members co-operate to establish a collaborative community that creates and shares good practice. The AI Pact members do not solely comprise representatives of the Technologists' Guild, but are drawn from a much wider pool. This breadth of expertise must be applauded – and maintained!

In January 2025, the UK government published the *AI Opportunities Action Plan*, which is largely a statement of hope and intention.[40] In March 2025, the Artificial Intelligence (Regulation) Bill was proposed (via a Private Member's Bill originating in the House of Lords), which would see a statutory body similar to the EUAI Office, called the (UK) AI Authority, established. That Authority would regulate the "safety, security and robustness of AI and the appropriate transparency and explainability of it" and establish "fairness; accountability and governance ... contestability and redress".[41] The proposed UK AI Authority would also house a super-catalogue of all third-party data and intellectual property used for training AI and ensure (via its regulatory powers) that all such data and IP are utilized with informed consent.

Whilst the AI Authority would house the back-catalogue of training data, this would not in itself assist in determining if a work was original or artistic – whether it be literary, musical, or computer-generated – under our national copyright definition. The repository is not intended to achieve this purpose, but it obviously could.

If the courts (and legislation) take the view that creativity is an essentially human characteristic, that characteristic – however it manifests, in organic humans *and* in AI – means that art should be protected if it contains originality of thought and expression and intention in its creation, without discrimination as to the means of creation or authorship. Opening the UK AI catalogue to review and interrogation might result in it becoming apparent that AI uses so many inputs that its work is indeed original and creative; it might also be used to demonstrate if a work is a bare copy. In this way, we ensure that all creativity of this type remains *capable* of protection if it meets the tests set down as far back as the Statute of Anne, honed, interpreted, refreshed, and rebooted for the post-digital age.

New laws enacted and proposed fall short of definitively answering the conundrum of "Is it art?" in respect of AI output. Law- and policymakers may perhaps be waiting to see how the technology is used and hope to apply the mischief rule when it becomes apparent that the drafting fell short in imagination and reach.

If we endow computers with human-like intelligence by training them on the output of human creators, enabling them thereby to produce work akin to that formed by humans, it is only a matter of time before we must grant full intellectual property rights to AI. By doing so, we reiterate that original works *should* be protected; that copyright is effective; that sanctions follow when the granted protection is breached; and that creation of works capable of copyright protection should still return value (and income) to the author – not simply to the owners of the printing press.

References

1 King, G., "Big Data Is Not About The Data!", Harvard University, 2016. See: https:/gking.harvard.edu/files/gking/files/prefaceorbigdataisnotaboutthedata_1.pdf.

2 Slashdot, "An Early History of Nupedia and Wikipedia", 2005. See: https://features.slashdot.org/story/05/04/18/164213/the-early-history-of-nupedia-and-wikipedia-a-memoir.

3 Perrigo, B., "Inside Anthropic, the AI company betting that safety can be a winning strategy", *Time*, 30 May 2024. See: https://time.com/6980000/anthropic/.

4 See my previous assessment of this: Brook, J., "Data bites back", *Modern Lawyer*, 2024, volume 7, issue 4, pp. 49–59.

5 Moore, G.E., "Cramming more components onto integrated circuits", *Proceedings of the IEEE*, 1998, volume 86, issue 1. https://www.cs.utexas.edu/~fussell/courses/cs352h/papers/moore.pdf.

6 Cottier, B., Rahman, R., Fattorini, L. et al, "How Much Does It Cost to Train Frontier AI Models?", Epoch AI, 13 January 2025. See: https://epoch.ai/blog/how-much-does-it-cost-to-train-frontier-ai-models.

7 United States District Court Southern District of New York, "Case 1:23-cv-08292-SHS: *Authors Guild, David Baldacci, Mary Bly, Michael Connelly, Sylvia Day, Jonathan*

Franzen, John Grisham, Elin Hilderbrand, Christina Baker Kline, Maya Shanbhag Lang, Victor Lavalle, George R.R. Martin, Jodi Picoult, Douglas Preston, Roxana Robinson, George Saunders, Scott Turow, and Rachel Vail V. Openai Inc., Openai Opco LLC, Openai Gp LLC, Openai LLC, Openai Global LLC, Oai Corporation LLC, Openai Holdings LLC, Openai Startup Fund ILP, Openai Startup Fund Gp I LLC, Openai Startup Fund Management LLC, And Microsoft CORPORATION", The Authors Guild, 14 April 2023. See: https://authorsguild.org/app/uploads/2023/12/Authors-Guild-OpenAI-Microsoft-Class-Action-Complaint-Dec-2023.pdf.

8 Allyn, B., "2023-12-27 NYT dkt 1 Complaint", DocumentCloud, 27 December 2023. See: https://www.documentcloud.org/documents/24241000-2023-12-27-nyt-dkt-1-complaint/?q=unlawful+&mode=search.

9 Royal Courts of Justice, "Case No: IL-2023-000007: (1) Getty Images (US) Inc (2) Getty Images International UC (3) Getty Images (UK) Limited (4) Getty Images Devco UK Limited (5) Istockphoto LP (6) Thomas M Barwick Inc and STABILITY AI LTD", Judiciary.co.uk, 14 January 2025. See: https://www.judiciary.uk/wp-content/uploads/2025/01/Getty-Images-and-others-v-Stability-AI-14.01.25.pdf.

10 Schaul, K., Chen, S.Y., and Tiku, N., "Inside the secret list of websites that make AI like ChatGPT sound smart", *The Washington Post*, 19 April 2025. See: https://www.washingtonpost.com/technology/interactive/2023/ai-chatbot-learning/.

11 Information Commissioner's Office, "The lawful basis for web scraping to train generative AI models", 2025. See: https://ico.org.uk/about-the-ico/what-we-do/our-work-on-artificial-intelligence/response-to-the-consultation-series-on-generative-ai/the-lawful-basis-for-web-scraping-to-train-generative-ai-models/.

12 European Data Protection Board, "EDPB opinion on AI models: GDPR principles support responsible AI", Europa.eu, 18 December 2024. See: https://www.edpb.europa.eu/news/news/2024/edpb-opinion-ai-models-gdpr-principles-support-responsible-ai_en.

13 *Andersen v. Stability AI Ltd.* (3:23-cv-00201).

14 Thomson Reuters Enter. *Centre GmbH v. Ross Intelligence Inc.*, 694 F.Supp.3d 467.

15 *Andersen v. Stability AI Ltd.* (3:23-cv-00201).

16 Intellectual Property Office, Department for Science, Innovation and Technology and Department for Culture, Media and Sport, "Closed consultation: Copyright and Artificial Intelligence", Gov.uk, 17 December 2024: See: https://www.gov.uk/government/consultations/copyright-and-artificial-intelligence/.

17 Scott, E., "Copyright and artificial intelligence: Impact on creative industries", House of Lords Library, 27 January 2025. See: https://lordslibrary.parliament.uk/copyright-and-artificial-intelligence-impact-on-creative-industries/#:~:text=Currently%2C%20developers%20are%20subject%20to,this%20material%20could%20be%20used.

18 Department for Science, Innovation and Technology, "AI Opportunities Action Plan", Gov.uk, 13 January 2025. See: https://www.gov.uk/government/publications/ai-opportunities-action-plan/ai-opportunities-action-plan.

19 Parliamentary Bills, "Artificial Intelligence (Regulation) Bill [HL]: Private Members' Bill (Starting in the House of Lords)", UK Parliament, 5 March 2025. See: https://bills.parliament.uk/publications/59353/documents/6094.

20 Slashdot, "An Early History of Nupedia and Wikipedia", 2005. See: https://features.slashdot.org/story/05/04/18/164213/the-early-history-of-nupedia-and-wikipedia-a-memoir.

21 Copyright, Designs and Patents Act 1988.

22 *Ibid.*, section 9(3).

23 *Ibid.*, Chapter 4.

24 *Ibid.*

25 Directive 2009/24/EC of the European Parliament and of the Council of 23 April 2009 on the legal protection of computer programs [2009] OJ L 111; Article 2(1).

26 Directive 96/9/EC of the European Parliament and of the Council of 11 March 1996 on the legal protection of databases [1996] OJ L 77; Article 4(1).

27 Fritz, J., "The notion of 'authorship' under EU law—who can be an author and what makes one an author? An analysis of the legislative framework and case law", *Journal of Intellectual Property Law & Practice*, 2024, volume 19, issue 7, pp. 552–556. https://doi.org/10.1093/jiplp/jpae022.

28 EUR-Lex, "Judgment of the Court (Fifth Chamber) of 11 June 2020. *SI and Brompton Bicycle Ltd v Chedech / Get2Get*. Request for a preliminary ruling from the tribunal de l'entreprise de Liège. Reference for a preliminary ruling — Intellectual and industrial property — Copyright and related rights — Directive 2001/29/EC — Articles 2 to 5 — Scope — Utilitarian object — Concept of 'work' — Copyright protection of works — Conditions — Shape of a product which is necessary to obtain a technical result — Folding bicycle. Case C-833/18", 11 June 2020. See: https://eur-lex.europa.eu/legal-content/EN/TXT/?uri=celex:62018CJ0833.

29 Li v Liu Beijing Internet Court Civil Judgment (2023) Jing 0491 Min Chu No. 11279. See: https://english.bjinternetcourt.gov.cn/2023-12/28/c_688.htm.

30 *Ibid.*

31 Asimov, I., *Runaround*, New York (NY): Street & Smith; 1942. The Laws of Robotics were codified in later works.

32 Asimov, I., *Caves of Steel*, New York (NY): Del Rey/Ballantine Books; 1953.

33 Brand, S., *The Media Lab: Inventing the Future at MIT*, New York (NY): Viking Press; 1987.

34 This consists of 44,000,000,000,000,000,000,000 bytes.

35 A historic view on this can be found here: Leberknight, C.S., Chiang, M., Poor, H.V., and Wong, F., "A Taxonomy of Internet Censorship and Anti-Censorship", Princeton University, 31 December 2010. See: https://www.princeton.edu/~chiangm/anticensorship.pdf. A current position on internet censorship can be found here: Wendzel, S., Volpert, S., Zillien, S., Lenz, J., and Caviglione, L., "A Survey of Internet Censorship and its Measurement: Methodology, Trends, and Challenges", arXiv, 20 February 2025. https://doi.org/10.48550/arXiv.2502.14945.

36 Ha, A., "Jack Dorsey and Elon Musk would like to 'delete all IP law'", TechCrunch, 13

April 2025. See: https://techcrunch.com/2025/04/13/jack-dorsey-and-elon-musk-would-like-to-delete-all-ip-law/.

37 A response to Jack Dorsey's statement can be found here: Newton-Rex, E., "Tech execs declaring all-out war on creators who don't want their life's work pillaged for profit", Blue Sky, 12 April 2025. See: https://bsky.app/profile/ednewtonrex.bsky.social/post/3lmmv4x7gps2a.

38 Atilla, S., "Dealing with AI-generated works: lessons from the CDPA section 9(3)", *Journal of Intellectual Property Law & Practice*, 2023, volume 19, issue 1, pp. 43–54. https://doi.org/10.1093/jiplp/jpad102.

39 Regulation (EU) 2024/1689 of the European Parliament and of the Council of 13 June 2024 laying down harmonised rules on artificial intelligence and amending Regulations (EC) No 300/2008, (EU) No 167/2013, (EU) No 168/2013, (EU) 2018/858, (EU) 2018/1139 and (EU) 2019/2144 and Directives 2014/90/EU, (EU) 2016/797 and (EU) 2020/1828 [2024] OJ L 2024/1689.

40 Department for Science, Innovation and Technology, "AI Opportunities Action Plan", Gov.uk, 13 January 2025. See: https://www.gov.uk/government/publications/ai-opportunities-action-plan/ai-opportunities-action-plan.

41 Parliamentary Bills, "Artificial Intelligence (Regulation) Bill [HL]: Private Members' Bill (Starting in the House of Lords)", UK Parliament, 5 March 2025. See: https://bills.parliament.uk/publications/59353/documents/6094.

Chapter 5:
The legal technology playbook: a step-by-step guide to implementing legal technology

By Justin Turman, founder, Automate Office Work

The legal profession stands at a crossroads. As client expectations evolve, caseloads grow, and regulatory landscapes shift, law firms and legal departments face unprecedented pressure to deliver faster, more precise, and cost-effective services. However, many organizations remain tethered to outdated workflows – manual document reviews, disjointed communication channels, and error-prone billing practices – that drain resources and stifle innovation. This chapter is not merely about adopting technology; it is about reimagining how legal work *gets done*. The rise of artificial intelligence, cloud computing, and automation has ushered in a new era of possibilities. Tools that once seemed futuristic – like AI-driven contract analysis, predictive legal analytics, and secure client portals – are now within reach. However, the true challenge lies not in accessing these tools, but in implementing them *strategically*. Too often, firms invest in flashy solutions, only to grapple with poor adoption, integration headaches, or unmet promises.

This chapter is designed for legal professionals who recognize that technology is not a magic bullet, but a catalyst for meaningful change. Whether you are a managing partner steering firm-wide transformation, a paralegal seeking to streamline daily tasks, or an IT leader tasked with safeguarding data, this chapter offers a structured, human-centered approach to legal technology implementation.

You will discover:

- A step-by-step framework grounded in real-world examples, from conducting needs assessments to measuring return on investment (ROI);
- Practical strategies to overcome common pitfalls, such as resistance to change or misaligned vendor partnerships; and
- Actionable insights on tailoring tools to your firm's unique workflows, ensuring technology amplifies – not complicates – daily work.

Technology alone cannot transform a practice; *people* do. This chapter also emphasizes the importance of fostering a culture where innovation thrives. You will learn how to empower "technology champions", communicate value to skeptics, and celebrate wins that inspire organization-wide buy-in.

Who should read this chapter?

- Law firm leaders seeking to future-proof their practice;
- In-house legal teams aiming to reduce costs and improve compliance;
- IT and operations professionals navigating integrations and security; and
- Forward-thinking practitioners eager to reclaim time for high-value, client-centered work.

Implementing legal technology is not a one-time project, but an ongoing journey of adaptation and growth. The pages ahead will equip you with the tools to navigate this journey with confidence – transforming uncertainty into opportunity, and ambition into action. This will be achieved through a ten-step process:

1. Needs assessment, process mapping, and goal-setting;
2. Build vs buy analysis and vendor selection;
3. Pilot program or proof of concept;
4. Planning, customization, and integration;
5. Training and change management;
6. Implementation and rollout;
7. Monitoring, feedback, and continuous improvement;
8. Planning for updates, enhancements, and scalability;
9. Evangelizing success and expanding use; and
10. Evaluating and future planning.

The future of legal practice belongs to those who dare to innovate. Let this chapter be your roadmap.[1]

Phase 1: Needs assessment, process mapping, and goal-setting – a strategic approach

The successful implementation of legal technology requires more than selecting the latest software or trend. It demands a deliberate strategy, rooted in understanding your organization's unique challenges, mapping out existing workflows, and setting clear and actionable goals. By following a structured approach centered on needs assessment, process mapping, and goal-setting, you can ensure that technology becomes a catalyst for efficiency, innovation, and growth, rather than a costly misstep.

Understanding needs: the foundation of effective implementation

Every successful legal technology initiative begins with a thorough needs assessment. This process involves engaging stakeholders across the organization – from lawyers and paralegals to IT teams and finance departments –to identify pain points, inefficiencies, and aspirations. Start by conducting interviews, surveys, or focus groups to gather insights into daily workflows, technology usage, and unmet needs. For example, ask teams how they currently manage document storage, track billable hours, or communicate with clients. Are they bogged down by manual data entry, frustrated by disjointed systems, or concerned about compliance risks?

Dive deeper into specific areas like document management, where version control issues or inefficient retrieval processes might be slowing down casework. Explore timekeeping practices to uncover inaccuracies or delays that erode profitability. Assess client communication gaps, such as reliance on insecure email chains or missed updates that strain relationships. This phase should also evaluate how existing tools align with the firm's strategic objectives, whether these are improving client satisfaction, reducing operational costs, or scaling services. Crucially, consider future needs: will the technology adapt to emerging trends like AI-driven legal research or remote collaboration demands?

By the end of this stage, you will have a prioritized list of challenges and opportunities – perhaps the firm struggles with contract management delays or lacks analytics to track case outcomes. These insights will shape your technology requirements, ensuring solutions address root causes, rather than symptoms.

Mapping processes: visualizing the path to efficiency

With a clear understanding of needs, the next step is to map existing workflows. Process mapping involves documenting how tasks flow through the organization, from client intake to case resolution. Visual tools like flowcharts or diagrams can reveal redundancies, bottlenecks, and areas ripe for automation. For instance, a litigation team might discover that manual document review consumes 30 percent of their time, while a corporate law group might identify delays in contract approvals due to unclear hand-offs between departments.

Focus on high-volume, repetitive tasks, such as drafting standard contracts, calendaring deadlines, or inputting client data, where automation can save hours each week. Pinpoint error-prone steps, such as compliance checks or billing entries, where AI tools could enhance accuracy. Engage staff in this exercise. Their frontline experiences often highlight overlooked inefficiencies, like a paralegal's struggle to locate files across disconnected systems.

Process mapping also uncovers dependencies between teams and tools. For example, if the document management system does not integrate with the billing platform, attorneys waste time cross-referencing data. By visualizing these gaps, you can prioritize technologies that unify workflows. This phase is not just about fixing current issues; it is about designing a future-state workflow where technology streamlines collaboration, accelerates decision-making, and empowers remote teams.

Setting goals: turning vision into action

Armed with insights from needs assessment and process mapping, the final step is to define clear, measurable goals. Effective goal-setting bridges the gap between identifying problems and realizing solutions. Start by aligning technology objectives with the firm's broader mission. If the firm aims to enhance client satisfaction, a client portal for real-time case updates might be a priority; if reducing overhead is key, focus on automating billing or document assembly. Adopt the SMART framework:

- *Specific:* "Reduce contract review time by 25 percent through AI tools."
- *Measurable:* "Increase billable hours by 15 percent via automated time tracking."
- *Achievable:* Ensure goals account for budget, timelines, and staff capacity.
- *Relevant:* Tie objectives to critical pain points, like improving compliance or reducing data breaches.
- *Time-bound:* "Implement e-discovery software within six months."

Balance short-term wins, like piloting a document automation tool, with long-term visions, such as firm-wide digital transformation. Break ambitious goals into phases: train 25 percent of staff in Q1; expand to 75 percent by Q3; and measure adoption rates through user feedback. Establish key performance indicators (KPIs) to track progress, such as hours saved per week or client satisfaction scores, and collect baseline data to quantify improvements.

Engage stakeholders throughout this process. Lawyers resistant to change may embrace tools that simplify their workload, while IT teams need clarity on integration requirements. Communicate goals transparently, emphasizing how technology will alleviate daily frustrations. Finally, build flexibility into your plan. Legal tech evolves rapidly; a tool chosen today may need adjustments tomorrow. You must regularly revisit goals to incorporate new advancements or shifting priorities.

Conclusion: building a future-ready legal practice

Implementing legal technology is not a one-time project, but an ongoing journey. By rigorously assessing needs, mapping processes, and setting strategic goals, firms can avoid costly missteps and foster a culture of innovation. The outcome is a legal practice where technology amplifies human expertise, freeing professionals to focus on high-value work, deliver exceptional client service, and stay ahead in a competitive landscape. As you move forward, remember that success lies not just in the tools you choose, but in the clarity of your vision and the commitment of your team.

Phase 2: Build vs buy analysis and vendor selection – choosing the right path

The decision to build custom legal technology or purchase an off-the-shelf solution is a pivotal moment in any firm's digital transformation journey. This choice hinges on a careful analysis of your organization's unique needs, resources, and long-term vision; equally critical is selecting a vendor capable of aligning with your goals, whether you opt for a pre-built tool or a tailored system. By balancing cost, flexibility, and strategic alignment, you can navigate this crossroads with confidence.

The build vs buy dilemma: balancing customization and practicality

The first step is to assess whether your firm's challenges demand a bespoke solution or can be addressed by existing tools. Begin by revisiting the needs identified in your earlier assessment: are your pain points highly unique, such as a niche compliance requirement or a proprietary workflow that no off-the-shelf product accommodates? Or could a configurable platform, designed for the legal industry, meet your needs with minor adjustments?

Cost is a central factor. Building custom software involves significant upfront development expenses, ongoing maintenance, and the need for in-house technical expertise. Purchasing a solution, on the other hand, shifts the burden of updates and support to the vendor, but may involve recurring subscription fees or licensing costs. For example, a mid-sized firm aiming to automate complex contract workflows might find that a pre-built AI contract analysis tool, augmented with light customization, offers better value than developing a system from scratch.

Time is another consideration. Off-the-shelf solutions can often be deployed within weeks, whereas building custom software may take months or years. If your firm faces urgent inefficiencies, such as mounting client complaints about slow case updates, a faster implementation may justify opting for a ready-made client portal. However, if your long-term vision includes scalable, firm-specific features that evolve with your practice, a custom build might be worth the investment.

Scalability and integration further tip the scales. Purchased solutions must integrate seamlessly with your existing tech stack, such as document management or billing systems. If a vendor's product lacks robust application programming interfaces (APIs) or struggles with interoperability, it could create new inefficiencies. Conversely, custom software offers full control over integration, but requires ongoing development to adapt to future tools or regulatory changes.

Vendor selection: finding a partner, not just a product

Once the decision to buy is made, selecting the right vendor becomes paramount. Start by defining clear requirements grounded in your firm's pain points. Involve stakeholders from legal, IT, and operations to draft a detailed request for proposal (RFP) that outlines technical needs, compliance standards, and desired outcomes. For instance, a litigation-focused firm might prioritize e-discovery capabilities, while a corporate practice may emphasize contract lifecycle management.

Vendor demos are where theory meets reality. Arrange sessions that simulate real-world scenarios, such as drafting a motion or tracking billable hours, to evaluate usability and performance, and encourage attorneys and paralegals to participate. Their feedback on the interface's intuitiveness or workflow compatibility is invaluable. Scrutinize integration capabilities during demos; ask vendors to demonstrate how their tool interacts with your existing systems, like pulling data from your customer relationship management (CRM) system into a case management dashboard.

Beyond features, assess the vendor's long-term viability. A provider with a strong track record in legal tech, robust financial health, and a clear innovation roadmap is more likely to evolve alongside your firm. Investigate their customer support structure. Will you have a dedicated account manager, or are you relegated to a generic helpdesk? For global firms, 24/7 support might be non-negotiable.

Security and compliance cannot be overlooked. Legal professionals handle sensitive data, so vendors must adhere to standards like the European General Data Protection Regulation (GDPR), the US Health Insurance Portability and Accountability Act (HIPAA), or Systems and Organization Controls 2 (SOC 2), created by the American Institute of Certified Public Accountants (AICPA) in 2010. Probe their encryption practices, data storage policies, and disaster recovery plans. A vendor that offers multi-factor authentication and granular access controls demonstrates a commitment to safeguarding client confidentiality.

Negotiating for success: contracts, costs, and flexibility

Pricing models vary widely, ranging from subscription fees, per-user licensing, or one-time purchases. However, the true cost lies in the total ownership experience. Scrutinize hidden expenses, such as charges for API access or premium support tiers. Negotiate flexible contract terms, including exit clauses and trial periods, to avoid lock-in with an underperforming solution. For example, a clause allowing data export in standard formats ensures you retain control if you later switch vendors.

Conclusion: aligning technology with vision

The build vs buy decision and subsequent vendor selection shape your firm's technological trajectory. By prioritizing strategic alignment over flashy features, you ensure the chosen solution not only solves today's problems, but also adapts to tomorrow's challenges. Whether custom-built or off-the-shelf, the right technology becomes an invisible ally, streamlining workflows, fortifying compliance, and elevating client service. Remember: this decision is not merely transactional; it is the foundation of a partnership that will drive your firm's success in an increasingly digital legal landscape.

Phase 3: Pilot program or proof of concept – testing before scaling

Implementing legal technology without first testing its efficacy is akin to navigating uncharted waters without a compass. A pilot program or proof of concept serves as a critical safeguard, allowing your organization to validate the chosen solution's effectiveness, uncover potential pitfalls, and refine the approach before committing to a full-scale rollout. By testing in a controlled environment, you minimize risk, optimize user adoption, and ensure the technology aligns with both operational workflows and strategic objectives.

Defining the scope: start small, think big

The success of a pilot hinges on a well-defined scope. Begin by selecting a department or team whose workflows most acutely reflect the pain points that the technology aims to address. For instance, if the goal is to streamline contract management, the corporate legal team handling high-volume agreements might be an ideal candidate. Focus on one or two critical use cases that promise measurable impact, such as automating contract review or enhancing deadline tracking. This narrow focus ensures clarity and allows for in-depth analysis without overwhelming participants.

Equally important is establishing a realistic timeline. A pilot spanning four to six weeks provides sufficient time to gather meaningful data while maintaining momentum. Too short a period risks superficial insights; too long may delay broader implementation and dampen stakeholder enthusiasm. For example, a litigation team piloting an e-discovery tool sets a six-week window to assess its ability to reduce document review time during an active case.

Integration besting: ensuring seamless compatibility

A new tool's ability to integrate with existing systems is often the linchpin of its success. During the pilot, rigorously test compatibility with core platforms, such as document management systems, billing software, or client portals. Suppose the pilot involves a new AI-driven legal research tool: verify that search results can be seamlessly exported into case management software and that data format align with existing workflows.

Data migration is another critical consideration. If the pilot requires transferring historical case data into the new system, assess the process for accuracy and ease. For instance, migrating client intake records into a new CRM should preserve metadata and avoid duplication. Any hiccups here can signal broader challenges during full deployment.

Measuring success: quantifying impact through KPIs

Clear metrics transform subjective impressions into actionable insights. Define KPIs tailored to the pilot's objectives:

- *Time saved:* Track hours reclaimed by automating tasks like document drafting or legal research. For example, if associates previously spent 10 hours weekly manually redacting sensitive information, measure how much a new redaction tool reduces this effort.

- *Error reduction:* Monitor decreases in missed deadlines, data entry mistakes, or compliance oversights. A pilot for an AI contract analyzer might measure the reduction in overlooked clauses across 100 contracts.
- *Efficiency gains:* Evaluate productivity through task completion rates or user satisfaction surveys. If a pilot workflow management tool reduces email follow-ups by 40 percent, it signals stronger team coordination.
- *Cost savings:* Calculate operational savings, such as reduced overtime costs or lower outsourcing expenses for routine tasks.

These metrics not only validate the technology, but also build a compelling case for stakeholder buy-in during full deployment.

Gathering feedback: listening to the frontlines

End-users are the ultimate arbiters of a tool's practicality, so you should regularly collect feedback through surveys, focus groups, or one-on-one interviews. Ask targeted questions: is the interface intuitive? Does the tool disrupt or enhance daily routines? How steep is the learning curve? For example, paralegals testing a new document automation feature might praise its time-saving potential, but request additional training on template customization.

Simultaneously, monitor system performance for technical glitches; slow load times, integration errors, or mobile accessibility issues that could hinder adoption. Addressing these during the pilot phase prevents them from escalating post-launch. Training effectiveness should also be assessed. If users struggle despite initial sessions, consider refining onboarding materials or offering just-in-time support resources.

Communication: transparency builds trust

A well-structured communication plan keeps the entire organization invested in the pilot's success. Launch the initiative with a clear announcement explaining its purpose, scope, and anticipated benefits. Regular updates via emails, meetings, or internal newsletters should share progress, celebrate early wins, and acknowledge challenges. For instance, sharing a mid-pilot update highlighting a 20 percent reduction in document retrieval time reinforces the technology's value.

Conclude the pilot with a final report that synthesizes findings, including quantitative results and qualitative feedback. Present this to stakeholders with recommendations for scaling, adjusting, or, if necessary, reassessing the solution. Transparency about both successes and shortcomings fosters trust and prepares the organization for the next phase.

Conclusion: from validation to transformation

A pilot program is more than a trial run; it is a strategic investment in your firm's future. By validating the technology's impact, refining workflows, and engaging users early, you lay the groundwork for a smooth, confident rollout. The insights gained, whether they reveal a need for additional customization, training, or even a pivot to a different tool, are invaluable. Ultimately, a successful pilot transforms skepticism into advocacy, ensuring that when the technology scales, it does so with the precision and support needed to drive lasting change. In an era where legal tech evolves rapidly, this iterative, evidence-based approach is not just prudent – it is essential.

Phase 4: Planning, customization, and integration – crafting a cohesive solution

The true potential of legal technology lies not just in its features, but in how seamlessly it molds to your organization's unique workflows and coexists with existing systems. After validating a solution through a pilot program, the next phase – planning, customization, and integration – transforms a promising tool into a tailored asset. This stage bridges the gap between theory and practice, ensuring the technology aligns with operational realities while minimizing disruption.

Collaboration: harnessing expertise for precision customization

Effective customization begins with collaboration. Engage subject matter experts (SMEs) from across the organization, such as attorneys, paralegals, IT specialists, and operations managers, to dissect how the technology can adapt to daily demands. For example, litigation teams might require custom fields in a case management system to track deposition schedules, while corporate lawyers may need automated clause libraries for contract drafting. These SMEs provide granular insights into pain points that generic software often overlooks.

Work closely with developers or vendor consultants to tailor user interfaces (UIs) and features. A cluttered dashboard might overwhelm users, whereas role-based views, such as a simplified interface for paralegals and a data-rich panel for partners, can enhance productivity. Similarly, automate repetitive tasks specific to your workflows, like generating client intake forms pre-populated with matter-specific data. The goal is to make the tool feel less like an external product and more like a natural extension of your team's expertise.

Integration: weaving technology into the existing fabric

Even the most sophisticated tool falters if it operates in isolation. Map out how the new solution will integrate with core systems like document management platforms, CRMs, or billing software. For instance, ensure time entries logged in the new system automatically sync with the firm's billing software to prevent revenue leakage. APIs play a critical role here. Verify that data flows bidirectionally and in real time, avoiding manual exports or duplicate entries.

Consider a corporate law firm adopting AI contract analysis software. Seamless integration with the document management system allows attorneys to review contracts within their existing workflow, with AI-suggested edits appearing directly in familiar interfaces like Microsoft Word. Such cohesion reduces friction and accelerates adoption.

Timeline: balancing ambition with realism

A detailed implementation timeline is the backbone of this phase. Break the process into milestones, such as data migration, user training, integration testing, and assign clear deadlines. An example could be:

- Weeks 1–2: Finalize UI customizations and configure role-based access.
- Weeks 3–4: Integrate with document management and billing systems; conduct initial compatibility tests.
- Weeks 5–6: Migrate historical data and validate accuracy.
- Week 7: Begin phased training sessions.

Build buffer periods into the schedule to address unforeseen challenges, such as unexpected data formatting issues or delays in third-party vendor support. A realistic timeline respects the complexity of legal work while maintaining momentum toward deployment.

Communication: preparing the organization for change

Transparent communication is vital to mitigating resistance and fostering buy-in. Share a roadmap that outlines key milestones, expected changes to workflows, and how disruptions will be minimized. For example, if the new system will temporarily restrict access to case files during data migration, provide advance notice and workarounds.

Host town halls or workshops where SMEs demonstrate customized features, emphasizing how the tool simplifies tasks. You should address concerns head-on. If attorneys worry about the learning curve, highlight the personalized training plans. Use multiple channels, such as emails, intranet updates, and team meetings, to reinforce the message that the technology is designed with them, not for them.

Outcome: a solution that feels like home

By the end of this phase, the technology should feel intuitive, integrated, and indispensable. Custom workflows mirror the firm's best practices; integrations eliminate silos; and stakeholders understand both the "how" and "why" of the upcoming changes. This meticulous preparation lays the groundwork for a rollout that feels less like an upheaval and more like an evolution, a deliberate step toward a more agile, future-ready practice.

In the ever-evolving legal landscape, technology that adapts to your firm's rhythm is no longer a luxury, but a necessity. Through thoughtful customization and strategic integration, you ensure the solution does not just meet today's needs but becomes a foundation for tomorrow's innovations.

Phase 5: Training and change management – cultivating confidence and adaptability

The implementation of legal technology reaches its zenith not when the software is installed, but when it becomes an invisible thread woven into the daily fabric of your organization. Training and change management are the twin engines that drive this transition, transforming apprehension into proficiency and resistance into advocacy. By equipping teams with the skills to harness the technology and fostering a culture adaptable to change, firms can turn disruption into opportunity.

Tailored training: bridging knowledge gaps

Effective training begins with recognition that a one-size-fits-all approach seldom fits anyone. Segment users by role, such as attorneys, paralegals, and

IT staff, and design programs that speak directly to their workflows. For instance, attorneys might engage in workshops simulating AI-assisted contract review, while paralegals focus on automating document assembly. Interactive e-learning modules can cater to self-paced learners, whereas hands-on sessions with real-case scenarios reinforce practical application.

Consider a mid-sized firm rolling out a new case management system. Junior associates might benefit from step-by-step chapters on deadline tracking, while partners receive training on high-level analytics dashboards. Phased scheduling ensures everyone trains without overwhelming daily operations. Launch foundational sessions weeks before go-live, followed by advanced modules post-implementation. Refresher courses, paired with quick-reference chapters, address the inevitable "How do I...?" moments that arise post-launch.

Champions of change: empowering internal advocates

Technology champions are the unsung heroes of adoption. Select these individuals not solely for technical prowess, but for their influence and enthusiasm. A senior paralegal respected for their problem-solving skills, or a partner open to innovation, can inspire peers more effectively than any top-down mandate. Arm champions with deep training, enabling them to troubleshoot issues and model best practices.

A regional law firm facing resistance to a new billing platform designates champions in each practice area. These champions host "lunch-and-learn" sessions, demonstrating how the tool reduced administrative burdens. Their peer-to-peer support creates a ripple effect, turning skeptics into advocates and surfacing workflow tweaks that IT had not anticipated.

Navigating resistance: flexibility as a catalyst

Resistance often stems from fear of the unknown, not defiance. Proactively identify concerns through surveys or focus groups. Did the pilot reveal anxiety about AI replacing jobs? Address these head-on with transparent dialogue. Offer flexible adoption paths. Allow attorneys to start with basic features, like automated time entry, before gradually introducing advanced analytics.

A corporate legal department, for instance, mitigates pushback against a contract lifecycle management tool by letting teams choose their onboarding timeline. Early adopters receive recognition, while hesitant users access sandbox environments to experiment risk-free. Personalized coaching sessions bridge skill gaps, ensuring no one felt left behind.

Leadership and inclusion: the bedrock of buy-in

Visible leadership commitment is non-negotiable. When senior partners actively use the technology, say, logging into a client portal during meetings, it signals its strategic importance. Involve employees early. A firm developing a document automation tool can form a cross-functional committee to co-design templates, fostering ownership and preempting critiques.

Sustaining momentum: beyond the launch

Post-implementation support turns initial success into lasting habit. Establish a help desk staffed by IT and super-users to resolve issues swiftly. Continuous learning opportunities, like monthly webinars on new features, or a repository of video tutorials, keep skills sharp. Feedback loops, such as quarterly surveys, uncover pain points and spark iterative improvements.

Communication: weaving a narrative of progress

A strategic communication plan amplifies every effort. Regular updates celebrating milestones – for example, "85 percent of motions now drafted using AI tools" – reinforce the technology's value. Champions share success stories in internal newsletters, highlighting how the tool saved time on a high-stakes case. Transparently address concerns through FAQs or town halls, ensuring anxieties are heard and alleviated.

Outcome: from adoption to advocacy

When training and change management are executed with empathy and precision, technology ceases to be a disruption and becomes a reflex. Teams no longer "use" the tool; they rely on it. Resistance gives way to curiosity, as even the most hesitant partner discovers newfound efficiencies. The result is a resilient organization where innovation is not feared, but embraced, and where the human element – the attorney's judgment, the paralegal's diligence – is amplified, not replaced, by technology. In this environment, legal tech doesn't just succeed; it becomes indispensable.

Phase 6: Implementation and rollout – executing with precision

The culmination of months of planning, testing, and preparation rests on the moment of truth: deploying legal technology across your organization. A successful rollout hinges on meticulous execution, balancing urgency with caution. Whether phased or comprehensive, the implementation must prioritize seamless integration, user readiness, and adaptability. By structuring the process with clarity and transparency, you transform anticipation into action, ensuring the technology delivers on its promise.

Choosing the right deployment strategy: phased vs full-scale

The scale of your rollout depends on organizational size, complexity, and risk tolerance. For larger firms or intricate systems, a phased approach minimizes disruption. Begin with a pilot department or practice area, such as litigation or corporate services, to refine the process before expanding. For example, a global firm might roll out a new e-discovery tool first in its New York office, addressing region-specific compliance needs, and then adapt lessons learned for London and Singapore.

Smaller firms or straightforward tools, like a client portal, may opt for full deployment. This "big bang" approach demands rigorous preparation, with all integrations tested, data migrated, and staff trained simultaneously. A boutique IP firm, for instance, might deploy a document automation system firm-wide after a successful pilot, relying on pre-established super-users to shepherd adoption.

Regardless of strategy, a detailed schedule is critical. You must map milestones, such as data migration completion, training wrap-up, go-live date, with buffer periods for unforeseen delays. Allocate resources strategically, such as IT teams focusing on technical execution, while department leads manage workflow adjustments.

Integration: the silent backbone of success

A flawless technical integration ensures the new tool does not operate in isolation. Revisit compatibility with core systems. Does the AI contract analyzer pull clauses from the document management system? Do time entries sync automatically with billing software? For example, a family law firm implementing a case management system must ensure that custody schedules and client communications integrate with its calendaring tool to avoid missed court dates.

Data migration demands precision. Transferring decades of case files or client records requires validation checks to prevent corruption or loss. A firm migrating to a cloud-based system may discover mid-rollout that metadata from older PDFs are not indexing properly, necessitating a pause to reformat files. Pre-emptive testing mitigates such risks.

Support: the safety net during transition

Even the smoothest rollout encounters hiccups. A dedicated support team armed with playbooks for common issues prevents minor glitches from spiraling. Establish a helpdesk with tiered escalation paths: Level 1 staff resolve password resets, while Level 2 tackles integration errors. For instance, when a litigation team's new deposition tool crashes during a critical prep session, immediate access to a dedicated engineer can restore functionality within hours, preserving trust in the system.

Monitoring and adaptation: listening in real time

Post-launch metrics reveal more than pre-deployment projections. Track usage patterns: are attorneys bypassing the automated brief drafting feature? Is the client portal underutilized? Real-time dashboards can highlight adoption gaps. A corporate law department notices paralegals are manually inputting data into both old and new systems "just in case", signaling a need for reinforced training on data integrity.

Feedback loops are equally vital. Regular surveys, focus groups, or "office hours" with champions uncover pain points. For example, when users at a mid-sized firm report that the new AI research tool's alerts are overwhelming, developers simplify notifications, boosting satisfaction by 40 percent.

Communication: the thread that connects the process

Transparent communication transforms uncertainty into confidence. Launch the rollout with a clear announcement: what's changing, when, and why. Regular updates, via email, intranet, or town halls, highlight progress. Celebrate wins: "The new billing system processed 95 percent of invoices error-free this month!" Acknowledge challenges openly, outlining fixes. For example, when a document management upgrade temporarily slows retrieval times, leadership explain the bottleneck and provide workarounds, maintaining credibility.

Outcome: from blueprint to reality

A well-executed rollout is not the end, but the beginning, of a new operational rhythm. When integrations hum quietly in the background, support is responsive but rarely needed, and teams instinctively reach for the tool; the technology has ceased to be "new". It is simply how work gets done. This seamless transition, chaptered by structure and empathy, positions the organization to reap the full benefits of innovation: heightened efficiency, sharper compliance, and a culture poised to embrace the next wave of legal tech. In the end, the measure of success is not just a successful deployment, but a team that feels equipped, heard, and ready for what's next.

Phase 7: Monitoring, feedback, and continuous improvement – sustaining success

The launch of legal technology is not the finish line; it is the start of an ongoing journey. To ensure long-term success, organizations must treat their tools as living systems, evolving in tandem with shifting workflows, user needs, and industry advancements. By embedding a culture of continuous improvement, rooted in rigorous monitoring, candid feedback, and agile adjustments, firms can transform technology from a static solution into a dynamic asset that grows alongside their ambitions.

Monitoring performance: the pulse of progress

KPIs are the compass guiding this journey. Revisit the metrics established during goal-setting, such as time saved, error reduction, user adoption rates, and track them relentlessly. For instance, a firm that implemented AI-driven legal research tools might monitor the average time attorneys spend locating precedent cases, aiming to reduce it by 30 percent. Dashboards displaying real-time data, such as automated reports on billing accuracy or document retrieval speeds, turn abstract goals into tangible insights.

Consider a corporate legal department that introduces a contract lifecycle management platform. By tracking metrics like contract turnaround time and approval bottlenecks, they identify that sales teams are bypassing the system for simple agreements. This prompts targeted training, boosting compliance from 65 percent to 92 percent within months.

Feedback: the voice of the user

Quantitative data tell only half the story. Regularly solicit feedback through surveys, focus groups, or "innovation labs" in which users brainstorm enhancements. For example, after rolling out a new client portal, a family law firm discovers, through anonymous feedback, that clients find the interface confusing; simplifying the layout and adding video tutorials increases engagement by 50 percent.

Create channels for continuous dialogue, such as a suggestion box in the intranet, monthly "tech check-in" meetings, or pulse surveys, after major updates. For instance, a mid-sized firm notices recurring complaints about its e-discovery tool's search functionality; it convenes a cross-functional team of attorneys and IT staff to co-design improvements, resulting in a 40 percent drop in support tickets.

Iterative optimization: bridging gaps, seizing opportunities

Feedback without action breeds cynicism. Partner with vendors or internal developers to prioritize and implement changes. This might involve refining features (e.g., adding bulk editing to a case management system), addressing bugs, or scaling integrations. For example, a litigation firm using predictive analytics software works with the vendor to incorporate judge-specific ruling tendencies into case strategy templates, enhancing its strategic edge.

Agile methodologies shine here. Break enhancements into sprints, releasing updates incrementally. For example, a regional firm updates its document automation tool quarterly, with each iteration informed by user feedback. This approach keeps the tool aligned with evolving practice areas, from merger agreements to GDPR-compliant privacy policies.

Communication: fueling trust through transparency

Continuous improvement thrives on transparency. Share performance reports and system updates through multiple channels: quarterly all-hands meetings, email digests, or interactive dashboards accessible to all staff. For example, a firm's monthly "Tech Pulse" newsletter highlights metrics like reduced administrative hours, user adoption rates, and upcoming features.

Celebrate wins and acknowledge setbacks. When a cybersecurity upgrade temporarily slows document access times, leadership explains the trade-off between security and speed, outlining steps to optimize performance. This honesty preserves trust and underscores the organization's commitment to balancing priorities.

Outcome: a system that grows with you

The result of this relentless focus on improvement is a technology ecosystem that feels perpetually fresh. Users no longer tolerate clunky tools; they expect – and drive – enhancements. A global firm's contract management system, for instance, evolves from a basic repository into an AI-powered negotiation platform, all through iterative updates shaped by attorney feedback.

This cycle of monitoring, feedback, and adaptation does more than refine technology. It cultivates a culture of innovation. Teams become proactive problem-solvers, confident that their voices shape the tools they use daily. Clients, in turn, benefit from faster, more precise service, as the firm's tools stay ahead of regulatory changes and market demands.

In the end, legal technology's value is not measured by its initial launch, but by its capacity to evolve. By embracing continuous improvement, firms ensure their investments do not just solve today's challenges, but unlock tomorrow's opportunities. The journey never truly ends – and that's the point.

Phase 8: Planning for updates, enhancements, and scalability – future-proofing your legal tech

The lifespan of legal technology is not defined by its initial implementation, but by its ability to evolve. As laws, client expectations, and business strategies shift, so too must the tools that support them. Proactive planning for updates, enhancements, and scalability ensures that your solution remains a strategic asset, not a relic. By aligning vendor roadmaps with organizational goals, anticipating growth, and fostering a culture of continuous innovation, firms can turn technology into an enduring competitive advantage.

Collaborative evolution: partnering for progress

Technology thrives when treated as a partnership, not a purchase. Establish a rhythm of regular updates by collaborating closely with vendors or internal developers. Define a schedule for enhancements, such as quarterly feature releases or biannual security patches, and agree on testing protocols to avoid disruptions. For example, a mid-sized firm using a cloud-based case management system might coordinate with its vendor to deploy updates during low-activity periods, minimizing downtime.

User feedback fuels this cycle. Create channels for attorneys and staff to submit feature requests and then prioritize them based on impact. A corporate legal team, for instance, lobbies for bulk-editing capabilities in their contract management tool after manual updates slowed merger negotiations. By integrating this feature into the next update, the vendor reinforces the tool's relevance while deepening client trust. Rigorous testing remains critical. A family law firm may avoid a potential disaster by catching a calendar integration bug in a pre-release sandbox before it can affect court deadlines.

Scaling with purpose: building for tomorrow's demands

Scalability is the bridge between current efficiency and future growth. Assess whether your solution can handle a 50 percent increase in caseloads or a surge in data volume. For instance, a litigation firm anticipating class-action suits may ensure its e-discovery tool can scale horizontally by adding cloud servers during peak demands, avoiding performance lag.

Monitor system performance to pre-empt bottlenecks. For example, a real estate practice using AI for due diligence can implement dashboards tracking processing times and error rates. When transaction volumes spike, the data reveal server strain, prompting a preemptive upgrade to vertical scaling with higher-capacity servers. Infrastructure planning, such as adopting hybrid cloud storage for sensitive documents, ensures elasticity without compromising security.

Strategic alignment: synchronizing visions

A vendor's roadmap should mirror your firm's aspirations. Schedule regular reviews to ensure their planned features align with your long-term goals, whether that is expanding into new practice areas or bolstering compliance. When a global firm aims to reduce its carbon footprint, it partners with its document management vendor to prioritize energy-efficient data centers and paperless workflow enhancements.

Stay attuned to legal tech trends, such as AI-driven analytics and blockchain for smart contracts, and assess how the vendor's innovations can keep your firm ahead. A healthcare law group, for example, may align its vendor's roadmap with upcoming HIPAA updates, ensuring its client portal will automatically encrypt new data types.

Communication: the catalyst for confidence

Transparency transforms updates from disruptions into opportunities. Announce enhancement schedules through multiple channels: email bulletins, team huddles, or a dedicated Slack channel. When a new AI research feature launches at a criminal defense firm, the IT team hosts "innovation showcases" to demo its impact on case prep time, coupling the rollout with bite-sized training videos.

Highlight how each update ties to broader goals. A firm's quarterly tech newsletter might explain how a new billing automation feature supports its strategic priority to reduce administrative costs by 20 percent. Celebrate user-driven improvements. When a paralegal's suggestion for a document tagging system went live, leadership spotlights their contribution, reinforcing that innovation is a team sport.

Outcome: a living system, not a static tool

The result of this forward-thinking approach is a legal tech ecosystem that grows alongside your firm. Updates will feel less like mandatory overhauls and more like natural progressions. Scalability becomes effortless, whether expanding to new jurisdictions or absorbing a merger. Most importantly, the technology remains invisible – not because it is unused, but because it is so seamlessly ingrained that it feels like an extension of the team's expertise.

In an industry where change is the only constant, the ability to adapt is the ultimate differentiator. By planning not just for today's needs, but for tomorrow's unknowns, firms future-proof their operations, ensuring that their technology investments yield dividends for years to come. The path forward is not about predicting the future; it is about building a system resilient enough to thrive in it.

Phase 9: Evangelizing success and expanding use – igniting a culture of innovation

The true measure of legal technology's success lies not just in its initial adoption, but in its ability to spark curiosity, inspire creativity, and permeate every corner of the organization. By spotlighting wins, empowering advocates, and exploring new frontiers, firms can transform a single solution into a catalyst for organization-wide transformation. This phase is about momentum, turning early victories into sustained innovation.

Amplifying success: stories that resonate

Success thrives in the spotlight. Begin by documenting tangible wins: a 40 percent reduction in contract review time; a 25 percent drop in billing errors; or client praise for real-time case updates. Quantifiable metrics lend credibility, while anecdotes humanize the impact. For instance, a personal injury firm might highlight how AI-driven document analysis helped to secure a landmark settlement by uncovering a critical precedent in hours instead of weeks.

Transform these stories into compelling case studies. Detail the challenge, solution, and outcome, such as a corporate legal team automating NDAs, slashing turnaround from days to minutes. Include testimonials: "The system cut our discovery costs by 30 percent," or "Clients now receive updates before they even ask." Distribute these narratives through newsletters, intranet spotlights, and all-hands meetings. A monthly "Innovation Digest" video series featuring attorneys and staff sharing their experiences can be a catalyst for organic adoption across departments.

Champions: the heartbeat of advocacy

Technology champions are the bridge between potential and practice. Empower these influencers, such as partners who embraced the tool early and paralegals who streamlined workflows, to mentor peers. Champions can host "lunch-and-learn" sessions demonstrating how AI legal research tools have transformed their case prep. A litigator's story of winning a motion by leveraging predictive analytics can inspire a surge in tool usage among junior associates.

Create peer-learning forums, such as a Slack channel for tips, or a "Tech Innovator of the Month" award. Imagine a family law team developing a template library in their document automation system, and then champions leading workshops to replicate this success in estate planning and immigration practices.

Expanding horizons: from tool to transformation

Innovation thrives when technology transcends its initial use. Analyze workflows for untapped opportunities: could the e-discovery tool's AI classify regulatory risks in M&A due diligence? Might chatbot client intake forms be adapted for internal HR policies? A healthcare law firm expanded its compliance tracking system to automate audit responses, reducing manual work by 50 hours monthly.

Pilot new applications with the same rigor as the initial rollout. A boutique IP firm tests AI for trademark similarity searches and then scales it firm-wide after the pilot cuts search time by 70 percent. Document each experiment's lessons, whether success or setback, to refine future efforts.

Communication: fueling the fire of engagement

Sustained enthusiasm demands relentless communication. Launch an internal campaign celebrating milestones: "Our client portal reduced follow-up calls by 200 hours this quarter!" Use varied channels, such as animated infographics in elevators or quick-hit videos in team huddles, to keep the message fresh. For instance, at a global firm, a "Tech Trek" roadshow visits offices worldwide, showcasing regional success stories and crowdsourcing ideas for new use cases.

Recognition is rocket fuel: publicly honor teams who innovate. For example, a real estate group that automated lease reviews, or a pro bono team using the system to track 500+ cases. Tie rewards to strategic goals, such as bonuses for reducing manual tasks, or promotions for leading tech-driven process overhauls.

Outcome: from adoption to revolution

When success is celebrated, champions are empowered, and innovation is relentless, technology becomes more than a tool. It becomes a mindset: a corporate department's AI contract analyzer evolves into a negotiation ally; a litigation team's e-discovery tool becomes a strategic intelligence platform. Clients notice the shift, praising faster, more precise service, while employees thrive in a culture where curiosity is rewarded.

The journey from implementation to evangelism is where technology's ROI multiplies. By spotlighting wins, nurturing advocates, and daring to reimagine possibilities, firms do not just adopt technology; they redefine what's possible. In this environment, every challenge becomes an invitation to innovate, and every success becomes a stepping stone to the next breakthrough. The result? A future where the organization does not just keep pace with change – it leads it.

Phase 10: Evaluation and future planning – reflecting to propel forward

The implementation of legal technology is not a finite project, but a dynamic process that demands reflection and foresight. Evaluating outcomes and planning for the future ensures that investments continue to deliver value amid evolving challenges and opportunities. By systematically assessing impact, measuring returns, and staying attuned to innovation, organizations can cultivate a proactive stance, turning hindsight into foresight and lessons into strategy.

Post-implementation review: measuring against the compass

A formal review begins by revisiting the goals set during the planning phase. Did the AI contract review tool reduce drafting time by the targeted 30 percent? Has the client portal improved satisfaction scores as projected? For example, a mid-sized litigation firm compares pre- and post-implementation data, discovering that their e-discovery platform has slashed document review time by 40 percent, surpassing initial expectations.

Gather feedback through surveys, interviews, and focus groups. A corporate legal department, after rolling out a matter management system, conducts anonymous surveys revealing that, while attorneys praise centralized tracking, paralegals find the interface cumbersome. This duality highlights the need for holistic insights. Success in one area may coexist with friction in another.

Identify both gaps and opportunities. A family law practice uncovers that their automated calendaring tool reduced missed deadlines, but struggles with syncing external court dates. This insight spurred collaboration with the vendor to refine integration features, turning a partial win into a comprehensive solution.

ROI: quantifying value beyond dollars

ROI extends beyond financial metrics. Define KPIs aligned with strategic goals: time savings, error reduction, client retention. A personal injury firm tracking ROI finds that their client intake chatbot not only saved 15 hours weekly, but also increased case acceptance rates by 20 percent due to faster response times.

Collect data rigorously. For instance, a real estate practice using time-tracking software finds that automated document assembly reclaimed 25 percent of associates' billable hours, which became time redirected toward client counseling. Comparing pre- and post-implementation billing records, they quantify a 15 percent revenue increase that was attributable to efficiency gains.

Analyzing these results informs future decisions. When a compliance team's AI tool flagged 50 percent more risks than manual reviews, the firm reallocated audit budgets to expand the tool's use across departments, amplifying its impact.

Horizon scanning: anticipating tomorrow's tools

Legal tech's rapid evolution demands vigilance. Monitor trends through webinars, industry consortia, and peer networks. Imagine a boutique IP firm, for instance, joining a legal tech incubator, gaining early exposure to AI-driven trademark analytics, which they later adopt to expedite global filings.

Assess emerging tools against organizational needs. A corporate firm notes rising demand for environmental, social, and governance (ESG) compliance and pilot a blockchain solution for tracking supply chain ethics, transforming a trend into a competitive edge.

Plan enhancements strategically. A national firm, recognizing the surge in remote courts, integrates video conferencing tools with their case management system, ensuring seamless virtual hearings. Roadmaps should balance innovation with stability, prioritizing upgrades that align with long-term objectives.

Communication: bridging insight and action

Transparent sharing of evaluation outcomes fosters collective ownership. Present findings through detailed reports and town halls. A regional firm's post-review webinar showcases how client portal adoption correlated with a 35 percent drop in follow-up calls, reinforcing the tool's strategic value.

Engage stakeholders in future planning. For instance, when a litigation team's feedback reveals demand for predictive analytics, leadership hosts workshops to co-design the next phase of tech investments. Recognition programs, like awarding "Innovation Champions", sustain momentum by celebrating contributors.

Outcome: from reflection to roadmap

The culmination of evaluation and planning is a roadmap that is both informed and agile. A global firm's review reveals that, while their document automation system excels in routine tasks, it lags in complex transactions. This leads to a targeted upgrade, integrating generative AI for bespoke clauses, which reduces negotiation cycles by 25 percent.

By marrying data-driven insights with visionary thinking, organizations transform technology from a static tool into a strategic ally. The process ensures that every investment not only addresses today's needs, but also lays the groundwork for tomorrow's breakthroughs. In this cycle of reflection and reinvention, firms do not just adapt to change – they anticipate it, setting a course where innovation becomes habitual and growth becomes inevitable.

Conclusion: Embracing the future of legal practice

The legal profession has always been defined by its ability to adapt: to new laws, shifting client demands, and societal changes. Today, that adaptability must extend to technology. This chapter has guided you through the complexities of legal tech implementation, from identifying pain points to fostering a culture of continuous innovation. However, the journey doesn't end here; it evolves.

Key takeaways

1. *Technology is a means, not an end:* Tools like AI and automation are most powerful when they serve your firm's strategic goals, whether that is reducing overhead, improving client experiences, or mitigating risk.
2. *People drive success:* Even the most advanced system fails without buy-in. Empower your team through tailored training; celebrate their wins; and listen to their feedback.
3. *Agility is survival:* The legal landscape will keep changing. Future-proof your practice by building scalable systems, staying attuned to trends, and iterating relentlessly.

A call to action

The challenges of modern legal practice, such as mounting caseloads, cyber-security threats, and demands for transparency, are also opportunities to streamline workflows, deepen client trust, and redefine what it means to practice law.

Imagine a future where attorneys spend less time on administrative tasks and more on strategic counsel; paralegals harness AI to uncover insights hidden in decades of case law; and clients feel heard, not billed. This future is not a distant ideal; it is within reach for firms willing to innovate thoughtfully.

Final thoughts

Legal technology is not about replacing the human element; it is about amplifying it. By marrying expertise with innovation, your firm can transcend the limitations of tradition and lead in a digital-first world. The tools are here; the roadmap is in your hands. Remember: the greatest minds do not fear change – they shape it. Your journey starts with a single step. What will yours be?

Reference

1 Author's note: I began writing this chapter in a more condensed format of bullet lists at https://legaltechready.com. I have attended legal technology conferences where it is often noted that somewhere between 70 and 90 percent of legal technology implementations fail. This is absolutely appalling. As a community of users and vendors, we need to do better. I, therefore, made it my mission to compile information on every single pitfall and every piece of advice on how to overcome those pitfalls – in short, everything we can and must do to increase the chances of

ensuring success when implementing legal technology. This chapter is written as a long-form narrative. If you would like to give your team the plain checklists, send them to www.legaltechready.com. It is a living website, so if you see any areas where you can lend your experience and expertise, send me an email at: justin@automateofficework.com. I'd love to hear from you.

Chapter 6:
Managing expectations: practical steps to achieve successful AI implementation

By Mark Gediman, senior research analyst, Alston & Bird

I'm sitting at my desk, thinking about AI. Should I use CoPilot, Gemini, or ChatGPT to find a place with a good pastrami-on-rye sandwich? Does AI really know what goes into a good pastrami sandwich? I know, I know... it will figure out which places to recommend from the reviews and comments it finds on the internet. However, will it capture subtleties, like taste and expertise?

AI has been portrayed in books and motion pictures as a semi-sentient artificial construct with human emotions and thoughts. Think of C-3PO™, HAL™, and Commander Data™ as examples. Legal publishers produce ads touting how AI can help you cut hours, days, and even weeks from the document preparation process. These images color the expectations of attorneys when using AI products for research. The reality (with one possible exception, which will be discussed later) does not come close to this.

So that you know what to expect, this chapter will not get too far into the algorithms and learning that goes into the creation of an AI legal research tool. AI tools have now been in the law firm environment for at least a year, which is enough time to get a sense of the challenges inherent in rolling these out for routine use, as well as how to make this rollout successful. The term "AI" as used in this chapter refers to generative artificial intelligence, and products will only be named specifically when necessary. The focus of this chapter will be on the ways in which these tools are used day-to-day in the law firm and legal department environments.

There are many AI tools on the market. A deliberative process should be used when selecting an AI product. The firm should develop an outline of what needs the product would address prior to selecting the products for evaluation. Narrow the available products down, with three options being an optimal number; three products provide the firm with a broad platform to compare and contrast, with a greater likelihood of finding the one that meets their needs. Since budgets are limited, using a proof-of-concept process, with a trial group of attorneys and research staff, will allow the firm to test several use cases to find the product's strength and weaknesses before committing financial resources. As a participant in these test groups, I have learned several important things along the way:[1]

- Users approach AI with preconceived assumptions. For more on users' AI assumptions, I recommend that you look at the Law360 2025 AI Survey.[2] Generally speaking, these preconceptions can be summarized by the statements below:
  - AI tools can intuitively understand legal concepts;
  - AI tools recognize legal terms of art;
  - AI tools understand the questions asked, as well as the context;
  - AI tools are the same;
  - These tools are only good for legal research or document analysis; and
  - AI tools are a good replacement for basic legal research.
- Output format needs to be specified;
- News reporting of AI issues influences perceptions; and
- Security concerns are a big worry with third-party AI services. It is extremely difficult for law firms to provide their proprietary information to AI tools, given their duty to safeguard their clients' information and their own work product.

This last point presents a bit of a conundrum. Due to these concerns, training an AI to produce results that align with the unique cultural and intellectual demands of a firm remains an existential challenge in the legal industry. Until this issue is adequately addressed, AI-generated results will likely be somewhat generic. Reportedly, some firms have successfully addressed this issue by developing their own internal AI tool or securely storing a copy of a third-party AI tool within their network. Both solutions can be cost-prohibitive for firms lacking the extensive financial, technical, or support resources as their larger brethren.

Preconceived notions about AI inherently limit the use of these tools and can create frustration among the users. Frustration can easily lead to a lack of trust, which can be the kiss of death to new technology, and result in a failed rollout of expensive software. To counter this, it is necessary to consider the users' assumptions, as well as the software's limitations, and develop a plan to manage expectations and train the users how to realistically get the most from the software. Looking at both the assumptions and the limitations in more detail can help a user to understand the challenges of using these tools in day-to-day legal research.

AI cannot replace good old-fashioned legal research... yet

Legal research requires attention to detail. First, let's quickly review the research process without AI:

1. Determine where to search. Even running a global search on Lexis, Westlaw, or Bloomberg requires you to determine where you want to start your research. Is it better to search for cases to start with, or look for a treatise for a discussion of a particular point of law and/or fact pattern.
2. Create a query using Boolean search terms ("AND", "OR", "w/n").
3. Review the search results, looking for the most relevant items. If there are many hits for your search, it may be necessary to filter based on courts, additional terms, or specific sources.
4. When you find the right case, check that case for additional cases that discuss the same point of law and may also contain similarities to the fact pattern, using tools such as Shepard's or Keycite. Both Steps 3 and 4 require that the researcher read the cases closely for applicability to their argument.
5. Repeat Step 3 and 4 until you are confident you have the best cases to support your argument or thesis.

When users are first presented with an AI tool that is built specifically for legal research, the assumption is that the tool will replace Steps 1–4 above. The problem is that there is more to using these tools than just asking them a question and relying on the results.

AI tools will not provide relevant answers to just any question. In fact, I have come across occasions in which "unable to answer" is the system reply. Reviewing the search results is an important part of the due diligence process in AI research.

AI systems are notorious for their inaccuracies[3] and "hallucinations". "Hallucinations" are defined by the Stanford University Human-Centered Artificial Intelligence simply as the fabrication of false information.[4] Examples of this in the legal context can be as egregious as the creation of a fake citation to a non-existent case, or as subtle as misinterpreting the holding of a case. For this reason, case citations should be checked for accuracy. Do they actually exist? If so, does the AI's summary match the case?

Legal AI users should expect these hallucinations to occur and be vigilant. The vendors of AI tools have taken steps to reduce the occurrence of these hallucinations, with varying degrees of success. Some have implemented retrieval augmented generation (RAG), which, in theory, "would allow a system to first retrieve the relevant source material and then use it to generate the correct response".[5] Without going into too much detail on this, it suffices to say that, while RAG may reduce the occurrence of hallucinations, it does not eliminate them.[6]

It is not enough to know that these errors can occur; instead, this knowledge should form part of the preparation process prior to the rollout of AI products. It is important to include discussions of the tendency of AI to embellish or just be plain wrong before users ever type their first prompt. Note that this applies to potential end users of this information, as well as the "hands-on" researchers. The potential consumers of AI reports should receive a proper, consistent briefing into the basics and possible pitfalls of using AI. There are several organizations that offer pre-packaged video tutorials to ensure that prospective users are properly prepared.

Going one step further with AI results is not a bad idea. Incorporating a standard disclaimer into the transmittal of AI results will reinforce the nature of the information that is being provided. The disclaimer I use reads: "Please note that this is only meant as a starting point for your research and the information contained in this report should be vetted." This places the responsibility of ensuring the information provided by AI actually exists and is relevant squarely on the requestor. This is an area where collaboration between the research staff and the requestor can achieve better outcomes.

Determining the best AI tool(s)

You cannot just put any AI tool into a firm. My experience with onboarding AI tools has taught me that the legal tools currently on the market all have strengths and weaknesses. The challenge is putting a process into place to evaluate each tool and find the one that best meets your needs.

The evaluation process should use a test group that encompasses different specialties and different experience levels. Litigators and transactional attorneys each have unique requirements. How case summaries, points of law research, and document drafting are handled is important to each group, and each is handled differently by varying AI systems. Including people with varying levels of technical expertise is also important. A comfort with technology may give a group member unreasonable expectations, both positive and negative, for the tools and the end results. Their expectations most likely come from years of typing in Boolean and natural language searches on Lexis, Westlaw, Bloomberg, or similar legal research platforms. In fact, since natural language processing is a rudimentary form of AI, I was not surprised by how many attorneys have expected comparable results. Inexperienced researchers may understand the law, but do not understand the system. All group members may be influenced by news stories detailing the issues of AI tools in legal research, especially their tendency to "hallucinate".

I recently took part in a panel discussion in which the panelists[7] assessed three selected AI tools.[8] This was hosted by the Southern California Association of Law Libraries (SCALL) 2025 Institute, with the assessment questions reflecting the local jurisdiction of California. Three generic prompts were created, and the results were evaluated using this six-factor test:

- Accuracy of answer;
- Depth of answer;
- Cited primary sources;
- Secondary sources cited;
- Format of answer; and
- Iterative options.

The three prompts asked of each AI tool were:

1. What is the timeframe to seek certification of an interlocutory appeal from the district court in Ninth Circuit?
2. Is there a private right of action under the California Reproductive Leave Loss for Employees Act?
3. What is the standard for appealing class certification? (California)

The evaluated products were Westlaw Precision AI, Lexis+ AI, and Vincent AI from vLex. I have placed links to a few of the write-ups of this program in the endnotes to give you an idea of how it was viewed by the legal library/research/tech community.[9] This panel was composed of researchers who are familiar with using AI tools in the law firm environment, rather than the vendor representatives. The program was crafted from the point of view that hearing the unvarnished views of the end users of these products would have value to an audience of people with similar backgrounds.

After running the three prompts on each of the three AI tools, we found the results varied based on the question. For example, Question 2 concerned a statute (the California Reproductive Leave Loss for Employees Act (SB 848)) that only went into effect on 1 January 2024.[10] Due to the statute's limited time in effect, I did not expect there to be a lot of related information, whether cases, codes, or secondary materials. In this, I was not disappointed. Here are the summarized conclusions from each service:

- Lexis + AI: No explicit private right of action under this statute.
- Westlaw Precision AI: No explicit right of action under this statute. However, it does allow for a *possible* right of action under the California Private Attorney General Act (PAGA).
- Vincent AI (vLex): Found that a private right of action *did* exist by:
  - Interpreting the language at Cal. Gov. Code § 12945.6 (where the act is codified); and
  - Finding a related regulation: Cal. Code Regs. Title 2, § 14050. This regulation explicitly allows for a civil action in federal or state court.

I found the differences between the three AI tools interesting. Although using basically the same databases of primary law, each service came to a different conclusion. Westlaw Precision AI was able to find a possible path to a right of action using a different statute, while Lexis+ AI concluded that the private right of action did not exist. It is notable that Vincent AI came to a different conclusion from both Lexis and Westlaw. Vincent AI found a regulation that appeared to be directly applicable to this statute. It is unusual for a regulation to be issued this quickly for a statute this recent and, in full transparency, I did not find it in my research – and I am not inexperienced when it comes to researching these types of issues. In this case, I preferred the answer provided by Vincent AI. Vincent AI's answer was a supportable argument, grounded in both statutory and regulatory law.

This does not mean that any of these tools were wrong. Different systems are trained on a distinct set of resources, and each company has a different collection of intellectual property that can create unique paths of reasoning and result in different conclusions.

Table 1 summarizes how these tools measured up.

Table 1: Results from the "AI smackdown", hosted by the SCALL Institute. Created by Cindy Guyer and reproduced with permission here.

	Evaluation factors					
	Accuracy	**Depth**	**Cited sources**	**Secondary sources**	**format**	**Iterative options**
WL	Yes	Medium depth	22	6 (some irrelevant)	Paragraphs and list	Follow-up questions
LX	Yes	Least depth	91	25 (some irrelevant)	Paragraphs	Most options for users
VLEX	Yes	Most depth	36	11 (most federal)	Paragraphs in sections	Modify source lists, follow-up questions

As you can see, each tool had its strengths and weaknesses. Some points that stuck out to me during the process of putting this presentation together with my colleagues were:

- The most cited sources in a search result did not translate to the most in-depth discussion;
- The ability to modify and follow-up searches was an important feature of all these tools, with Vincent's unique ability to adjust the search by adjusting the results making refining the research much easier; and
- As the chart shows, they each had their own unique features.

AI due diligence

Here are my recommendations for proper AI due diligence:

1. *Ask yourself if the result makes sense.*
   Why? Your legal experience is the result of years of education and practical experience. If it does not make sense, it should not be relied upon.
2. *Never take the research report at face value.*
   Why? Read the research carefully and review the cited cases, codes, and regulations to confirm that the citations actually say what the AI system thinks they say. AI systems are programmed to find you an answer; this means that the system is trying to please you by finding

results to your query, but this does not guarantee that these results will be relevant. Another advantage to checking the citations is confirming that they do, indeed, exist.

3. *Check the status of the case.*
   Why? Some AI tools do not provide comprehensive case flags (like the type used for case law on Lexis and Westlaw) to show whether the points of law discussed in these cases are still valid. Check the current status of the case, even if there is a flag to confirm.
4. *Try posing your research question in a couple of different ways.*
   Why? One issue with AI is the fact that even asking the same question two different times can give you different results. Asking your question in a different way can confirm the results from the first question, even if the same perfect case is buried in one, but ranked highly in the other.

Conclusion

It is important to note that the American Bar Association[11] and at least three state bar associations (California,[12] New York,[13] and Florida[14]) have all released guidance on lawyers' duty of supervision over work product created with AI tools. More than 30 federal judges[15] have issued standing orders instructing attorneys to disclose or monitor the use of AI in their courtrooms. As if that's not enough, some corporate counsel are requiring firms disclose and – in some cases – get pre-approval when using AI on their matters.

Despite these concerns, 78 percent of respondents in a recent Thomson Reuters survey[16] said they believe AI is a force for good in the legal profession. Think about that for a moment – even when taking the possible negatives into consideration, attorneys still see this as a net positive for the industry. The potential to reduce write-offs from inefficient research, as well as the ability to spend their valuable time more productively researching legal concepts, such as crafting an argument based on the information found in Question 2 above, are strong entries on the positive side of the ledger.

I cannot say I disagree with the Thomson Reuters respondents. When AI first came upon the scene, I was skeptical. There I was, a researcher who spent decades honing my craft; I wield Boolean searches with surgical precision. All of a sudden, a tool is then invented that replaces the need for this type of research. However, I have been made a believer: my research time is much better spent reviewing the search results and getting the most relevant items as quickly as possible. As for there being less work because of these tools, I am finding the opposite to be true: I am busier than ever, conducting more interesting research. Plus, I'm hoping that – with a little bit of help – I can find that perfect pastrami-on-rye.

References

1 Please note that the opinions stated in this chapter are my conclusions and reflect my personal experience with these tools. They do not reflect the attitudes, perceptions, opinions, or assumptions of Alston & Bird, its employees, the membership of the American Association of Libraries (AALL), AALL affiliate the Southern California Association of Law Libraries, or the owners of the AI tools referenced in this chapter.

2 Law360 Pulse, "AI Survey: Expanded Use and the Legal Industry's Response", March 2025. See: https://www.law360.com/pulse/articles/2299612?utm_source=Social+General+Option+2+Large+Law&utm_medium=Social&utm_campaign=2025+Pulse+AI+Survey&es_id=f64ac4c3c3.

3 Surani, F. and Ho, D.E., "AI on Trial: Legal Models Hallucinate in 1 out of 6 (or More) Benchmarking Queries", Stanford University Human-Centered Artificial Intelligence, 23 May 2024. See: https://hai.stanford.edu/news/ai-trial-legal-models-hallucinate-1-out-6-or-more-benchmarking-queries.

4 *Ibid.*

5 *Ibid.*

6 Magesh, V., Surani, F., Dahl, M. et al, "Hallucination Free? Assessing the Reliability of Leading AI Legal Research Tools", arXiv, 30 May 2024. https://doi.org/10.48550/arXiv.2405.20362.

7 My fellow panelists in the AI Smackdown were Tanya Livshits, Manager Research at DLA Piper, and Cindy Guyer, senior knowledge and research analyst at O'Melveny.

8 Please note that these were tools that the panelists had access to and were chosen for that reason.

9 Tromans, R.," vLex Does Well At 'AI Smackdown' + Ed Walters Interview", Artificial Lawyer, 13 February 2025. See: https://www.artificiallawyer.com/2025/02/13/vlex-does-well-at-ai-smackdown-ed-walters-interview/; Ambrogi, B., "In 'AI Smackdown,' Law Librarians Compare Legal AI Research Platforms, Finding Distinct Strengths and Limitations," LawSites, 14 February 2025. See: https://www.lawnext.com/2025/02/in-ai-smackdown-law-librarians-compare-legal-ai-research-platforms-finding-distinct-strengths-and-limitations.html; and Meyers, E., "Wrestling with New AI Tools: An Overview of the 'AI Smackdown' at the Institute," *SCALL Newsletter*, 2025, volume 52, issue 3, pp.1–16. See: https://scallnet.org/wp-content/uploads/2025/03/SCALL-Newsletter-Spring-Issue-2025-color.pdf.

10 SB-848 Employment: leave for reproductive loss. Senate Bill No. 848 (Chapter 724): An act to add Section 12945.6 to the Government Code, relating to employment.

11 American Bar Association, "Formal Opinion 512: Generative Artificial Intelligence Tools", 29 July 2024. See:

https://www.americanbar.org/content/dam/aba/administrative/professional_responsibility/ethics-opinions/aba-formal-opinion-512.pdf.

12 The State Bar of California, "Standing Committee on Professional Responsibility and Conduct: Practical guidance for the use of generative artificial intelligence in the practice of law", 2025. See: https://www.calbar.ca.gov/Portals/0/documents/ethics/Generative-AI-Practical-Guidance.pdf.

13 New York State Bar Association, "Report and Recommendations of the New York State Bar Association Task Force on Artificial Intelligence", April 2024. See: https://nysba.org/wp-content/uploads/2022/03/2024-April-Report-and-Recommendations-of-the-Task-Force-on-Artificial-Intelligence.pdf.

14 The Florida Bar, "Florida Bar Ethics Opinion: Opinion 24-1", 19 January 2024. See: https://www.floridabar.org/etopinions/opinion-24-1/.

15 Law360 Pulse, "Tracking Federal Judge Orders On Artificial Intelligence", 2025. See: https://www.law360.com/pulse/ai-tracker.

16 Thomson Reuters, "Future of Professionals Report: AI-powered technology & the forces shaping professional work", July 2024. See: https://www.thomsonreuters.com/content/dam/ewp-m/documents/thomsonreuters/en/pdf/reports/future-of-professionals-report-2024.pdf.

Chapter 7:
The global impact of the European Union's AI Act on the legal profession

By Itsiq Benizri, counsel, WilmerHale

The European Union's Artificial Intelligence Act[1] (AI Act) is the world's first comprehensive horizontal legal framework for AI. With challenging requirements and significant extraterritorial effects and fines, the AI Act will have a profound impact on the legal profession that extends far beyond the EU.

While the AI Act will generally apply from 2 August 2026, some provisions are already applicable at the time of writing, with other requirements to be enforced before August 2026. Legal professionals should start their compliance programs as soon as possible, as it will take time to understand the technology and set their own risk thresholds to be able to navigate compliance effectively.

This chapter will outline:

- Key aspects of the AI Act for the legal profession;
- Its impact on non-EU laws; and
- How the legal profession should prepare for compliance.

Although this chapter focuses on compliance with the AI Act, it is important to note that the EU General Data Protection Regulation (GDPR)[2] and the ePrivacy Directive on privacy and electronic communications[3] continue to apply to the processing of personal data in connection with the AI Act.

Essentials of the AI Act for the legal profession

The AI Act is relevant to the legal profession both within and outside the EU due to its broad scope from a material, personal, and territorial perspective. The AI Act relies on a risk-based approach and includes significant penalties. Additionally, the timeline is quite challenging. Finally, the AI Act is intended to have a relatively dynamic approach. This chapter focuses on the most relevant aspects of these points for the legal profession.

Scope

Material scope

The AI Act applies to AI systems and specific AI models.[4]

An AI system is a "machine-based system designed to operate with varying levels of autonomy, that may exhibit adaptiveness after deployment and that, for explicit or implicit objectives, infers, from the input it receives, how to generate outputs such as predictions, content, recommendations, or decisions that can influence physical or virtual environments."[5] This definition may be more complex than it appears and has been addressed by the European Commission in recent guidelines.[6] For the purposes of this chapter, it is sufficient to highlight that this definition emphasizes two key characteristics of AI systems: their autonomy and their ability to infer how to generate outputs.

AI models are part of AI systems and serve as the engines providing functionality. To become complete AI systems, AI models need additional components, like a user interface. While the AI Act generally does not subject AI models to legal obligations, it defines a general-purpose AI model (GPAI model) as "an AI model, including where such an AI model is trained with a large amount of data using self-supervision at scale, that displays significant generality and is capable of competently performing a wide range of distinct tasks regardless of the way the model is placed on the market and that can be integrated into a variety of downstream systems or applications."[7] A GPAI model, therefore, has three main characteristics: significant generality; the ability to perform various tasks; and potential for integration into downstream services.

The AI Act does not apply to any research, testing or development activity regarding AI systems or models before their market release or entry into service within the EU. However, testing in real-world conditions is not covered by this exemption.[8]

Personal scope

The AI Act identifies several key players, all of which can be natural or legal persons. For the purposes of this discussion, the most relevant players are providers and deployers. Providers develop or have developed AI systems or GPAI models and make them available in the EU or supply them for first use in the EU under their own name or trademark, whether for payment or free of charge. Deployers use AI under their authority in the course of their professional activities. Most legal professionals are likely to qualify as deployers. The largest, most innovative, or ambitious law firms, legal organizations and bodies may qualify as providers.

The AI Act includes a reclassification clause for high-risk AI systems, which can turn any deployer of such systems into a provider – subject to providers' obligations – if they engage in certain actions.[9] For law firms and legal organizations and bodies, these actions include placing their name or trademark on a system already marketed or in service in the EU; making substantial modifications to such a system that maintains its high-risk status; or altering its intended purpose in a way that renders it high-risk. In such cases, the original provider is no longer considered the provider, but must instead cooperate with the new provider by making the necessary information available and providing the reasonably expected technical access and assistance required to fulfil the obligations set out in the AI Act.

Territorial scope

The AI Act has significant extraterritorial effects, as it applies to providers who make AI systems or models available in the EU or supply them for first use in the EU, regardless of their location or establishment.[10] The AI Act also applies to providers and deployers established or located outside the EU if the output of the system or model is used in the EU.[11] For instance, legal professionals might be subject to the AI Act if they use AI outside the EU and the legal advice or research produced by that AI is used in the EU.

Risk-based approach

The AI Act relies on a risk-based approach, meaning that different requirements apply based on the level of risk. AI systems posing unacceptable risk are prohibited, while high-risk AI systems must comply with strict requirements. Many sources also refer to limited-risk AI systems, which must comply with transparency requirements. However, this classification is misleading, as these transparency requirements apply to certain AI systems, irrespective of their risk level. Similarly, the requirements for GPAI models apply, irrespective of the risk level. Lastly, there are no restrictions for what is commonly referred to as "minimal-risk AI systems", such as AI-enabled video games or spam filters, unless the general transparency requirements apply.

Penalties

EU Member States must establish the rules on penalties applicable to infringements of the AI Act and take all measures necessary to ensure their implementation. Administrative fines will be determined based on an undertaking's global revenue if the calculated amount exceeds the fine cap.

Noncompliance with the AI Act's requirements regarding prohibited AI systems is subject to administrative fines of up to €35 million or up to seven percent of revenue. Failing to comply with the requirements for limited-risk and high-risk AI systems and GPAI models will incur administrative fines of up to €15 million or up to three percent of revenue. Providing incorrect, incomplete or misleading information in response to authorities' requests will attract fines of up to €7.5 million or one percent of revenue.

Timeline

The timeline is complex and follows a progressive application of the rules. The most relevant dates for the legal profession are as follows. The AI Act's provisions concerning prohibited AI practices and the obligation to ensure a sufficient level of AI literacy of staff entered into application on 2 February 2025.[12] The provisions related to GPAI models will be applicable starting 2 August 2025.[13] Most other provisions, including those pertaining to high-risk and limited-risk AI systems, will enter into application on 2 August 2026.[14]

Dynamism

The EU's regulatory framework approach for AI compliance is structured to be adaptable in response to technological developments and challenges encountered during the implementation of the AI Act. However, not all adaptations will stem from these developments; the evolving political landscape is also expected to influence these adjustments.

Technological developments

The EU legislature has recognized the need to adapt the AI Act in response to rapid technological developments and the technical expertise required for its effective application.[15] This is reflected in provisions for the review, adaptation, and specification of the AI Act. Whether this will be sufficient to ensure that the AI Act will keep pace with rapid technological developments remains an open question.

First, the European Commission will evaluate and review the AI Act in its entirety by August 2029 and every four years thereafter.[16] Second, the European Commission can adopt acts and guidelines regarding specific provisions of the AI Act to ensure the regulatory framework is adjusted as needed.[17] The European Commission will annually assess the need to amend the list of prohibited practices.[18] It will also develop guidelines for implementing the AI Act's provisions on prohibited AI systems.[19]

The European Commission can also amend the list of high-risk AI systems and the exemptions to such classification.[20] The Commission is required to assess the need to amend the list of high-risk AI systems annually,[21] and must consider extending this list by August 2028 and every four years thereafter.[22] The Commission will provide guidelines on the classification rules for high-risk AI systems, including conditions for exceptions, by February 2026.[23] Specifically, the Commission can amend the requirements for the technical documentation that demonstrates compliance of high-risk AI systems with the AI Act;[24] the content of the EU declaration of conformity with the requirements associated with high-risk AI systems;[25] and the provisions regarding the conformity assessment procedure leading to such a declaration.[26] The Commission will also specify the requirements for post-market monitoring plans of high-risk AI systems.[27]

The European Commission will assess the necessity to update the list of limited-risk AI systems by August 2028 and every four years thereafter.[28] The Commission will promote EU-wide codes of practice for implementing AI Act requirements on detecting and labelling artificially generated or manipulated content. The Commission can approve these codes of practice and, if it considers them inadequate, specify common rules for implementing the AI Act's obligations.[29]

Finally, the European Commission can amend the criteria for the designation of GPAI models with systemic risk;[30] the technical documentation for providers of GPAI models;[31] and the transparency information for providers of such models.[32]

Implementation challenges

The European Commission will assess the need to amend the AI Act to ensure the enforcement mechanisms remain effective by August 2028 and every four years thereafter. Similarly, in July 2023, five years after the GDPR came into effect, the European Commission proposed a regulation with additional procedural rules to ensure proper enforcement of the GDPR, addressing criticisms in this respect.[33] Comparable initiatives may be undertaken concerning the AI Act in the next few years, if required.

Political developments

As a general-purpose technology – a transformative innovation that has widespread effects across multiple sectors of the economy, much like the printing press, electricity, or the internet – AI is inherently highly political.

Political developments are, therefore, expected to influence the regulatory landscape and enforcement of AI.

At the AI Action Summit in Paris in February 2025, many global leaders, including US vice president J.D. Vance, advocated for a lighter touch on tech regulation. French President Emmanuel Macron called for a simplification of the EU AI regulatory framework, noting that "at the national and European scale, it is very clear that we have to resynchronize with the rest of the world."[34] The president of the European Commission, Ursula von der Leyen, insisted that the AI Act adds value, as it provides for a unified set of safety rules across the EU instead of 27 different national regulations. However, she also stated: "We have to make it easier; we have to cut red tape. And we will."[35] Henna Virkkunen, the European Commission's executive vice president in charge of digital policy, further emphasized that the "digital work can't be a Wild West where there are no rules", but confirmed that the European Commission is "very committed to cut bureaucracy and red tape."[36] Virkkunen noted that the EU's deregulatory efforts are driven by its own competitiveness goals and are not "dependent on the US."[37]

At of the time of writing, the European Commission has already withdrawn its proposal for an AI liability directive, which was intended to provide a feasible avenue for victims under fault-based liability law.[38]

Impact on non-EU laws

As previously explained, the EU's approach to AI regulation is influenced by international political pressure, mainly from the US. However, the EU is also expected to inspire other regions, much like it did with the GDPR. Many countries may use the EU's approach as a reference when developing their own regulations, particularly considering the substantial effort the EU has invested in the AI Act. However, adopting from the AI Act does not imply exact replication. Similarly to the GDPR, non-EU countries will likely select specific EU rules that align with their needs and discard those that do not. Some countries might even delay implementation until they observe the outcomes in Europe, making adjustments to avoid any identified drawbacks.

While the AI Act is more prescriptive than other legislations, we observe relatively similar principles at its core being adopted in various regions and international organizations. In particular, non-binding guidelines and upcoming mandatory regulations for generative AI are already emerging outside the EU.

The UK currently does not plan to adopt a horizontal AI regulatory approach. Instead, it aims for a principles-based framework, focusing on safety, security and robustness; transparency and explainability; fairness; accountability and governance; and contestability and redress.[39] This framework will not be codified into law at present,[40] although there is consideration for future legislation targeted at the small number of developers of the most powerful general-purpose systems.[41] This approach would involve establishing dynamic thresholds based on forecasts of capabilities using two proxies: the amount of computation power used for model training and high capabilities resulting in high risk.[42] The prospective obligations under such legislation would build upon the aforementioned principles and could incorporate transparency measures related to the data on which systems are trained; risk management; accountability; corporate governance obligations; and actions to address potential harms, such as those caused by misuse or unfair bias, both pre- and post-training.[43]

The US does not currently have a federal law explicitly designed to regulate AI. Although executive orders issued by President Biden have paved the way for such legislation, many of these initiatives were revoked by President Trump.[44] Nevertheless, several US states have either adopted or are in the process of adopting AI-related legislation. For example, California has enacted laws that require developers to disclose information about the data used to train their generative AI systems,[45] provide AI detection tools, and offer users the possibility to identify content as AI-generated.[46] Colorado was the first state to adopt a comprehensive AI law based on a risk-based approach, drawing some inspiration from the AI Act.[47] The Colorado Act focuses on high-risk AI and imposes requirements for documentation, risk assessment and mitigation, governance, and transparency. The Colorado Act also mandates that consumers be informed when they are interacting with AI systems, irrespective of the risk level. Interestingly, the Colorado Act incorporates some terminology from the AI Act, such as "deployers".

Australia is considering mandating guardrails for high-risk AI, focusing on testing, transparency, and accountability based on the AI system's risk profile.[48] Options include adapting existing regulations or creating new ones, such as an Australian AI Act.[49] The focus is on GPAI models and high-risk AI.[50] At the time of writing, Australia is still gathering feedback on this approach.

Japan has issued AI guidelines based on non-binding principles that include human-centric AI, safety, fairness, privacy, security, transparency, accountability, literacy, fair competition, and innovation.[51] Japan is also evaluating the regulation of GPAI models, with an emphasis on ensuring safety and transparency.[52] However, Japan's ambitions are very clear, as it aspires to become "the world's most AI-friendly nation."[53]

China issued the first regulation on the management of generative AI services in August 2023, addressing aspects such as lawful data processing, intellectual property rights, data labeling, training, content moderation, and mechanisms for complaints and reporting.[54]

Drawing upon Organisation for Economic Co-operation and Development (OECD) principles, G7 leaders representing Canada, France, Germany, Italy, Japan, the UK, the US, and the EU have adopted a code of conduct for organizations developing "advanced AI systems".[55] This code is based on 11 principles, including risk assessment and mitigation, transparency (particularly in the identification of AI-generated content), incident reporting, governance, and cybersecurity.

Finally, the OECD definition of AI largely inspired the one adopted in the AI Act. The OECD's AI principles encompass key principles such as human-centric and fair AI, transparency and explainability, safety, and accountability. However, these principles are not legally binding.[56] Furthermore, the Council of Europe, which is distinct from the EU and includes 46 countries, has adopted the first international AI treaty, known as the Council of Europe's *Framework Convention on Artificial Intelligence and Human Rights, Democracy and the Rule of Law.*[57] This Convention applies only to AI systems used by public authorities that have the potential to affect human rights, democracy, and the rule of law. The Convention requires signatories to adopt a risk-based approach and focuses on principles similar to those mentioned above.

Impact on compliance requirements for legal professionals

Most lawyers consider that AI will have a significant or transformational impact on their work by 2030 and will be a force of good in the legal profession.[58] Rapid adoption of AI, and generative AI specifically, is predicted, as reported usage of these technologies continues to increase.[59] In this context, ensuring compliance with AI regulations will be of utmost importance, especially concerning the AI Act. This is due to its extensive material scope, early entry into application, and extraterritorial impact. Legal professionals will, therefore, need to ensure compliance with the AI Act's requirements regarding prohibited practices, high-risk AI systems, limited-risk AI systems, and GPAI models.

Prohibited systems

The AI Act bans AI systems that materially distort behavior or raise serious concerns in democratic societies.[60] Some prohibitions directly impact legal professionals, while others primarily concern governments or law enforcement, indirectly affecting the legal profession.

Specifically, the AI Act bans AI systems that infer emotions in the workplace, except for medical or safety uses.[61] Employers, including legal professionals, should, therefore, avoid using these systems in their offices.

Furthermore, the legal profession should be aware of the AI Act's prohibitions regarding AI systems employed for social scoring purposes or for making risk assessments to identify or predict an individual's likelihood of committing a criminal offense based solely on profiling or evaluating their personality traits and characteristics.[62] Save exceptions, the AI Act also prohibits the use of real-time remote biometric identification systems in publicly accessible spaces for law enforcement purposes.[63]

High-risk AI systems

The AI Act identifies two categories of high-risk AI systems. The first category pertains to products and has limited relevance for the legal profession.[64] We will, therefore, focus on the second category, which includes a specific list that encompasses relevant AI use cases for legal professionals.[65]

Legal professionals, as employers, should be aware that high-risk AI systems include those used for recruitment purposes, such as placing targeted job advertisements, analyzing and filtering job applications, and evaluating candidates.[66] High-risk AI systems also cover AI systems used to make decisions affecting terms of employment relationships, such as promotions or terminations, task allocation based on individual behavior or personal traits or characteristics, and monitoring and evaluating performance and behavior in these relationships.[67]

Legal professionals, as practitioners of law, should focus on AI systems intended to be used by judicial authorities (or on their behalf) or in alternative dispute resolutions to assist in researching, interpreting facts and law, and applying legal principles to specific cases.[68] This, therefore, applies to courts, arbitrators, and arbitral institutions. It is important to note that not every application of AI in this context constitutes a high-risk scenario. The use of AI qualifies as high-risk only if it is meant to research or interpret facts and the law or to apply the law to a defined set of circumstances.

Legal professionals will also need to become familiar with high-risk AI systems used by or on behalf of law enforcement authorities or the EU to assess the risk of an individual becoming a victim of criminal offences; evaluate the reliability of evidence in the course of the investigation or prosecution of criminal offences; for profiling purposes in this context; or to assess the likelihood of an individual committing offences.[69]

These AI systems will not be considered high-risk if they do not pose a significant risk of harm to individuals' health, safety or fundamental rights, including by not materially influencing decision-making outcomes. This exemption applies if one of the following conditions is satisfied: the AI system is intended to perform a narrow procedural task; to improve the result of a previously completed human activity; to detect decision-making patterns or deviations from prior decision-making patterns without replacing or influencing prior human assessments without proper human review; or to perform preparatory tasks relevant for assessments in high-risk use cases.[70]

The exemption never applies if the AI system profiles individuals. Profiling is defined as any form of automated processing of personal data consisting of the use of personal data to evaluate certain personal aspects relating to a natural person, particularly to analyze or predict aspects concerning that natural person's performance at work, economic situation, health, personal preferences, interests, reliability, behavior, location, or movements.[71]

If a provider determines that an AI system qualifies for the exemption, it must document its assessment before placing that system or putting it into service in the EU. The provider must also register the system in an EU database for high-risk AI systems, which is set up and maintained by the European Commission.[72]

We will now discuss the requirements for high-risk AI systems and the relevant obligations for providers and deployers of such systems.

Requirements for high-risk AI systems

High-risk AI systems must comply with a significant number of requirements in consideration of their intended purposes, the generally acknowledged status of AI and AI-related technologies, and the risk management system put in place. Legal professionals, whether employing high-risk AI systems themselves or encountering their use by judicial authorities, alternative dispute resolution bodies, or law enforcement must ensure that these systems comply with the requirements outlined below. The same obviously applies, in particular, to judicial authorities and alternative dispute resolution bodies.

High-risk AI systems require a risk management system operating throughout their entire lifecycle. This concerns only risks that may be reasonably mitigated or eliminated through the development or design of high-risk AI systems or the provision of adequate technical information.[73] The training, validation, and testing data used to develop high-risk AI systems must also be subject to appropriate data governance and management practices suitable for the intended purpose of these systems.[74] Technical documentation demonstrating that high-risk AI systems comply with the AI Act must also be drawn up before placing the system or putting it into service in the EU.[75] High-risk AI systems must enable the automatic recording of events (logs) over their lifetime to ensure the traceability of the functioning of the systems, appropriate to their intended purpose.[76] Deployers must be provided with sufficiently transparent information to interpret the system's output and use it appropriately. In particular, the system must be accompanied by instructions for use.[77] High-risk AI systems must be designed and developed in such a way that they can be effectively overseen by humans.[78] Finally, high-risk AI systems must be designed and developed in such a way that they achieve an appropriate level of accuracy, robustness and cybersecurity, and perform consistently in those respects throughout their lifecycle.[79]

Obligations for providers of high-risk AI systems

It is relatively unlikely that law firms or legal organizations and bodies will qualify as providers of high-risk AI systems, although it is not impossible. Most of the time, the obligations outlined below will primarily be relevant for legal professionals, so they are able to ensure that the high-risk AI systems they may encounter are compliant with the AI Act.

Providers of high-risk AI systems must ensure that their systems comply with the requirements associated with such systems and demonstrate such compliance to national competent authorities upon request.[80] Additionally, providers must clearly indicate their name, registered trade name or trademark, and their contact address on the system itself; if that is not feasible, this information must be displayed on the packaging or accompanying documentation.[81]

In addition, providers must comply with the following requirements: putting in place a quality management system to ensure compliance;

keeping the required documentation for 10 years after the system has been placed on the market or put into service in the EU; keeping the logs automatically generated by the system to the extent they are under the providers' control; ensuring that the system undergoes the conformity assessment procedure before being placed on the market or put into service in the EU; drawing up an EU declaration of conformity with the requirements associated with high-risk AI systems; affixing the CE marking to the system to indicate conformity with the AI Act; registering themselves and their systems in the EU database; ensuring post-market monitoring; reporting serious incidents; and follow-up on such incidents.[82]

If providers consider that a high-risk AI system is not in conformity with the AI Act, they must immediately take corrective action to bring that system into conformity or withdraw, disable, or recall it, as appropriate.[83] In any event, providers must also cooperate with competent authorities.[84]

Prior to making high-risk AI systems available on the EU market, providers established outside the EU must appoint an authorized representative established in the EU. This representative can be addressed, in addition to or instead of the provider, by the competent authorities on all compliance issues.[85]

Finally, the provider of a high-risk AI system and the third party that supplies such a system or the tools, services, components, or processes used or integrated in such a system must, through a written agreement, specify the necessary information, capabilities, technical access, and other assistance based on the generally acknowledged status of AI and AI-related technologies. The objective is to enable the provider to comply with its obligations. However, this requirement does not extend to third parties offering tools, services, processes, or components to the public, excluding general-purpose AI models, under a free and open license.[86]

Obligations for deployers of high-risk AI systems

Lawyers in private practice are more likely to be considered deployers of high-risk AI systems when they use such systems in their role as employers. They are less likely to use such systems in their professional roles, but these individuals should be aware of the obligations outlined below to ensure that judicial authorities or alternative dispute resolution bodies use high-risk AI systems in compliance with the AI Act. Judicial authorities and alternative dispute resolution bodies, however, likely to qualify as deployers of the high-risk AI systems identified above.

Deployers have several obligations in light of the provider's instructions for use.[87] They must implement appropriate technical and organizational measures for use of high-risk AI systems, in accordance with the instructions. They must monitor the system's operation based on these instructions and inform the provider where relevant. If deployers believe that following the instructions could harm individuals' health, safety or fundamental rights, they must, without undue delay, inform the provider or distributor and the relevant market surveillance authority. They should also suspend use of the system. In the event of a serious incident, deployers must first immediately inform the provider, followed by the importer or distributor and the relevant market surveillance authorities. If the deployer is unable to contact the provider, it must inform the market surveillance authority of the European country where the incident occurred. This should be done immediately after establishing or reasonably suspecting a causal link between the AI system and the serious incident, but no later than 15 days after becoming aware of the incident.[88] Deployers of high-risk AI systems must retain automatically generated logs under their control for a duration appropriate to the system's intended purpose and for at least six months, unless otherwise specified by applicable EU or national law.[89] If the deployer exercises control over the input data, it must ensure that such data are relevant and sufficiently representative for the system's intended purpose.[90]

Deployers must assign human oversight to individuals with the necessary competence, training, authority, and support. Deployers may organize their resources and activities as needed to implement the oversight measures specified by the provider.[91] EU or national law can impose additional obligations. The above requirement regarding input data also applies.

Before a high-risk AI system is put into service or used in the workplace, employers must notify workers' representatives and the affected workers about its usage.[92]

Deployers of specific high-risk AI systems mentioned above, who make decisions or assist in decision-making related to individuals, must inform them that such systems are being used.[93]

Finally, deployers must cooperate with the relevant national competent authorities in any action those authorities take in relation to the high-risk AI system to implement the AI Act.[94]

Limited-risk AI

The AI Act establishes transparency obligations for providers and deployers of certain AI systems, irrespective of the risk level. These obligations apply to AI systems and GPAI systems (i.e., AI systems based on a GPAI model and which has the capability to serve a variety of purposes, both for direct use as well as for integration in other AI systems).[95] In practice, these obligations are the ones most likely to directly apply to legal professionals.

Obligations for providers

Providers must ensure that AI systems intended to directly interact with individuals, such as chatbots, are designed and developed in such a way that individuals are informed that they are interacting with an AI system. This requirement does not apply where this is obvious for reasonably well-informed, observant, and circumspect individuals, taking the circumstances and the context of use into account.[96]

In addition, providers of AI systems – including GPAI systems – which generate synthetic audio, image, video, or text content must ensure that their systems' outputs are marked in a machine-readable format and detectable as artificially generated or manipulated. This obligation does not apply to AI systems performing an assistive function for standard editing or that do not substantially alter the input data provided by deployers, or the semantics thereof.[97]

Finally, providers of AI systems must take measures to ensure, to their best extent, a sufficient level of AI literacy among their staff and other people dealing with the operation and use of AI systems on their behalf. These measures should consider their technical knowledge, experience, education, and training and the context in which the AI systems will be used, as well as the individuals impacted by these systems.[98] AI literacy encompasses the skills, knowledge, and understanding that allow providers, deployers, and affected individuals – taking into account their respective rights and obligations under the AI Act – to make an informed deployment of AI systems, as well as to gain awareness about the opportunities and risks of AI and possible harm it can cause.[99] This obligation applies to all AI systems – not just certain AI systems – irrespective of the risk level.

Obligations for deployers

Deployers using AI-generated or manipulated image, audio, or video content that resembles existing persons, objects, places, or other entities or events and would falsely appear to a person to be authentic or truthful ("deepfakes") must disclose that the content has been artificially generated or manipulated. This obligation does not apply where the use is authorized for law enforcement purposes.[100]

Deployers of AI systems that generate or manipulate text published to inform the public on matters of public interest must also disclose that the text has been artificially generated or manipulated. This obligation does not apply where the use is authorized for law enforcement purposes, or where the text has undergone a process of human review or editorial control, and where a natural or legal person holds editorial responsibility for the publication of the content.[101]

The AI literacy requirement also applies to deployers of all AI systems, regardless of the risk level.[102]

GPAI models

Obligations regarding GPAI models apply only to providers and not to deployers. This reduces the likelihood of legal professionals being directly affected by these obligations. However, it is important for legal professionals to be aware of key compliance requirements under the AI Act, as many are expected to use GPAI models.

GPAI model providers must draft and keep the technical documentation of the model up to date, including training, testing processes, and evaluation results, and share it with authorities upon request.[103] They must also draft, keep up to date, and make available information and documentation on the capabilities and limitations of the model to downstream providers.[104] Providers must establish a policy for compliance with EU copyright and publish a summary of the content users for training their AI model, following a template from the European Commission's AI Office.[105] Finally, the aforementioned cooperation and EU representative requirements also apply here.[106]

Providers of free and open-license AI models must only comply with the copyright and training requirements. This exception is not applicable if the AI model poses a systemic risk.[107]

A GPAI model poses systemic risk if the provider or the European Commission determines that it has high-impact capabilities, meaning that it has a significant impact on the EU market – due to the model's reach or due to actual or reasonably foreseeable negative effects on public health, safety, public security, fundamental rights, or society as a whole – and this impact can be propagated at scale across the value chain.[108] A GPAI model is presumed to have high-impact capabilities where the cumulative amount of computation used for training a GPAI model is greater than 10^25 floating point operations per second (FLOPs).[109] The European Commission may also consider that a GPAI model has high-impact capabilities by taking various criteria into account, such as the number of parameters of the model; the quality or size of the dataset; the amount of computation used for training the model; whether the model has a high impact on the EU internal market due to its reach; and the number of registered end users.[110]

In addition to the obligations mentioned above, providers of GPAI models with systemic risk must perform model evaluations in accordance with standardized protocols and tools reflecting the generally acknowledged status of AI and AI-related technologies, including conducting and documenting adversarial testing of the model with a view to identifying and mitigating systemic risks.[111] Providers must assess and mitigate possible systemic risks at the EU level; track, document, and report serious incidents and possible corrective measures to the European Commission's AI Office and relevant national authorities; and ensure an adequate level of cybersecurity protections for the model and its physical infrastructure.[112]

Conclusion

The AI Act will be highly significant for the legal industry, given its global impact and the broad range of professions encompassed within its umbrella. While the Act will undoubtedly present challenges, it should also be seen as an opportunity.

First, the AI Act's requirements may apply to legal professionals acting in their capacity as employers, private practice lawyers, legal organizations, judicial authorities, or alternative dispute resolution bodies. Furthermore, legal professionals must be cognizant of the AI Act's requirements given their pivotal role in democratic societies and the judicial system.

Second, legal professionals will need to familiarize themselves with the AI Act's requirements even if they are located outside the EU, either because they fall within its scope, due to its extraterritorial effects, or to anticipate similar requirements in their own jurisdictions. Although the EU's approach to AI regulation is influenced by the shifting global political landscape, the AI Act is still expected to inspire other lawmakers around the world to some extent. It might not be replicated by others, but it will likely serve as a global benchmark.

Third, understanding the AI Act's requirements will be challenging due to its complexity and evolving nature. It will be important – but difficult – to keep track of the various acts and guidelines that the European Commission will need to adopt to ensure that the AI Act remains aligned with rapid technological developments; the technical expertise required for its effective application; and potential implementation challenges.

Finally, the AI literacy requirement, effective since February 2025, applies (or will apply) to nearly all legal professionals and illustrates the challenges ahead. It is essential that all legal professionals possess an appropriate understanding of AI technology and compliance. This requirement is not merely a legal obligation. It is crucial for legal professionals to continue practicing law effectively, maintain competitiveness, and adhere to the highest professional and ethical standards in the 21st century.

References

1 Regulation (EU) 2024/1689 of the European Parliament and of the Council of 13 June 2024 laying down harmonised rules on artificial intelligence [2024] OJ L 130.

2 Regulation (EU) 2016/679 of the European Parliament and of the Council of 27 April 2016 on the protection of natural persons with regard to the processing of personal data and on the free movement of such data [2016] OJ L 119.

3 Directive 2002/58/EC of the European Parliament and of the Council of 12 July 2002 concerning the processing of personal data and the protection of privacy in the electronic communications sector [2002] OJ L 201.

4 Regulation (EU) 2024/1689 of the European Parliament and of the Council of 13 June 2024 laying down harmonised rules on artificial intelligence [2024] OJ L 130.

5 *Ibid.*

6 European Commission, "Commission Guidelines on the definition of an artificial intelligence system established by Regulation (EU) 2024/1689 (AI Act)", 2 February 2025. See: https://digital-strategy.ec.europa.eu/en/library/commission-publishes-guidelines-ai-system-definition-facilitate-first-ai-acts-rules-application.

7 Regulation (EU) 2024/1689 of the European Parliament and of the Council of 13 June 2024 laying down harmonised rules on artificial intelligence [2024] OJ L 130; Article 3(63).

8 *Ibid.*, Article 2(8).

9 *Ibid.*, Article 25(1). See the section on high-risk AI systems under Impact on compliance requirements for legal professionals, located later in this chapter.

10 *Ibid.*, Article 2(1)(a).

11 *Ibid.*, Article 2(1)(c). The AI Act obviously also applies to deployers who are established or located in the EU (Article 2(1)(b)).

12 *Ibid.*, Article 113(a).

13 *Ibid.*, Article 113(b).

14 *Ibid.*, Article 113.

15 *Ibid.*, Recitals 173 and 174.

16 *Ibid.*, Article 112(3).
17 In addition to the examples listed here, see also Recital 173 of the EU AI Act.
18 *Ibid.*, Article 112(1).
19 *Ibid.*, Article 96(1)(b).
20 *Ibid.*, Articles 6(6), (7), and (8).
21 *Ibid.*, Article 112(1).
22 *Ibid.*, Article 112(2)(a).
23 *Ibid.*, Article 6(5).
24 *Ibid.*, Article 11(3).
25 *Ibid.*, Article 47(5).
26 *Ibid.*, Articles 43(5) and (6).
27 *Ibid.*, Article 72(3).
28 *Ibid.*, Articles 112(2)(b).
29 *Ibid.*, Article 50(7).
30 *Ibid.*, Article 51(3).
31 *Ibid.*, Articles 53(1)(a) and (6).
32 *Ibid.*, Articles 53(1)(b)(ii) and (6).
33 European Commission, "Proposal for a Regulation laying down additional procedural relating to the enforcement of GDPR", 4 July 2023. See: https://commission.europa.eu/publications/proposal-regulation-laying-down-additional-procedural-rules-relating-enforcement-gdpr_en.
34 Breeden, A., and Alderman, L., "Macron pitches lighter regulation to fuel A.I. boom in Europe", *The New York Times*, 10 February 2025.
35 European Commission, "Speech by President von der Leyen at the AI Action Summit", 11 February 2025, https://ec.europa.eu/commission/presscorner/api/files/document/print/en/speech_25_471/SPEECH_25_471_EN.pdf.
36 Moens, B., and Foy, H., "EU scales back tech rules to boost AI investment, says digital chief", *Financial Times*, 14 February 2025.
37 *Ibid.*
38 European Commission, "Commission work programme 2025. Moving forward together: A bolder, simpler, faster Union", COM(2025) 45 final, 11 February 2025; Annex 4.
39 Department for Science, Innovation and Technology and Office for Artificial Intelligence, "AI regulation: A pro-innovation approach", 3 August 2023, para. 10. See: https://www.gov.uk/government/publications/ai-regulation-a-pro-innovation-approach.
40 Department for Science, Innovation and Technology, "Consultation outcome. A pro-innovation approach to AI regulation: Government response", 6 February 2024, para. 16. See: https://www.gov.uk/government/consultations/ai-regulation-a-pro-innovation-approach-policy-proposals/outcome/a-pro-innovation-approach-to-ai-regulation-government-response.
41 *Ibid.*, para. 73.
42 *Ibid.*, para. 73.

43 *Ibid.*, para. 74.
44 The White House, "Removing barriers to American leadership in artificial intelligence", 23 January 2025. See: https://www.whitehouse.gov/presidential-actions/2025/01/removing-barriers-to-american-leadership-in-artificial-intelligence/.
45 AB 2013: Generative artificial intelligence: training data transparency, 28 September 2024.
46 CA SB942: California AI Transparency Act, 19 September 2024.
47 SB24-205: Concerning consumer protections in interactions with artificial intelligence systems, 17 May 2024.
48 Australian Government: Department of Industry, "Security and Resources, "Safe and responsible AI in Australia: Proposals paper for introducing mandatory guardrails for AI in high-risk settings", September 2024, p. 30. See: https://consult.industry.gov.au/ai-mandatory-guardrails.
49 *Ibid.*
50 *Ibid.*
51 Japanese Ministry of Internal Affairs and Communications and Ministry of Economy, Trade and Industry, "AI guidelines for business, version 1.0", 19 April 2024. See: https://www.meti.go.jp/english/press/2024/0419_002.html.
52 Shiozaki, A., "自民党AIの進化と実装に関するプロジェクトチーム [Project team on the evolution and implementation of AI]", Note.com, 16 February 2024. https://note.com/akihisa_shiozaki/n/n4c126c27fd3d.
53 Sakamaki, S., "Japan's light-touch regulatory plans back 'most AI-friendly nation' ambitions", Mlex, 27 February 2025. Additionally, see: Liberal Democratic Party Headquarters for the Promotion of Digital Society, "AI White Paper 2024. New strategies in Stage II: Toward the world's most AI-friendly country", 11 April 2024. See: https://www.taira-m.jp/AI%20White%20Paper%202024.pdf.
54 Cyberspace Administration of China, "Interim measures for the management of generative artificial intelligence services", 10 July 2023. See: https://www.chinalawtranslate.com/en/generative-ai-interim/.
55 G7, "Hiroshima Process International Code of Conduct for Organizations Developing Advanced AI Systems", 30 October 2023. See: https://g7g20-documents.org/fileadmin/G7G20_documents/2023/G7/Japan/Leaders/2%20Leaders'%20Annex/Hiroshima%20Process%20International%20Code%20of%20Conduct%20for%20Organizations%20Developing%20Advanced%20AI%20Systems_30102023.pdf.
56 Organisation for Economic Co-operation and Development, "Recommendation of the Council on artificial intelligence", OECD/LEGAL/0449, 22 May 2019. See: https://oecd.ai/en/assets/files/OECD-LEGAL-0449-en.pdf. This Recommendation has been adopted by 46 governments.
57 Council of Europe, "The Framework Convention on Artificial Intelligence and Human Rights, Democracy and The Rule of Law", CETS no. 225, 17 May 2024. See: https://www.coe.int/en/web/artificial-intelligence/the-framework-convention-on-artificial-intelligence. At the time of writing, this Convention has been signed by

Andorra, Georgia, Iceland, Montenegro, Norway, Moldova, San Marina, the UK, Canada, Israel, Japan, the US, and the EU.

58 Thomson Reuters, "Future of Professionals report: AI-powered technology & the forces shaping professional work", July 2024. See: https://www.thomsonreuters.com/content/dam/ewp-m/documents/thomsonreuters/en/pdf/reports/future-of-professionals-report-2024.pdf.

59 *Ibid.*

60 Regulation (EU) 2024/1689 of the European Parliament and of the Council of 13 June 2024 laying down harmonised rules on artificial intelligence [2024] OJ L 130; Article 5. Additionally, see: European Commission, "Commission Guidelines on prohibited artificial intelligence (AI) practices on prohibited artificial intelligence practices established by Regulation (EU) 2024/1689 (AI Act)", 4 February 2025. See: https://digital-strategy.ec.europa.eu/en/library/commission-publishes-guidelines-prohibited-artificial-intelligence-ai-practices-defined-ai-act.

61 Regulation (EU) 2024/1689 of the European Parliament and of the Council of 13 June 2024 laying down harmonised rules on artificial intelligence [2024] OJ L 130; Article 5(1)(f).

62 *Ibid.*, Article 5(1)(c).

63 *Ibid.*, Article 5(1)(h).

64 *Ibid.*, Article 6(1).

65 Regulation (EU) 2024/1689 of the European Parliament and of the Council of 13 June 2024 laying down harmonised rules on artificial intelligence [2024] OJ L 130; Article 6(2) and Annex 3. We will not discuss high-risk AI systems in migration, asylum, and border control management here, although they might be relevant for some law firms, legal organizations, and bodies, depending on their practice (Article 7 of Annex 3).

66 *Ibid.*, Article 4(a) of Annex 3.

67 *Ibid.*, Article 4(b) of Annex 3.

68 *Ibid.*, Article 8(a) of Annex 3. Additionally, see: *Ibid.*, Recital 61.

69 *Ibid.*, Article 6 of Annex 3.

70 *Ibid.*, Article 6(3).

71 Regulation (EU) 2016/679 of the European Parliament and of the Council of 27 April 2016 on the protection of natural persons with regard to the processing of personal data and on the free movement of such data [2016] OJ L 119; Article 4(4).

72 Regulation (EU) 2024/1689 of the European Parliament and of the Council of 13 June 2024 laying down harmonised rules on artificial intelligence [2024] OJ L 130; Article 6(4).

73 *Ibid.*, Articles 9(1) and (3).

74 *Ibid.*, Article 10.

75 *Ibid.*, Article 11.

76 *Ibid.*, Article 12.

77 *Ibid.*, Article 13.

78 *Ibid.*, Article 14.
79 *Ibid.*, Article 15.
80 *Ibid.*, Article 16(a).
81 *Ibid.*, Article 16(b).
82 *Ibid.*, Article 16.
83 *Ibid.*, Articles 16(j) and 20.
84 *Ibid.*, Article 21.
85 *Ibid.*, Article 22.
86 *Ibid.*, Article 25(4).
87 *Ibid.*, Article 26(1).
88 *Ibid.*, Article 26(5).
89 *Ibid.*, Article 26(6).
90 *Ibid.*, Article 26(4).
91 *Ibid.*, Articles 26(2) and (3).
92 *Ibid.*, Article 26(7).
93 *Ibid.*, Article 26(11).
94 *Ibid.*, Article 26(12).
95 *Ibid.*, Article 3(68).
96 *Ibid.*, Article 50(1).
97 *Ibid.*, Article 50(2).
98 *Ibid.*, Article 4.
99 *Ibid.*, Article 3(56).
100 *Ibid.*, Article 50(4).
101 *Ibid.*, Article 50(4).
102 *Ibid.*, Article 4.
103 *Ibid.*, Article 53(1)(a).
104 *Ibid.*, Article 53(1)(b).
105 *Ibid.*, Articles 53(1)(c) and (d) and Directive (EU) 2019/790 of the European Parliament and of the Council of 17 April 2019 on copyright and related rights in the Digital Single Market [2019] OJ L 130/92.
106 Regulation (EU) 2024/1689 of the European Parliament and of the Council of 13 June 2024 laying down harmonised rules on artificial intelligence [2024] OJ L 130; Articles 53(3) and 54.
107 *Ibid.*, Article 53(2).
108 *Ibid.*, Articles 51(1)(a) and 3(65).
109 *Ibid.*, Article 51(2).
110 *Ibid.*, Articles 51(1)(b) and Annex 13.
111 *Ibid.*, Article 55(1)(a).
112 *Ibid.*, Articles 55(1)(b), (c), and (d).

Chapter 8: Navigating regulatory frameworks: building ethical and compliant AI in the legal sector

By Harry Borovick, general counsel, Luminance

Too often, AI is discussed in an ethical vacuum as a neutral technology – neither good nor bad. The framing of this implies that only the outcomes of AI can potentially cause harm, while the underlying technology is absent from social dynamics. Of course, when digging beyond even the finest of surface-level arguments, this is clearly and simply wrong. AI developers are faced with significant ethical considerations and related practical challenges throughout a technology's development stages. However, it is important to keep in mind that simply navigating the base requirements of the law is not the same as acting ethically.[1]

What is ethical AI?

Ethical AI has no agreed definition, in the same way that there is no standardized approach to "being ethical". Geographical, cultural, or even religious factors impact individual perceptions of ethical or unethical behavior and action. However, there are established ethical standards that are somewhat widespread in most modern legal systems. It is common to talk about AI ethics in the more operational vein of "responsible AI". Responsible AI can be best described as the ongoing process of building ethical principles (such as fairness, reliability and safety, privacy and security, inclusiveness, transparency, and accountability) directly into AI systems.[2] So, whenever we mention ethical AI systems at a practical level, we may be best served referring to it as responsible AI. Nevertheless, for the purposes of this chapter, we will use "ethical" rather than "responsible", as a reminder of the intentions.

A reasonable guiding principle for AI to be considered ethical in its creation, operation, and deployment is that its providers and users are able to recognize, address, and minimize potential societal and human harms that may directly or indirectly arise from its existence and use. Ethical AI requires an approach that considers fairness, accountability, and transparency from the development phase through to deployment and usage.

One major challenge is algorithmic opacity, where even developers may struggle to fully explain how complex AI models reach conclusions. This lack of interpretability inherently poses risks in legal applications, where justification and traceability are often essential.[3]

> *"Bias, security vulnerabilities, misinformation risks are all shaped by how an AI model is trained, the data it is exposed to, and the controls (or lack thereof) placed on it before it ever reaches an end user. If regulation only focuses on application-level enforcement, it's inherently reactive, it assumes we can fix problems after they happen. But history shows that by the time an issue is widespread enough to require enforcement, it's often too late to mitigate the harm."*[4]

Any legal service provider or legal professional should also understand, unequivocally, that this matters. What comes into AI systems affect what comes out. Therefore, when using AI systems to accelerate or even automate legal processes and advisory services, the level of consideration applied to the AI system's legal and ethical design and data content is critical. It is likely to directly affect the quality of service delivery and compliance with legal and professional standards (further discussed later in this chapter).

Similarities between AI and big data

As I discuss in greater depth in my book *AI and the Law: A Practical Guide to Using AI Safely* (2024), an early example of this, which started in earnest in the early 2000s before what many would consider the present "AI era", is the collection, usage, and manipulation (in the strict technical sense) of personal data by "big tech" to achieve targeted advertising outcomes. Much early scrutiny regarding targeted advertising centered around exactly that – the outcome, which was targeted adverts. However, many of the more serious ethical complexities are, in reality, found in how data have been gathered and categorized/profiled.

The outputs and outcomes may, in some cases, be ethically questionable (e.g., predatory targeted advertising to vulnerable consumers) because of how the underlying data are gathered and then sorted within the relevant systems. The core of the ethical challenge rests almost entirely in the building and operation of such technologies, including how to embed ethical values (e.g., combatting historic bias) into the fabric of the technology and the culture of the companies who make it. A focus on the outputs and outcomes is mostly superficial.

Similar ethical challenges arise in legal AI applications when systems process sensitive client information. Inadequate safeguards may lead to misuse of sensitive client information, privacy and legal privilege breaches, or biased legal recommendations. The principle of "informed consent" is increasingly relevant in AI ethics, as legal professionals and clients should understand the implications of AI-driven decisions on matter management, delivery of legal advice, or even case outcomes. The probability and severity of potential harms deriving from outputs and resulting outcomes is likely to be materially greater when the AI systems are used for the delivery of legal advice or other legal processes by members of the public without legal training or education.[5]

What about when the AI systems make the decisions?

Complexity and challenges are greater when AI systems are not passive tools. As agentic AI systems become more commonplace, or even the norm, these systems may be active participants in decision-making processes and execution.

> *"If machines engage in human communities as quasi-autonomous agents, then those agents must be expected to follow the community's social and moral norms. Embedding norms in such quasi-autonomous systems requires a clear delineation of the community in which they are to be deployed."*[6]

What is legally compliant AI?

"Legally compliant AI" in the legal sector refers to AI systems that adhere to – or at least acknowledge and somewhat comply with – relevant regulatory frameworks, ethical guidelines, and professional responsibilities governing legal practice. In addition to cross-industry considerations, such as data protection, intellectual property, and consumer rights, legal AI must navigate additional layers of professional regulation, including legal privilege, duties of competence and standards of care, and broader principles of justice and fairness.

Insufficient "algorithmic accountability" for legal AI applications is a potentially significant risk for regulatory compliance.[7] As insurance policies are typically designed to cover errors and omissions, rather than breach of regulatory obligations, it is worth noting that the use of AI in a way which may breach any professional regulatory frameworks could invalidate or neuter relevant insurance policies. This is critically important, as one of the "dirty" facts which lawyers hate to acknowledge is that the value of external advisory lawyers (less of a factor for in-house lawyers) is the reassuring safety net for clients of their professional indemnity insurance.

One way to manage this is through periodic audits of AI models used in legal practice to ensure they align with the relevant principles (which may vary between jurisdictions). Compliance frameworks should also incorporate mechanisms to detect and correct biases in AI-generated legal analyses. Simple "human in the loop" verification and audits, even if only on a sample of outputs, may materially reduce risk of bias, inaccurate, unfair, or poor-quality outputs and outcomes. It is also possible to use complementary AI systems to check each other's homework through automated bias assessment or other forms of targeted verifications.[8] Although this may not be as confidence-inducing as human verification in many circumstances, it may be a practical safety net at scale and is likely to become more common as AI verification tools aimed at regulating other AI systems become more adept at testing the cracks in each other's logic and source data.

Regulatory frameworks governing AI in legal practice

AI in legal services operates within an evolving regulatory landscape that varies across jurisdictions. AI doesn't exist in a legal or regulatory vacuum; existing international and territory-specific regimes applicable to key areas of law (IP, privacy, financial regulatory, etc.) all still may apply to AI use cases in legal practice. However, with respect to AI-specific legal considerations, relevant frameworks are still very much in their infancy.

European Union AI Act

The EU AI Act (EUAIA) categorizes AI applications by risk level, imposing strict requirements on high-risk AI systems, including those used in legal decision-making. Transparency, accountability, and human oversight are key principles of the regulation. Notably, AI frontier "general purpose" models (think the various large models of OpenAI, Anthropic, Mistral, Meta, Google, Deepseek, etc.) are essentially regulated with greater scrutiny and burden in their own risk category, irrespective of the risk of the relevant application to a task or circumstance.

Due to the potential risks to the fundamental rights of EU citizens, some AI systems may be considered "high risk" under the EUAIA when applied to some forms of legal services or processes, such as law enforcement and administration of justice.[9] This may be regardless of whether the relevant AI system is itself ordinarily or otherwise categorized as high risk under the EUAIA. It is currently unclear and untested as to whether legal professionals in law firms, or outside of government and law enforcement but working with or against them, would fall under the scope of the EUAIA when using AI systems.

AI governance in the United States

The US does not yet have a comprehensive AI law, but agencies such as the Federal Trade Commission (FTC), which is capable of regulating deceptive and unfair business practices (including anti-trust and consumer protection), are increasingly scrutinizing AI transparency and fairness[10] both from a strict legal perspective as well as an ethical standpoint. Additionally, the Biden administration's (non-binding) Blueprint for an AI Bill of Rights provides guidance on ethical AI practices.

Many individual states have passed AI regulations aimed to cover specific risks. Colorado was the first to move, but states such as California have driven hard at complex issues around labelling AI, with a heavy focus on misinformation.

The United Kingdom's approach to AI regulation

The UK emphasizes pro-innovation AI regulation. What this really means is aligning AI governance with existing data protection laws, such as the Data Protection Act 2018 and the General Data Protection Regulation (GDPR), as well as existing intellectual property frameworks.[11]

It is likely that the UK will continue to diverge from existing frameworks (notably around intellectual property rights) in order to facilitate an environment which increasingly favors AI companies generally when considering the existing rights of creative industries.[12] On certain flagship concerns, such as labelling of AI, the UK approach generally remains aligned with that of the EU, even if not entirely codified in law.

Other jurisdictions and international approaches

Countries including Canada, China, South Korea, and Australia have introduced AI governance frameworks that emphasize fairness, transparency, and accountability. While many jurisdictions have replicated or improved upon the EUAIA's approach of risk categorization, most have not aligned to the EUAIA's direct, distinct, and more burdensome approach to frontier general-purpose AI models.

As governments and regulators develop their AI strategies, a patchwork of complex regulatory contradictions is likely to form for any international company seeking to build or deploy AI across numerous territories – in a similar, although likely more complex, manner than those seen with the international boom of post-GDPR privacy laws.

Key compliance considerations for legal AI

Data protection and privacy

AI systems must comply with regulations such as the GDPR (EU) and the California Consumer Privacy Act (CCPA) (US). This means that personal data used in AI training should be lawfully obtained, stored, and processed. As AI systems deployed in the legal industry often rely on large datasets, even when utilizing smaller models, they may include sensitive or personal information. As such, ensuring conformity with data protection regulations is a major challenge. The complexity grows when the same or similar AI system(s) is deployed across multiple territories, which may each have their own applicable laws and regulations to cover data processing.

Ideally, the obtaining, storage, and processing of data should be more than legal; it should be ethical. Practically, this usually means that there should be a legitimate basis (or explicit consent) for the ways in which the data are gathered and used. Data must be stored to a secure standard that would be considered reasonable or justifiable – to either/both the data subject and a competent authority, such as a data regulator. Something that is often practically forgotten is that the data should also be minimized or deleted when possible. So, periodic deletion of old data, or data which are not in regular use, may be advisable. It is also worth clarifying that commercial or otherwise non-personal data (i.e., data that do not relate to the personal information or characteristics of individuals or groups of people) are subject to far fewer legal or ethical considerations, as privacy/data laws are primarily designed to protect human beings and commercial data pose less direct potential harm to the fundamental rights of human beings.

Bias and fairness

Legal AI tools must mitigate biases in training data and algorithmic decision-making to avoid reinforcing discriminatory practices.

Some forms of bias in AI system data or outcomes are strictly illegal, depending on the jurisdiction. For example, under the EUAIA, it is considered an "unacceptable risk" to fundamental rights for an AI system to be designed for, or applied to, social scoring of any kind. The legal sector is not exempt from these rules. In practice, this would mean that classifying people in any way (e.g., using AI to classify individuals as at a high risk of committing fraud) based on their behavior, socio-economic status, or personal characteristics would be illegal – even if this may be done for the benefit of those individuals.[13]

Transparency and explainability

Legal professionals must be able to understand and explain AI-generated decisions, particularly in litigation and regulatory compliance.

Liability and accountability

Determining responsibility for AI-driven legal errors remains a key challenge, especially in cases of automated contract analysis and predictive legal analytics. However, put simply, legal practitioners providing legal process and advice services or legal advice are required to be insured. That insurance may not provide protection to legal practitioners if they act outside of the scope of their insurance policies, including with respect to dependence on AI systems, without appropriate guardrails.

Reliance without verification on AI systems, as with any technology, does not bypass that requirement. In short, the excuse that "We trusted the AI" is unlikely to ever be sufficient justification for the provision of a legal services to a negligent standard, and excessive reliance without appropriate verification may well be a cause of action for negligence in and of itself.

Most providers of AI systems carry prominent and explicit disclaimers that they are not providing legal advice on which reliance should be placed. Of course, when an AI output is provided direct to a consumer, this means that there is no regulated individual or firm involved; the most important thing in this instance is for clear disclaimers to be visible to members of the public to warn them to avoid "betting the house" solely on advice from AI outputs and to seek verification of the information provided from a regulated professional.

Professional conduct

Complementary to the point above, AI use must align with ethical duties, including a duty of competence. Legal practitioners should understand AI's capabilities and limitations, including when confidentiality and legal privilege may be compromised through the use of an AI system. We are already approaching an era where it may be sensible to suggest that a legal professional has acted contrary to their duties (such as those set out by the ABA, SRA, etc.[14]) by neglecting available technology.

In general, unsecured and free-to-use AI systems pose a greater risk to the professional duties of legal professionals, as data are more likely to be readily available to the AI system provider or mingled with the data of others. Remember that AI systems that are free or cheap are also those most likely to be used outside of official company policies, by individuals acting outside of approved internal governance, as they are the most accessible and may be useful for their specific needs. However, the law firm or organization for which those individuals act or are employees of will still bear the public and customer-facing brunt of potential negative outcomes.

The rule of law and legal independence

The interaction between the providers of AI systems and governments should not be underestimated. It is already well-understood that technology companies providing products or services in some jurisdictions may be required to compromise or adapt the nature of the outputs or access to specific information, if it is not in line with local regulations, executive orders, or government policies. The ability of AI systems to provide legal and ethical outputs, or take action, may be further limited where the outputs are likely to be directly political.[15]

Chinese-made AI systems often refuse to provide answers on specific events, ethical matters, or legal questions which are undesirable to the Chinese authorities.[16] Specifically of concern to law firms would be the increasing pressure placed on the legal sector in 2025 by President Donald Trump in the US. The issue of executive orders against several prominent law firms, accusing them of partisan activities and discriminatory practices, created sudden ethical and legal challenges to the practice of law, which may also feed into AI systems in the long term.

Accusations by tech companies of government pressure is nothing new,[17] but it may be the case that AI companies will become progressively interested in close relationships with governments for a variety of reasons (e.g., protection over ongoing issues regarding copyright infringements). It remains unclear what may be happening behind the scenes between the providers of AI systems and governments, but there is a real risk that legal practitioners using AI may have their access to objective information limited in future under government pressure in many jurisdictions.

In practice, available options/choices for legal practitioners may be limited, but it is important to at least be cognizant that the information or conclusions provided by AI systems may be subtly or overtly limited to meet government demands, so verification through additional sources may be required. In some extreme scenarios, access to AI resources by law firms who challenge doctrine may even be limited by providers and governments.

Strategies for ensuring AI compliance in the legal sector

To maximize compliance with legal and ethical standards, law firms and legal tech providers should implement the measures set out below. However, before doing so, the most important principle is to have a proper internal understanding amongst relevant stakeholders as to what the expected value of the use of an AI system is. It is rarely successful, both in terms of return on investment and legal/ethical compliance, to buy a piece of technology and then consider the specific points of value it might add in hindsight.

Start with identifying the potential value (often a pain-point for legal professionals, end-clients, or other stakeholders within the organization) and then seek out tools to deliver that value. Do not start by buying technology and then discovering its potential applications.

Implementing governance and compliance programs

Establishing internal policies and processes is critical to facilitate the effective, safe, and ethical use of AI systems responsibly and in compliance with legal and regulatory requirements.[18]

This includes legal, ethical, and compliance risk assessment and ongoing monitoring combined with robust security assessment. Request for proposals (RFPs) are a simple way of gathering information from third parties, such as the vendors of the AI systems. Some AI system providers may not provide information as part of RFPs, selling on a "take it or leave it" basis. It may still make sense to buy tech without RFPs, but this likely adds greater importance to the need for ongoing governance and monitoring.

Governance, compliance, and AI literacy programs should include initial trainings (i.e., at the onboarding of new joiners and/or deployment of new AI systems), as well as on an ongoing basis.[19] For example, it may make sense for a legal contracts manager within a law firm or in-house team to schedule 6-monthly or annual refresher training sessions from an internal AI governance lead or team (often overlapping with the General Counsel and/or Security functions) on key points of risk, such as how to handle sensitive data; the practical limitations and applications of each approved AI tool; where a list of internally approved AI systems, as well as other key policies, can be found; and what happens if employees make a mistake that contravenes internal policies.

Additionally, it should be considered that some AI systems can help to solve the problems of other AI systems. For example, in addition to reliance on third parties (such as law firms and industry groups, as discussed below), many AI tools exist on the market specifically to help identify, register, and manage AI legal and compliance risks, such as changes to legal regimes.[20]

Conducting AI risk assessments

Evaluating AI tools for risks related to bias, data security, and legal liability before deployment is often critical to supporting a successful governance and compliance program.

There is a delicate balancing act to perform regarding the breadth and depth of risk assessments. If risk assessments, particularly the elements reliant on third parties or others within your legal practice, are too frequent, extensive or burdensome, contribution and commitment or adherence to processes may be weaker. Simplicity and concision are often best. A framework based on a "red light, yellow light, green light" approach can help companies streamline AI governance and decision-making.[21]

If your legal practice is using AI tools blindly or with limited information, justifying that such an approach falls within expected professional competence and client care would be difficult. It may even be the case that neglecting proper consideration of risk assessment could breach strict legal obligations (e.g., with respect to data privacy).

Below is a simple example of an initial AI system risk assessment form, which should be populated by a mixture of stakeholders as appropriate (based on relevant expertise) and owned by the individual stakeholder or team who is driving the rollout.

Table 1. An example AI risk assessment intake form

Key questions to be asked for every AI model used by [name of legal practice]	Details
Summary	
Market name of AI system	e.g., OpenAI GPT 4.0, Claude Sonnet 2.5, Deespseek R1, Cursor
Intended purpose(s) of and task(s) of AI system	e.g., Contract analysis or legal research
Desired/estimated deployment date	e.g., Already deployed, or from [x date]
How will this be hosted?	e.g., Azure, AWS, GCP, direct API to provider, local appliance
Will the deployment be easily reversible? If so, please describe approach to reverse.	e.g., Yes, through [give example of practical mechanism]
Will any elements of the model, its weights, or code directly interact with our organization's data?	e.g., Yes, almost certainly
Will any elements of the model, its weights, or code directly interact with our customers' data?	e.g., Yes, almost certainly/possibly/no
Who/where from?	
Authors (e.g., names)	e.g., OpenAI, Google, Meta, Anthropic, Perplexity, Deepseek
Geography, if known, of authors	e.g., US, China, France, UK
Weblink to information for verification	e.g., https://huggingface.co/[...]
Licensing and restrictions	
Type of license	e.g., Apache 2.0
Any known restrictions other than the license?	e.g., This is for non-commercial or non-production use only

With all of the above information in hand, it is possible to approve, ask for further information, or reject the use of an AI system (i.e., green light, yellow light, red light). Consequently, an inventory/register of approved and reviewed AI can be built and maintained.

AI audits and continuous monitoring

Regularly assess the real-world performance and capabilities of AI systems to identify and mitigate emerging risks. Without regular assessment, any AI governance program can only operate with one eye open. Accordingly, performance testing should therefore be frequent and thorough, and include comparative technology.

Benchmarking may be best achieved through enticement – if vendors are offered the genuine ability to demonstrate the capabilities and value of their AI systems, this can be mutually beneficial for all involved. A common red flag to watch out for when assessing AI systems, even when a vendor has participated in an RFP, is when the technology is not immediately (a delay not greater than 24 hours) accessible for testing. Pilot testing should be mutually beneficial to vendor and buyer, if the technology is right for the use case.[22] Of course, it would be unreasonable to expect any piece of technology be set up to 100 percent of its potential capabilities right away, but there should be clear value in the technology at the "plug and play" stage.[23]

Collaboration with oversight organizations, industry groups and academia

Engaging with bar associations, regulators, policymakers, and industry stakeholders to help understand and shape AI regulations and standards. Engaging with these bodies provides a free or relatively low-cost opportunity to stay abreast of legal and practical changes, as well as events which impact daily ethical compliance.

Many of these bodies provide free or cheap guidance notes (such as the 2025 AI guidance by the Chartered Institute of Arbitrators), newsletters, or educational resources and training on AI governance best practice.[24] Much of this AI governance includes ethical considerations. Of note, the International Association of Privacy Professionals' AI governance professional (AIGP) training courses and materials place a heavy emphasis on navigating ethical tripwires through various existing frameworks.[25] Many universities also provide training schemes, qualifications, and guidance notes. Law firms, positioning themselves as AI advisors beyond the strictly legal (straying into the ethical), are often freely providing additional guidance, newsletters, and advice to further contextualize relevant rules and guidance notes.

Tech stacks and end-to-end solutions

It is crucial for legal professionals and legal service firms to approach technology like a chief technology officer (CTO) would; better yet, involve a CTO (or a similar professional) with real technical understanding to balance legal needs in your AI decision-making. A common issue when building a technologically-enabled legal practice is the desire to acquire a panacea to all the legal function's problems. However, this desire is simply detached from reality. Technology is typically specialized by design, in order to achieve specific outcomes, which technologists usually understand.

Broad-purpose tools, such as ChatGPT, can do a decent job of many tasks. They typically cannot (yet) perform a truly excellent job of any tasks, at least not from a qualitative perspective. However, even specialist GPTs built on these foundational models can provide far greater reliability, accuracy, and specificity to problem-solving. The level of success can be further improved when using a truly specialist AI system, although this often comes at greater cost.[26] The greater the level of understanding by the end user (i.e., the legal professional) regarding the limitations of a specific AI system, the greater the probability that it can be used in a responsible, ethical, and legal manner that complies with professional standards.

Accordingly, for some use cases (e.g., contracting), an end-to-end solution designed for that workflow, even if it does many things, may be an excellent option. However, the same system is likely to be compromised somewhere in its performance should it also offer unrelated functions, such as legal research. So, for a legal practice with a finite budget, identifying the greatest value tasks balanced against the lowest risk and applying a multi-tool approach may be best.

Bringing it all together

Legal compliance in the assessment, acquisition, deployment, usage, and risk management of AI should not just be a checklist. Instead, this requires an ongoing commitment to ethical responsibility, understanding existing and new legal frameworks, and acting with "common" sense in the practical day-to-day.

As AI systems continue to evolve in both predictable (increased speed and accuracy) and unpredictable (unknown agentic capabilities) ways, the need for AI governance in the legal profession grows. Legal professionals, in private practice and in-house, taking the lead directly or working with stakeholders dedicated to AI governance, must proactively address these challenges to support the delivery of AI-powered services as a tool for justice and for the ultimate benefit of internal and external clients in a manner that is both legal and ethical.

References

1 Fuchs, I., "Law vs. Ethics: The Debate Over What's Legal and What's Right", American Public University, 23 December 2024. See: https://www.apu.apus.edu/area-of-study/security-and-global-studies/resources/law-vs-ethics/.

2 International Standards Organisation, "Building a responsible AI: How to manage the AI ethics debate", 2025. See: https://www.iso.org/artificial-intelligence/responsible-ai-ethics.

3 Hasan, R., "Tackling Legal Issues with AI: A Guide for Modern Law Firms", TimeSolv, 2025. See: https://www.timesolv.com/blog/legal-issues-with-ai/?referrer=Ronald-Reinart-ron.reinart%2540timesolv.com.

4 Mahapatra, R., "... and why Europe's biggest problem isn't regulation", LinkedIn, 20 February 2025. See: https://www.linkedin.com/pulse/why-europes-biggest-problem-isnt-regulation-raj-mahapatra-przbe/?trackingId=4%2BQAmcoS7gzY8yq5Y1u04Q%3D%3D.

5 Kauffman, B., "The Implications of Generative AI: From the Delivery of Legal Services to the Delivery of Justice", Institute for the Advancement of the American Legal System, 29 March 2024. See: https://iaals.du.edu/blog/implications-generative-ai-delivery-legal-services-delivery-justice.

6 IEEE Standards Association, "The IEEE Global Initiative 2.0 on Ethics of Autonomous and Intelligent Systems", 25 March 2024. See: https://standards.ieee.org/content/ieee-standards/en/industry-connections/ec/autonomous-systems.html.

7 Nightfall AI, "Algorithmic Accountability Act", 2025. See: https://www.nightfall.ai/ai-security-101/algorithmic-accountability-act.

8 Tokmakov, S., "AI Bias Risk Assessment Tool", Terms Law, 23 March 2025. See: https://terms.law/2025/03/23/ai-bias-risk-assessment-tool/?utm_source=chatgpt.com.

9 European Parliament, "EU AI Act: first regulation on artificial intelligence", 8 June 2023. See: https://www.europarl.europa.eu/topics/en/article/20230601STO93804/eu-ai-act-first-regulation-on-artificial-intelligence?utm_source=chatgpt.com.

10 DiResta, A.E. and Sherman, Z., "The FTC Is Regulating AI: A Comprehensive Analysis", Holland & Knight, 25 July 2023. See: https://www.hklaw.com/en/insights/publications/2023/07/the-ftc-is-regulating-ai-a-comprehensive-analysis?utm_source=chatgpt.com.

11 Ponomarov, K., "How to Navigate UK AI Regulations", Legalnodes.com, 24 June 2024. See: https://legalnodes.com/article/uk-ai-regulations?utm_source=chatgpt.com.

12 Intellectual Property Office, Department for Science, Innovation and Technology, and Department for Culture, Media and Sport, "Closed consultation: Copyright and Artificial Intelligence", Gov.uk, 17 December 2024. See: https://www.gov.uk/government/consultations/copyright-and-artificial-intelligence/copyright-and-artificial-intelligence.

13 European Parliament, "EU AI Act: first regulation on artificial intelligence", 8 June 2023. See: https://www.europarl.europa.eu/topics/en/article/20230601STO93804/eu-ai-act-first-regulation-on-artificial-intelligence?utm_source=chatgpt.com.

14 Solicitors Regulation Authority Board, "SRA Code of Conduct for Solicitors, RELs and RFLs", Solicitors Regulation Authority, 16 December 2024. See: https://www.sra.org.uk/solicitors/standards-regulations/code-conduct-solicitors/.

15 Zeff, M., "Google still limits how Gemini answers political questions", TechCrunch, 4 March 2025. See: https://techcrunch.com/2025/03/04/google-still-limits-how-gemini-answers-political-questions/?guccounter=1&guce_referrer=aHR0cHM6Ly93d3cuZ29vZ2xlLmNvbS8&guce_referrer_sig=AQAAAAGqGURnzKaHQx7OMeEn7t9YGpvVcuAzZVoeQmIv4Tt8kof3eMZMG_uh6CmGP4wurfKnMO9Xgagy4aqojftDFtm23i6laZ4YYLnDO7BjXud_p8nQMndTKYXgNyRXEKiRp8g9q4pFpUEIsZyKg7Gv8802XlCynyot3QyQiq_CY4Of.

16 Lu, D., "We tried out DeepSeek. It worked well, until we asked it about Tiananmen Square and Taiwan", *The Guardian*, 28 January 2025. See: https://www.theguardian.com/technology/2025/jan/28/we-tried-out-deepseek-it-works-well-until-we-asked-it-about-tiananmen-square-and-taiwan.

17 Rajan, G. and Bose, N., "Zuckerberg says Biden administration pressured Meta to censor COVID-19 content", Reuters, 27 August 2024. See: https://www.reuters.com/technology/zuckerberg-says-biden-administration-pressured-meta-censor-covid-19-content-2024-08-27/.

18 Porter, A., "AI Governance Best Practices: Transparency in AI Systems", BigID, 15 May 2024. See: https://bigid.com/blog/what-is-ai-governance/.

19 Pappu, N., "AI Governance 101: Understanding the Basics and Best Practices", Zendata, 2025. See: https://www.zendata.dev/post/ai-governance-101-understanding-the-basics-and-best-practices.

20 Truyo,"AI Inventory: Discover Active AI Risks", 2025. See: https://truyo.com/solutions/by-use-case/ai-inventory/.

21 Stackpole, B., "A framework for assessing AI risk", MIT Sloan School of Management, 3 January 2024. See: https://mitsloan.mit.edu/ideas-made-to-matter/a-framework-assessing-ai-risk.

22 Terzo, "Why RFPs Are Outdated: A Case for Hands-On Software Evaluation in Enterprise Companies", 24 March 2025. See: https://terzo.ai/blog/why-rfps-are-outdated-a-case-for-hands-on-software-evaluation/.

23 Ridhawi, I.A., Otoum, S., Aloqaily, M., and Boukerche, A., "Generalizing AI: challenges and opportunities for plug and play AI solutions", *IEEE Network*, 2021, volume 35, issue 1, pp.1–8. https://doi.org/10.1109/mnet.011.2000371.

24 Haley, G. and Wong, B., "AI in International Arbitration: CIARB Guideline on the Use of AI in Arbitration (2025)", JD Supra, 3 April 2025. See: https://www.jdsupra.com/legalnews/ai-in-international-arbitration-ciarb-9250686/.

25 IAPP, "Artificial Intelligence Governance Professional training: Why you should take Artificial Intelligence Governance Professional training", 2025. See: https://iapp.org/train/aigp-training/.

26 Getronics, "GenAI vs specialised AI: Which is the right fit for your business?", 14 April 2024. See: https://www.getronics.com/types-of-ai-which-is-the-right-fit-for-your-business/.

Chapter 9: AI in the legal arena: navigating ethics, confidentiality, and professional responsibility

By Erick Robinson, partner, Brown Rudnick LLP

Artificial intelligence (AI) is changing how attorneys work, helping lawyers review documents, predict case outcomes, conduct legal research, and draft legal papers faster than ever before. However, use of AI creates privacy, confidentiality, and accuracy risks that lawyers must understand.

AI in the legal profession: navigating confidentiality and privacy concerns

Client confidentiality risks

When lawyers use AI tools, client information might be stored on third-party servers, which means sensitive data leaves attorney and law firm control. Many AI companies keep input data to improve their systems, and your client's private information could become part of the AI's training data (and appear in responses to inquiries by other parties) without proper safeguards.

These concerns are not theoretical. In April 2023, Samsung Electronics reported three incidents in which employees had inadvertently leaked sensitive company information by inputting it into ChatGPT.[1] In one case, an employee shared proprietary source code; in another, internal meeting notes were uploaded; and, in a third, equipment test data were entered. OpenAI's privacy policy at the time allowed user inputs to be utilized for model training unless users opted out, raising concerns that this sensitive data could be stored on OpenAI's servers or accessed by human reviewers. In another instance, several law firms discovered in 2024 that Microsoft's Azure OpenAI Service, which provides access to OpenAI's AI models, included a term of service which allowed Microsoft to retain and manually review user prompts.[2] This raised alarms among lawyers, as prompts containing client information could be accessed by Microsoft employees, potentially breaching confidentiality obligations and break privilege. Attorneys and law firms must make sure that privilege and confidentiality are maintained by whatever AI vendor they or their employees use.

The American Bar Association's (ABA) Model Rule of Professional Conduct 1.6(c) requires lawyers to "make reasonable efforts to prevent the inadvertent or unauthorized disclosure of, or unauthorized access to, information relating to the representation of a client".[3] This obligation extends to AI usage. The ABA's Formal Opinion 483 further clarifies that lawyers must employ reasonable efforts to monitor for data breaches and ensure their technology providers maintain reasonable security measures.[4]

Some AI systems might share information between users. Imagine if your case strategy was accidentally made available to opposing counsel because you both use the same AI platform. This would be a serious breach of confidentiality and could harm your client's interests. The case of *Harleysville Insurance Company v. Holding Funeral Home, Inc.* demonstrated how improper file sharing technology could potentially lead to a waiver of attorney–client privilege when confidential information was accidentally made available to opposing counsel.[5] Although the trial court's decision that privilege and work product were waived were ultimately overturned in *Harleysville Ins. Co. v. Holding Funeral Home, Inc.*,[6] the risk remains clear.

Another concern is that AI systems often need an internet connection to work. This creates more vulnerabilities which hackers could potentially exploit to access confidential information, with each connection representing a potential security weakness. For example, the District of Columbia Bar's Ethics Opinion 388 on attorney use of AI requires that "[c]ompetence includes understanding enough about any technology the lawyer uses in legal practice to be reasonably confident that the technology will advance the client's interests in the representation".[7]

Data security vulnerabilities

Legal documents often contain highly sensitive information. When attorneys upload case files to AI platforms, this data may not have the same protections as information stored on law firm servers. Different AI providers have different security standards: some may store data for long periods or in countries with weaker privacy laws.

The Health Insurance Portability and Accountability Act (HIPAA) of 1996 imposes criminal penalties for wrongful disclosure of individually identifiable health information.[8] Similarly, the Gramm–Leach–Bliley Act (alternatively known as the Financial Services Modernization Act of 1999) also protects financial information that often appears in litigation.[9] AI tools that do not comply with these regulations could expose attorneys to liability.

Many AI tools require broad terms of service agreements. These agreements might give the AI company broad rights to use data. In reviewing AI terms of service, attorneys should specifically look for:

- *Data retention policies.* How long does the service keep your information? Can you request deletion?
- *Training clauses.* Does the company use your data to train their AI models?
- *Third-party sharing.* Are your data shared with other companies or organizations?
- *Confidentiality provisions.* What specific protections are in place for attorney–client materials?
- *Jurisdiction and governing law.* Which country's laws apply to data disputes?

Failure to protect client data and meet these disclosure requirements has resulted in legal action against law firms. For example, in 2024, the New York Attorney General fined midsize law firm Heidell, Pittoni, Murphy & Bach $200,000 over a security lapse that caused a 2021 data breach.[10] Additionally, Orrick, Herrington & Sutcliffe "agreed to pay $8 million to settle class action claims from people who said their personal information was compromised in a breach of some of the firm's client data".[11] This is part of a growing trend in which law firms have been held responsible for security lapses.

Legal AI systems can also be attractive targets for cyberattacks, because they contain valuable information.

Privacy law compliance issues

Lawyers must follow many privacy laws like the General Data Protection Regulation (GDPR)[12] in Europe or the California Consumer Privacy Act of 2018 (CCPA). These laws set strict rules about how personal information must be handled. Using AI could make compliance more difficult.

Articles 5–7 of the GDPR establish core principles for data processing, including lawfulness, fairness, transparency, purpose limitation, data minimization, and accountability. Legal professionals must ensure their AI tools comply with these requirements. The CCPA Cal. Civ. Code § 1798.100 similarly provides consumers with rights to know about, delete, and opt out of the sale of their personal information.

The case of *Data Protection Commissioner v. Facebook Ireland Limited and Maximillian Schrems* invalidated the EU–US Privacy Shield framework, complicating the transfer of personal data from the EU to the US.[13] Law firms using US-based AI services for EU clients should maintain safeguards to ensure compliance. For example, clients have the right to know what personal data are being collected and how these are used. They also have the right to have their data deleted in certain situations. If a lawyer cannot explain how an AI system uses client data, the technology might violate these laws. In *Vizio, Inc. v. International Trade Commission*, the court established that companies must clearly disclose their data collection practices, which may extend to law firms using AI.[14]

International cases create additional challenges. Data transmitted to AI services may cross borders, triggering different privacy requirements; a solution that works in one jurisdiction might violate the laws of another. The European Court of Justice emphasized this in *Google Spain SL and Google Inc. v Agencia Española de Protección de Datos (AEPD) and Mario Costeja González*, establishing the "right to be forgotten" and highlighting the complexity of applying data protection laws across jurisdictions.[15]

Practical solutions for legal professionals

Despite these challenges, there are ways to use AI while protecting client confidentiality and privacy.

Evaluating AI providers and terms of service

Lawyers should select AI providers with strong security measures. Vendors should ideally specialize in legal services and have clear data policies with confidentiality provisions. The ABA's Formal Opinion 498 provides guidance on lawyers' virtual practice, including selection of technology providers.[16]

When reviewing AI terms of service, create a checklist which addresses:

- Data ownership (who owns the input and output data);
- Confidentiality provisions (specific protections for legal information);
- Subpoena and government request policies;
- Security standards (SOC 2 compliance; encryption methods);
- Ability to delete data permanently; and
- Breach notification procedures;

Document review of these terms as part of your due diligence. In *Bray & Gillespie Management LLC v. Lexington Insurance Co.*, the court examined the reasonableness of data retention policies, highlighting the importance of documenting technology decisions.[17]

Lawyers should be diligent in analyzing the underlying terms that govern the AI tools they use. They must make sure that their data are not used in further building LLMs and other AI tools, and that all data and output are maintained securely and confidentially. However, all this accomplishes is creating a breach of contract claim against the AI company if it violates the terms. To ensure that the AI company *cannot access* confidential data (the only way to truly ensure confidentiality), other methods and protocols are available.

Local AI implementation

Lawyers should use on-premises AI solutions whenever possible. Some AI tools can run locally on your own computers or servers, rather than on third-party cloud servers, which provides greater control over sensitive information. Local large language models (LLMs) offer significant privacy advantages:

- Even with Wi-Fi enabled, searches never leave your computer when using a locally-hosted LLM (I always turn off Wi-Fi, and even use a "sniffer" program to make sure that no data leaks after reconnection to the internet);
- Client information remains entirely within lawyer control;
- No third party has access to prompts/responses; and
- Compliance with specific jurisdictional requirements is maintained.

Setting up a local LLM requires some technical knowledge, but eliminates many privacy concerns. Options like LM Studio, Ollama, and self-hosted open-source models provide options for local deployment. Most of the models and software are free, but housing large-parameter (high-quality) LLMs on a local computer requires lots of computing power in terms of GPUs, RAM, and CPUs to a lesser extent. However, these initial set-up costs are offset by the elimination of subscription fees and enhanced security.

Finally, retrieval-augmented generation (RAG) is an AI-enabled approach in which a model fetches relevant external documents or data sources to generate more accurate and contextually appropriate responses. It enhances security by limiting AI outputs to verified, trusted content, reducing the risk of misinformation or hallucinated data.

Anonymization techniques

Use anonymization techniques when processing client data, such as replacing actual names with pseudonyms before uploading documents to AI services. Examples could be:

- Replace *"Microsoft Corporation v. Apple Inc."* with *"ABC Corp. v. XYZ Inc."*;
- Substitute "John Smith" with "Client A";
- Change specific locations to generic references;
- Modify dollar amounts while maintaining proportionality; and
- Remove or alter identifying details like dates, product names, and unique identifiers.

This approach complies with the data minimization principle under GDPR's Chapter 1, Article 5(1)(c),[18] while still allowing effective use of AI tools.

Client consent and governance

Create clear client consent procedures. Inform clients about how their information might be used with AI tools and get their permission before use. Make sure that you document this consent in your engagement letters.

Develop an AI governance policy for your practice and/or firm. This should include rules about what kinds of information can be processed using AI and what safeguards must be in place. Regular training will ensure everyone follows these policies. The Sedona Conference's Commentary on Defensible Disposition provides valuable guidance on information governance that can be applied to AI systems.[19]

Ongoing security measures

Perform regular security audits of your AI systems. Technology changes quickly, and new vulnerabilities appear all the time. Regular testing helps find problems before they lead to data breaches. Stay informed about AI developments. The technology and legal landscape around AI is evolving rapidly; continuing education about AI will help you make better decisions about which tools to use and how to use them safely. The ABA's Model Rule 1.1, Comment 8 notes that lawyers should "keep abreast of changes in the law and its practice, including the benefits and risks associated with relevant technology".[20]

The trade-off between technology and confidentiality

As AI becomes more integrated into legal practice, we will need new ethical guidelines and possibly new laws to address these issues. The current patchwork of regulations from state bar opinions to federal privacy laws creates uncertainty that must eventually be resolved. Until comprehensive guidance emerges, it falls to individual attorneys to use AI responsibly. By implementing the aforementioned safeguards – such as careful vendor selection, local implementations where feasible, anonymization, client consent, and robust governance – lawyers can navigate the current uncertainty while maintaining their ethical obligations.

The reality of AI

Along with the benefits of AI come significant risks concerning accuracy and AI's tendency to "hallucinate" (i.e., generate plausible yet incorrect information). For lawyers whose professional duties hinge on precision and reliability, these issues pose serious ethical and practical challenges. This section explores the critical implications of AI inaccuracy and hallucinations within the legal field, highlighting potential pitfalls, real-world consequences, and strategies to responsibly manage these emerging challenges.

Inaccuracy in legal research

When attorneys use AI for legal research, they often encounter a problem, known as a "hallucination", in which AI systems generate incorrect information with remarkable confidence. Hallucination refers to AI generating content that sounds well-informed, but is either incorrect, misleading, or completely imaginary.

To picture this clearly, imagine asking an AI chatbot a question about a historical event or for sources on a topic. The AI tool might confidently respond with dates, detailed descriptions, or even specific citations. However, once you try to verify this information, you discover these sources or details do not exist at all. This is hallucination. The answer as to why AI does this lies in the way AI models are trained and how they produce their outputs. AI systems, especially LLMs, are trained on vast amounts of textual data from books, articles, websites, and more. They learn patterns and structures in language, predicting what words or sentences come next, based on probabilities. However, they are not naturally equipped to verify their outputs against facts or real-time information. When faced with uncertainty or ambiguous prompts, AI tries to fill the gaps with predictions.

Prompt clarity also plays a significant role. When the AI receives vague or incomplete questions, it often tries to compensate by making assumptions or interpretations, which can inadvertently lead to hallucinations. Furthermore, because AI is designed to appear confident, these fabricated answers can be surprisingly convincing, making it harder for users to detect inaccuracies at first glance.

In my own practice, I have encountered cases cited by AI that do not exist and information about real-world cases that was either inaccurate or misleading. This creates serious professional liability concerns, as courts have begun sanctioning attorneys who rely on fabricated precedents. Recent sanctions in *Mata v. Avianca, Inc.*[21] and similar cases demonstrate the reputational and Federal Rules of Civil Procedure, Rule 11[22] exposure that follows when lawyers rely on unverified AI output.

Further, the use of AI in legal research presents opacity and explainability concerns, because AI systems often work like "black boxes" in the sense that AI produces results without explanation. This lack of transparency creates problems for attorneys who need to understand and explain the basis for their legal decisions. Lawyers have an ethical duty to supervise the technology they use. However, how can you properly supervise an AI if you cannot understand the ways in which it reached its conclusions? This creates a tension between using helpful technology and meeting professional responsibility standards.

Model Rule 5.3 requires lawyers to make reasonable efforts to ensure that non-lawyer assistance is compatible with the lawyer's professional obligations.[23] In the case of AI, this means attorneys must understand enough about the technology to ensure it complies with ethical standards. State Bar of California's Formal Opinion No. 2020-203 specifically addresses attorneys' ethical duties when using AI tools in legal practice, emphasizing the need for competent use of technology.[24]

The legal system values predictability and precedent. AI tools that cannot explain their reasoning process undermine these values and may reduce trust in the legal system over time. In *State v. Loomis*,[25] the court addressed concerns about using AI risk assessment tools in sentencing, highlighting the importance of transparency and the right to challenge algorithmic determinations. These also apply to utilization of AI in legal practice.

When a court, regulator, or client asks why the tool reached a conclusion, many commercial models cannot supply an audit trail. The EU AI Act technical documentation mandate forces providers and users to preserve detailed logs – an added cost for law firms.[26] Europe's first prohibitions under the AI Act took effect on 2 February 2025, implementing steep fines that can reach 7 percent of global turnover. US regulators (including the Federal Trade Commission, the Consumer Financial Protection Bureau, and the Securities and Exchange Commission) have also warned that existing consumer protection and securities rules apply to AI outputs.

How to minimize the risk of hallucination begins with understanding that AI is just a tool. Just as no experienced attorney would rely on a first-year associate's work without review before either sending it to a client or filing it with a court, neither should AI content be trusted without review. The risk of hallucination is minimized by implementing verification protocols. Lawyers should establish cross-checking procedures in which AI-generated research must be validated against traditional legal databases.

Additionally, users can help by providing clear, specific prompts, as clarity reduces ambiguity and minimizes room for the AI tool to guess. Integrating verification mechanisms, such as external databases or real-time fact-checking tools, also helps to ensure that AI-generated information aligns with reality. Finally, regular human oversight and specialized training can help AI systems become more reliable, reducing instances of unintended misinformation.

Inaccuracy in document review

The promise of AI to review thousands of documents in hours, rather than weeks, has transformed discovery practices. However, this efficiency comes with significant trade-offs in accuracy. I recently consulted on a patent infringement case in which an AI system missed critical technical documentation because the documents used terminology slightly different from the training examples. This oversight could have been catastrophic.

To address this challenge, lawyers should implement spot-checking protocols that manually review representative document subsets to validate AI performance. Hybrid approaches that pair human expertise with algorithmic efficiency maximize both safety and efficiency. Humans excel at contextual understanding, while machines excel at pattern recognition across large datasets. Furthermore, legal AI systems should be trained on industry-specific datasets and provide confidence scores with their classifications, allowing attorneys to prioritize human review for borderline determinations.

Professional responsibility concerns related to inaccuracy

The legal profession has always balanced technological advancement with ethical obligations. AI usage raises novel questions about attorney supervision requirements and delegation responsibilities. The Model Rules of Professional Conduct require lawyers to supervise non-lawyer assistance, but what constitutes adequate supervision of an algorithm? How can attorneys fulfill their duty of technological competence without becoming computer scientists? Additionally, the ABA's Formal Opinion 512 reminds lawyers that delegating work to software does not delegate responsibility; attorneys must understand a tool's limits, verify its work, and explain its use to clients when "material".[27] Importantly, using AI improperly may lead to malpractice. Bad AI advice given to a client, missed privilege flags in e-discovery, or reliance on biased analytics in settlement negotiations can all increase exposure to malpractice or other liability, often with an electronic papertrail documenting the lapse.

Additionally, unwise use of AI can lead to unauthorized practice of law (UPL) exposure. Many jurisdictions define the practice of law to include interpreting the law, applying legal principles to specific facts, and offering legal advice activities that some AI tools are now capable of performing. If an AI chatbot provides "instant legal answers" without licensed lawyer review, developers (and any lawyers who assist) may face UPL allegations and disciplinary action. If non-lawyers use AI to provide legal advice or services, they may be committing UPL. Similarly, lawyers who insufficiently supervise the use of AI by non-lawyers or who use AI to provide services in jurisdictions where they are not licensed also risk violating UPL rules. The risk is especially acute when AI tools autonomously generate legal documents, offer tailored legal advice, or otherwise perform tasks traditionally reserved for licensed attorneys.

The problem is the newness of AI and the varying definitions of UPL. The definition of the practice of law, and thus what constitutes UPL, varies significantly between states and countries. Some jurisdictions have begun to address these issues, but there is no uniform standard. Courts and regulatory bodies are still developing approaches to address the challenges posed by AI in legal services by balancing innovation and access to justice with consumer protection and the integrity of the legal profession.

Reasonable solutions include developing AI-specific competency standards for the profession. Bar associations should create certification programs for legal technology tools, similar to how certain practice specialties receive formal recognition. Law schools must incorporate legal technology literacy into their core curricula, rather than treating it as an elusive specialty. Additionally, courts and disciplinary authorities need to establish clear guidelines about when AI reliance constitutes reasonable professional judgment versus negligent delegation.

Bias in AI systems

The hidden prejudice in our digital tools

AI bias refers to the systematic and repeatable tendency of AI systems to produce unfair or prejudiced outcomes, often as a result of human biases embedded in the data or algorithms used to train them. This bias can arise from various sources, such as unrepresentative training data, flawed data collection methods, or the unconscious prejudices of those who design and deploy AI systems. For example, if an AI is trained primarily on data from one demographic group, it may perform poorly or unfairly when applied to other groups, leading to discriminatory results in areas like hiring, lending, healthcare, or law enforcement. AI bias not only mirrors existing societal inequalities, but can also amplify them, disproportionately affecting marginalized groups and reinforcing harmful stereotypes. Addressing AI bias is essential to ensuring that these technologies contribute to a more equitable and just society, rather than perpetuating or worsening existing discrimination.

Our legal history contains many examples of unfair treatment based on race, gender, and economic status. When AI systems learn from this data, they can reproduce these unfair patterns in their recommendations. For example, when AI reviews past judicial decisions to predict outcomes for new cases, it may suggest that certain groups deserve harsher treatment, simply because that is what happened in the past. The machine does not understand that those historical patterns reflect societal prejudice, rather than proper justice.

Consider a legal research tool trained on decades of court opinions. Such a system might give higher relevance rankings to arguments that succeeded historically, even when those successes partially resulted from biased judicial attitudes of previous eras. A lawyer using this tool might unknowingly build a strategy that reinforces outdated legal reasoning, missing opportunities to advance more equitable interpretations of the law.

The technical roots of legal AI bias

To understand bias in legal AI, we must understand how these systems work. Most modern AI tools use machine learning, where algorithms identify patterns in large datasets to make predictions or recommendations. These systems are only as good as the data they learn from.

The problem begins with data collection. Legal data are not neutral: court records reflect who had access to legal representation, which claims were pursued, and which cases were fully litigated rather than settled; cases involving wealthy clients or corporate interests are often better documented and more thoroughly litigated, creating an overrepresentation in the training data. Next comes data annotation, where humans label examples to teach AI systems. If the people performing this task bring their own biases or lack diverse perspectives, these limitations transfer to the AI. For instance, when classifying language in contracts as potentially problematic, annotators might miss cultural nuances or alternative interpretations.

Finally, algorithm design itself can introduce bias. Choices about which features to include, how to weight different factors, and what optimization goals to pursue all embed values into the system. An AI designed to maximize efficiency might sacrifice careful consideration of unique circumstances that could justify exceptions to general patterns.

Types of bias affecting legal AI

Several types of bias affect legal AI systems, each requiring specific attention. Historical bias occurs when past prejudice becomes encoded in AI recommendations. An AI tool analyzing past patent approvals might favor applications from large corporations or certain industries, simply because they received more approvals historically. This perpetuates advantages for established players and disadvantages newcomers, particularly those from underrepresented groups. The patent landscape demonstrates this problem clearly: a 2018 study found that patent applications for inventions developed by women were rejected more frequently than those developed by men, even when controlling for technology field and experience level.[28] If an AI system trained on historical patent data were to predict approval likelihood or suggest application strategies, it would likely reproduce this gender disparity.

Representation bias happens when certain groups have less available data. Legal AI may perform poorly for less common case types or for clients from underrepresented communities, simply because the system had fewer examples to learn from. This creates a dangerous cycle in which those already marginalized receive less effective legal assistance from AI tools. For example, immigration law AI tools might have limited training data for asylum seekers from smaller countries or those with recently emerged persecution grounds. This can lead to lower quality assistance precisely for those who may need it most, due to language barriers or limited resources.

Measurement bias arises when we choose which data to include. If legal AI only evaluates certain factors while ignoring others, it may miss important context. For instance, an AI predicting recidivism rates that does not consider rehabilitation programs may overestimate risk for defendants who participated in such programs. A notable example appears in pre-trial risk assessment tools. These systems often rely on factors like prior arrests, which themselves reflect biased policing practices. One widely used tool assigned higher risk scores to Black defendants even when they did not reoffend, while assigning lower scores to White defendants who later committed new crimes.

Aggregation bias occurs when AI systems make generalizations across diverse populations. Legal needs and circumstances vary significantly across different communities, yet AI systems often treat people as a homogeneous group, applying the same models and predictions to everyone. This creates systematic inaccuracies for anyone who does not match the majority pattern. Consider an AI tool that predicts jury verdicts based on historical case outcomes. If most historical trials occurred in predominantly White, suburban areas, the predictions may be inaccurate for cases in diverse urban settings or rural communities with different demographic compositions and social norms.

Real-world consequences in legal practice

Document review and discovery

AI-powered document review might miss important evidence related to cultural contexts outside the majority experience. In a discrimination case, an AI trained predominantly on mainstream corporate communications might fail to flag coded language or subtle patterns of bias that would be obvious to someone familiar with that specific workplace culture.

A multinational corporation defending against employment discrimination claims might use AI to review millions of emails and internal documents. If the AI was trained primarily on American business communications, it might miss culturally specific language patterns used in other countries that indicate problematic attitudes or behaviors.

Case outcome prediction

Predictive analytics tools increasingly help attorneys evaluate case strength and likely outcomes. These tools influence critical decisions about whether to litigate, settle, or pursue alternative dispute resolution. Biased predictions can lead to systematic undercompensation for certain clients. For example, AI systems predicting personal injury case outcomes might use geographic data, such as ZIP codes, to estimate settlement values. If historical settlements in certain areas – often correlated with socioeconomic or racial demographics – were lower, due to systemic inequities, the AI could perpetuate this by recommending lower payouts for claimants from those regions, even if their cases are comparable.[29] In short, the AI models accept the biases inherent in the data they were trained upon and will perpetuate such biases absent active intervention.

Judicial decision support

Judicial decision support tools might recommend harsher penalties for certain defendants based on factors correlated with, but not causally linked to, criminal behavior. Factors like zip code, education level, or employment history often serve as proxies for race or socioeconomic status, perpetuating historical patterns of discrimination.

In juvenile justice, risk assessment tools used to inform detention decisions have shown troubling patterns. As of 2021, Black youth were significantly more likely to be placed (i.e., detained or committed) in juvenile facilities than their white peers.[30]

Professional liability concerns

For attorneys, relying on biased AI could lead to professional liability. Imagine recommending a settlement amount based on an AI prediction that was systematically undervaluing claims for a particular demographic group. This could constitute malpractice.

Beyond malpractice concerns, attorneys have ethical obligations to provide competent representation and to avoid discrimination. The American Bar Association's Model Rule 1.1 requires lawyers to understand "the benefits and risks associated with relevant technology".[31] As AI becomes more prevalent, understanding algorithmic bias will likely become part of this competence requirement.

A law firm specializing in employment law might use AI to draft settlement agreements based on historical data. If the system consistently produces lower compensation figures for female employees compared to male employees with similar claims, the firm could face allegations of failure to provide equal representation to all clients.

The regulatory landscape

Legal professionals must navigate an evolving regulatory environment regarding AI use. Several jurisdictions have begun implementing AI regulation that directly impacts legal practice. For instance, the European Union's AI Act classifies AI systems used in legal settings as "high-risk" applications that are subject to strict requirements for transparency, robustness, and human oversight.[32] European law firms and legal departments must ensure their AI tools meet these standards or face significant penalties.

In the US, regulation remains fragmented. California has proposed regulations to address discrimination in employment resulting from the use of automated decision-making systems, including AI and algorithms.[33] New York City has implemented regulations requiring algorithmic audits for systems used in hiring decisions, which affects how law firms and legal departments select candidates.[34] The ABA has issued ethics opinions which suggest that attorneys must exercise reasonable care when using AI tools, including understanding their limitations and potential biases.[35] This creates a professional duty to evaluate AI systems before relying on them for client matters.

Addressing AI bias in legal practice

Legal professionals must take active steps to identify and address bias in our AI tools. This begins with demanding transparency from AI vendors. We need to understand what data were used to train the system and which measures were taken to identify and reduce bias. Legal professionals should request documentation relating to:

- The composition of training data, including its temporal and jurisdictional scope;
- Demographic representation within the data;
- Methods used to identify and mitigate potential biases;
- Performance metrics across different demographic groups and case types; and
- Limitations of the system and scenarios where it may be less reliable.

When evaluating an e-discovery platform, law firms should ask whether the system was tested on documents from various industries, languages, and communication styles. If a platform was primarily trained on financial services communications, it might perform poorly when reviewing healthcare or manufacturing industry documents.

Testing AI systems against diverse case examples helps reveal potential blindspots. If an AI performs differently when analyzing similar cases with merely demographic differences, this suggests bias. Law firms can implement "blind testing" protocols, in which identical legal scenarios are presented to AI systems with only the demographic details changed. For example, identical contract disputes could be presented with different client names suggesting different ethnicities, genders, or company sizes. Any variation in the AI's analysis would indicate potential bias.

Creating diverse legal teams to work alongside AI systems helps to catch biases the technology might miss. Different perspectives can identify when AI recommendations diverge from principles of fairness or when they fail to account for important contextual factors. A litigation team preparing for trial might include attorneys from different backgrounds to review an AI's jury selection recommendations. Team members might identify when the system's suggestions reflect outdated assumptions about juror attitudes based on demographics, rather than substantive views relevant to the case.

Human oversight remains essential. AI should support legal decision-making, not replace professional judgment. When an AI recommendation seems unusual, legal professionals should investigate why. Establishing clear review protocols helps to ensure AI outputs receive appropriate scrutiny. For high-stakes decisions, multiple attorneys might independently review AI recommendations, especially when they significantly impact client interests or legal strategy. A criminal defense practice might use AI to suggest sentencing alternatives based on case factors, but require attorney review before presenting any recommendation to a client. The reviewing attorney would evaluate whether the AI properly accounted for unique client circumstances and whether its suggestions align with current judicial attitudes in that particular court.

Documenting AI use and outcomes enables ongoing improvement. Legal professionals should track:

- When and how AI tools influenced decisions;
- Instances where human judgment overrode AI recommendations;
- Outcomes of cases where AI played a significant role; and
- Feedback from clients about AI-assisted services.

These data allow firms to identify patterns of bias and continuously refine their use of AI tools. It also creates an audit trail that can demonstrate due diligence if questions about AI use arise later.

The future of AI in legal practice: balancing innovation with ethics

AI presents both remarkable opportunities and significant challenges for the legal profession. The technology allows attorneys to work faster and handle more information than ever before, but it also introduces new risks to client confidentiality, data security, and the accuracy of legal work. Finding the right balance between embracing innovation and upholding our professional values will define the next chapter of legal practice.

The confidentiality concerns cannot be overlooked. When client information leaves our secure systems and enters third-party AI platforms, we create new vulnerability points. The cases of law firms facing significant financial penalties for data breaches remind us that these risks are not theoretical. Rather, these examples demonstrate that courts and regulators take data protection seriously. Our profession must do the same.

Perhaps most troubling is the tendency of AI systems to "hallucinate" or generate false information with remarkable confidence. Relying on AI-generated legal citations that do not exist can lead to professional sanctions. This undermines the foundation of our legal system, which depends on accurate information and genuine precedent. No technology efficiency is worth sacrificing the truthfulness that courts and clients expect from legal professionals.

The bias embedded in many AI systems presents another critical challenge. These tools learn from historical data that may reflect past discrimination in our legal system. Without careful oversight, AI can perpetuate these patterns, recommending different strategies or predicting different outcomes based on a client's demographics, rather than the merits of their case. This contradicts our professional obligation to provide equal representation to all clients.

Despite these challenges, there are practical paths forward. Local AI implementation keeps sensitive information under attorney control, never exposing it to third parties, even when connected to the internet. Anonymization techniques that replace real names and identifying details with generic substitutes protect client privacy while still allowing AI to process the legal concepts involved. Clear client consent procedures and comprehensive governance policies create transparency about how technology is being used.

The legal profession has always adapted to technological change, while preserving its core values. From the introduction of telephones to email to cloud computing, attorneys have found ways to balance innovation with ethical obligations. AI represents the next frontier in this ongoing journey.

Looking ahead, we need several developments to ensure responsible AI use in law. Bar associations and courts must establish clear guidelines about what constitutes appropriate AI use and adequate supervision. Law schools must incorporate technology ethics alongside traditional professional responsibility training. AI vendors serving the legal market must develop specialized tools that address the unique confidentiality and accuracy requirements of legal practice.

As individual attorneys, we must approach AI with both curiosity and caution. We should embrace its ability to handle routine tasks and process vast information quickly. However, we must maintain vigilant oversight, verifying critical outputs and never delegating our professional judgment. The future belongs to lawyers who can skillfully combine human wisdom with technological assistance, using each for what it does best.

By acknowledging both the promise and peril of legal AI, implementing appropriate safeguards, and maintaining our commitment to client protection, we can harness these powerful tools while preserving the integrity and trust that define our profession. The balance we strike today will shape legal practice for generations to come.

References

1 Kharpal, A., "Samsung bans use of A.I. like ChatGPT for employees after misuse of the chatbot", CNBC, 2 May 2023. See: https://www.cnbc.com/2023/05/02/samsung-bans-use-of-ai-like-chatgpt-for-staff-after-misuse-of-chatbot.html.

2 Coyer, C. and Marathe, I., "Legal industry players missed a Microsoft ai loophole that could expose confidential data", *LegalTech News*, 20 March 2024. See: https://www.law.com/legaltechnews/2024/03/20/legal-industry-players-missed-a-microsoft-ai-loophole-that-could-expose-confidential-data/?slreturn=2025050872304.

3 American Bar Association, "Rule 1.6: Confidentiality of Information", 2025. See: https://www.americanbar.org/groups/professional_responsibility/publications/model_rules_of_professional_conduct/rule_1_6_confidentiality_of_information/.

4 American Bar Association, "Formal Opinion 483: Lawyers' Obligations After an Electronic Data Breach or Cyberattack", 17 October 2018. See: https://www.americanbar.org/groups/professional_responsibility/publications/ethics_opinions/index_by_issue_dates/.

5 No. 1:15CV00057, 2017 WL 1041600, at *5 (W.D. Va. Feb. 9, 2017).

6 No. 1:15CV00057, 2017 WL 4368617, at *8 (W.D. Va. Oct. 2, 2017.

7 District of Columbia Bar, "Ethics Opinion 388: Attorneys' Use of Generative Artificial Intelligence in Client Matters", August 2024. See: https://www.dcbar.org/For-Lawyers/Legal-Ethics/Ethics-Opinions-210-Present/Ethics-Opinion-388.

8 42 U.S.C. § 1320d-6.

9 15 U.S.C. §§ 6801-6809.

10 Merken, S., "N.Y. Law Firm to Pay State $200K Over Data Breach", Reuters, 27 March 2023. See: https://www.reuters.com/legal/litigation/ny-law-firm-pay-state-200k-over-data-breach-2023-03-27/.

11 Thomas, D., "Law Firm Orrick Agrees to $8M In Settlement Over Breach of Client Data", Reuters, 11 April 2024. See: https://www.reuters.com/legal/litigation/law-firm-orrick-agrees-8-mln-settlement-over-breach-client-data-2024-04-11/.

12 Regulation (EU) 2016/679 of the European Parliament and of the Council of 27 April 2016 on the protection of natural persons with regard to the processing of personal data and on the free movement of such data [2016] OJ L 119.

13 CJEU Case C-311/18.

14 *Vizio, Inc. v. Int'l Trade Comm'n*, 605 F.3d 1330. (Fed. Cir. 2010).

15 CJEU Case C?131/12.

16 American Bar Association, "Formal Opinion 498: Virtual Practice", 10 March 2021. See: https://www.americanbar.org/groups/professional_responsibility/publications/ethics_opinions/index_by_issue_dates/.

17 259 F.R.D. 568 (M.D. Fla. 2009).

18 Regulation (EU) 2016/679 of the European Parliament and of the Council of 27 April 2016 on the protection of natural persons with regard to the processing of personal data and on the free movement of such data, and repealing Directive 95/46/EC (General Data Protection Regulation) [2016] OJ L 119; Chapter 1, Article 5(1)(c).

19 The Sedona Conference, "Commentary on defensible disposition, second edition", *The Sedona Conference Journal*, 2019, volume 20. https://thesedonaconference.org/sites/default/files/publications/Commentary%20on%20Defensible%20Disposition_1.pdf.

20 American Bar Association, "Rule 1.1: Competence – Comment", 2025. See: https://www.americanbar.org/groups/professional_responsibility/publications/model_rules_of_professional_conduct/rule_1_1_competence/comment_on_rule_1_1/.

21 678 F. Supp. 3d 443, 459 (S.D.N.Y. 2023).

22 Legal Information Institute, "Rule 11. Signing Pleadings, Motions, and Other Papers; Representations to the Court; Sanctions", Cornell Law School, 2025. See: https://www.law.cornell.edu/rules/frcp/rule_11.

23 American Bar Association, "Rule 5.3: Responsibilities Regarding Nonlawyer Assistance", 2025. See: https://www.americanbar.org/groups/professional_responsibility/publications/model_rules_of_professional_conduct/rule_5_3_responsibilities_regarding_nonlawyer_assistant/.

24 The State Bar of California Standing Committee on Professional Responsibility and Conduct, "FORMAL OPINION NO. 2020-201", 2020. See: https://www.calbar.ca.gov/Portals/0/documents/ethics/Opinions/Formal-Opinion-No-2020-203-Data-Breaches.pdf.

25 881 N.W.2d 749 (Wis. 2016).
26 Regulation (EU) 2024/1689 of the European Parliament and of the Council of 13 June 2024 laying down harmonised rules on artificial intelligence [2024] OJ L 130.
27 American Bar Association Standing Committee on Ethics and Professional Responsibility, "Formal Opinion 512: Generative Artificial Intelligence Tools", American BAR Association, 29 July 2024. See: https://www.americanbar.org/content/dam/aba/administrative/professional_responsibility/ethics-opinions/aba-formal-opinion-512.pdf.
28 Jensen, K., Kovács, B., and Sorenson, O., "Gender differences in obtaining and maintaining patent rights", *Nature Biotechnology*, 2018, volume 36, pp. 307–309. https://doi.org/10.1038/nbt.4120.
29 Obermeyer, Z., Powers, B., Vogeli, C., and Mullainathan, S., "Dissecting racial bias in an algorithm used to manage the health of populations", *Science*, 2019, volume 366, issue 6464, pp. 447–453. https://doi.org/10.1126/science.aax2342.
30 Sladky, C.T.J., and Kang, W., "Easy Access to the Census of Juveniles in Residential Placement", 2023. See: https://www.ojjdp.gov/ojstatbb/ezacjrp/.
31 American Bar Association, "Rule 1.1: Competence – Comment", 2025. See: https://www.americanbar.org/groups/professional_responsibility/publications/model_rules_of_professional_conduct/rule_1_1_competence/comment_on_rule_1_1/.
32 Regulation (EU) 2024/1689 of the European Parliament and of the Council of 13 June 2024 laying down harmonised rules on artificial intelligence [2024] OJ L 130.
33 Zheliabovskii, R., "Regulations to Ban Discriminatory AI Systems in California Move Ahead", SHRM, 1 May 2025. See: https://www.shrm.org/topics-tools/employment-law-compliance/regulations-to-ban-discriminatory-ai-systems-california.
34 NYC Consumer and Worker Protection, "Automated Employment Decision Tools: Frequently Asked Questions", 29 June 2023. See: https://www.nyc.gov/assets/dca/downloads/pdf/about/DCWP-AEDT-FAQ.pdf.
35 Fisher, K.R., "ABA Ethics Opinion on generative AI offers useful framework", *Business Law Today*, 3 October 2024. See: https://www.americanbar.org/groups/business_law/resources/business-law-today/2024-october/aba-ethics-opinion-generative-ai-offers-useful-framework/.

Chapter 10:
The human side of legal AI: leadership and value creation in in-house teams

By Rasmus Kirkeby Salling, head of transition, new markets, and Peter Kaas, head of digital legal and compliance, Falck

In this chapter, we will explore the human side of AI and – through the lens of a modern Nordic leadership approach – offer perspectives on selected leadership considerations for general counsels, CLOs, heads of legal, and other leaders in in-house teams ("legal leaders") as the transformative nature of generative AI (genAI) impacts their strategies and teams. We will offer some insights on how in-house teams might capture substantial benefits and value from implementing and using genAI in their daily work, drawing on our experiences over the last several years with Falck (a global provider of emergency response and healthcare services and with 25,000 employees across 25 countries).

We will then discuss perspectives on how in-house teams might measure the value of implementing genAI, including where such metrics are not financial.

Lastly, we will offer insights on why a focus on upskilling your in-house team might be the preferable leadership strategy, rather than recruiting new talent, on the AI journey.

Throughout this chapter, we will share what we have learned from a bold and experimentational strategy adopted by Falck, in which the in-house team has become one of the internal frontrunners in the adoption of genAI.

Leadership considerations

In the following, we aim to highlight a few crucial themes for the leadership of any in-house team to consider when embarking on or continuing an AI journey. Such considerations will eventually come to all in-house teams. A recent survey indicated that a significant majority of those in the legal industry are already engaged with genAI in one way or another, and most recognize its potential to bring value to organizations in the near future.[1]

The role of leadership in in-house teams is to ensure that the team delivers value to the business. However, while doing so, the key responsibility of the leadership is to take care of its people. This does not change with AI, and a people-centric approach should remain a focal point for the legal leader. However, what does change is the promise AI holds to create an even better work life for team members, which should be taken into consideration by the legal leader when developing their people leadership.

All in-house teams want to deliver value. However, great legal acumen will not suffice; it is only a foundation. GenAI does not change the fact that an excellent in-house team has a good understanding of the commercial strategy and drivers for the organization, as well as deep operational insight and financial literacy. An AI strategy should not focus less on the business. If anything, the focus should be increased.

The saying "data is the new oil" is well-known. Several profitable companies have built their business on data. For many organizations, however, data are often unstructured and scattered and, therefore, can be considered "crude oil" – not easily exploited for value. GenAI can become the refinery that can extract value from crude, unstructured data. Our work with genAI has revealed just how important such data are for legal teams.

One of the significant responsibilities of in-house teams is assessing risks. This will continue to be a focal point, with the addition of the inherent risks of genAI. In-house counsels typically assess risk in individual contracts, disputes, or other singular matters. However, with the support of genAI, there should be a focus on enterprise risk and portfolio risk, in which the legal team will not only consider such matters individually but focus on the bigger picture by looking across an entire portfolio. When considering portfolio risk, we have leveraged genAI inter alia to identify uncapped liability in contracts across our various businesses and services.

GenAI introduces new types of risk that are inherent in the technology: genAI is prone to inaccurate output ("hallucinations") and biases, and is often impossible to explain ("black box"). These are all concerns for a legal leader leading genAI adoption. It is crucial to ensure that mitigations, such as human-in-the-loop and output quality control, are implemented and encouraged in the in-house team. Some technological approaches, such as grounding and leveraging retrieval-augmented generation (RAG)-based setups, can improve the overall quality of the genAI models.[2]

The ethical aspects of the training data (data protected by various information regulations, such as data protection, trade secrets, and copyright) of the models raise a rather uncomfortable question: are the models fundamentally incompatible with existing legislation? Can we even use such technology? We cannot offer a simple answer to this – philosophical, to a certain extent – dilemma. Another dimension is the professional ethical standards applicable to lawyers.

The technology as a potential cost saver through FTE reduction also raises ethical concerns related to how genAI adoption is communicated. In times of such fundamental change, it is imperative that legal leaders provide comfort and direction to employees fearing for their jobs.

Additionally, genAI raises strategic concerns relevant to the environmental, social, and governance (ESG) agenda: organizations may be tied to tech giants delivering genAI services. In a geopolitically unstable world, legal leaders must devise strategies for mitigating risk of service disruption, sudden price increases, and data confidentiality concerns by sourcing alternative supply chains and considering near-shoring or in-sourcing. GenAI also raises concerns about energy consumption and carbon footprints; here, mitigation strategies can include reliance of vendors on green energy and use of small or narrow genAI models with lower energy consumption.

The way forward is to embrace and pay attention to these potential seismic developments and prepare for swift course correction. The market will likely also adapt and provide models with fewer legal or ethical considerations.

For the legal leader, it is, therefore, essential to ask these questions when adopting AI and integrating it into the work of a legal team: what is the worst thing that can happen? Where does it make sense to take risks? In Falck, we have focused our genAI adoption largely on the commercial legal and compliance documentation work, as the risks in these areas are fundamentally monetary in nature (e.g., a loss due to poor AI-based contract review) as opposed to some of the more profound risks affecting the livelihood and wellbeing of human beings. From our experience, advantages and development opportunities clearly surpass the risks, and legal leaders should consider leaning into a higher risk appetite, even if it requires moving out of one's comfort zone.

Capturing value

How do you capture value from AI as an in-house team? And what is value, by the way? Often, the initial reaction is that it is a monetary amount gained through either savings or revenue. However, value should be defined much more broadly. Many of the non-financial value parameters, traditionally considered "soft", often contribute to the progress of the in-house team and might impact financial performance indirectly or in the long run. This chapter will consider a wide range of such values, in combination with financial value.

Capturing non-financial value

One of the most convincing reasons to introduce genAI in legal teams is not the potential direct financial savings obtainable but, rather, how it can become an efficient leadership tool for the legal leader. An apparent opportunity is improving employee job satisfaction and retaining talent by enhancing in-house work, increasing value, and securing a seat at the table where decisions are made, thereby enhancing the feeling of purpose in the in-house team.

In-house counsel want to spend their time on high-value matters and other cases where they can make a difference. However, a frequent complaint from fellow legal professionals is a perception that in-house work too often involves low-value, routine, and repetitive tasks. Work lacking value or purpose negatively impacts the team, the organization, and overall performance.

Some might question why in-house teams would spend time on low-value tasks. A shift to high-value work is not always easy, and the legal leader must actively consider how to drive this shift. First, there might not be a coherent consensus on what is high-value; even if there is agreement on this definition, some tasks require at least a minimal degree of legal review. Lacking some form of automation, they will necessitate human review. Additionally, there will be instances where the business expects support, and it is essential to provide that as part of your business partnering strategy. Finally, you might not have earned the trust that secures your seat at the table and, therefore, access to the highest value work.

To deal with this, many legal teams have adopted a strategy of becoming business partners. However, there is an opportunity to move past that point and transition to embodying the business. A prerequisite, however, is a strong understanding of commercial, operational, and financial aspects, as argued above. GenAI has the potential to further support in-house counsels' focus on the more strategic and complex tasks, where sound judgment is a requirement, and allow the legal team to spend more time on what matters to internal and external customers, thereby embedding the legal team into the business.

It is not only internally that genAI will allow the in-house team to play a value-adding role. Traditionally, in-house counsel take a reactive role, focusing on contentious matters of the partnerships (at least after the signing of a contract), as they are usually consulted when a disagreement or conflict has materialized. In some cases, they are only involved at a point in time when the relationship is beyond repair. GenAI can provide better insights into the obligations of the relevant parties and means of adherence to a contract, which will allow the company to take appropriate actions at an earlier stage. This will help preserve relationships and de-escalate – or even prevent – later conflicts.

Finally, reputational value should not be overlooked. It will be important when attracting legal talent, which is something we have experienced in our own recruitment processes. While genAI might not be the sole nor primary driver for this, it will have an impact, as legal talent want to work in an environment that creates opportunities for the team and the individual. The reputational value can manifest both for the wider organization and the in-house team and will often translate into candidates asking themselves: "Do I want to work at this company, and do I want to be part of this team?" In turn, the legal leader should ask themselves: "Is my team perceived as a modern team that can work on things that matter and as an integral part of the business?"

Capturing financial value

Financial value can be captured in two ways: through cost-savings or increased revenue. Both of these hopefully lead to improved profitability.

Cost saving

The most obvious cost saving introduced by genAI is reduced FTEs in the legal team. This might either be through a reduction of the headcount, where fewer colleagues handle a static intake, or through a freeze in hiring despite increasing intake. While this is not the major driver of value of in-house teams, and not necessarily where the legal leader will find the true value of introducing genAI, it should not be disregarded, particularly for legal teams encountering budget constraints and hiring freezes.

To the extent that the legal team can automate, it might decrease the workload for the individual in-house counsel. Recent reports suggest that in-house teams can significantly increase the intake of cases without increasing the headcount.[3] Although this is not a cost saving, it yields the same effect.

This, of course, comes with the caveat that completed work often leads to more work. In many organizations, work will find its way to where it is solved. If the in-house team, through AI, can solve more tasks and have a quicker turnaround, it does not in itself mean that the workload will decrease, but it will hopefully lead to an adjusted and more strategic approach to its work and responsibilities.

Commercial contracts are a primary area in which we have experience in our work deriving value as cost-savings. We have created our own genAI tool for contract reviews and analyses, benchmarked against preferred and fall-back baselines. The analysis can help to assess risk, answer general questions on the contract, support re-drafting and redlining, and contract strategy. One of the most accessible value gains we identified early is auto-renewals of obsolete procurement contracts. The average company has hundreds – if not thousands of contracts – for procuring products and services, spanning from office supplies to IT, production equipment, and real estate. AI-powered contract management systems will allow the identification of products or services that are no longer needed. However, the prerequisite is sufficient data that link the contracts with the relevant aspects of the business, which enables consideration of whether it is obsolete or not. AI-driven contract management will allow you to pair invoices with products and services and unearth unnecessary usage or consumption.

Above, we discussed the opportunity for the legal team to engage actively in relationships with partners. Notwithstanding this, there will be situations where the organization fails to comply with contractual obligations, which will often lead to penalties and other sanctions, deteriorating the value of a contract in turn. AI can track the contractual performance. Similarly to what has been discussed above, the in-house counsel is uniquely positioned to advise on the degree of compliance and take appropriate actions, such as early settlement and dispute management.

Finally, procurement contracts may present opportunities for lower prices, such as volume discounts or discounts related to contract durations and renewals. While both parties typically have the obligation to ensure that pricing and invoicing are accurate, this is often overlooked. AI can assist in capturing contractually-entitled savings.

We have also had some good experiences introducing AI in our M&A work, where it can be utilized for a red flag to diligence reporting.

In addition to commercial contracts and M&A, we have positive experiences with using genAI in compliance. When a company has a myriad of policies within areas, such as code of conduct, GDPR, AI, and sanctions, it can – for the individual employee with little to no contact with compliance in their daily work – be difficult and daunting to determine which policy would apply to a specific situation, if they can find the policy at all. If they do not know where to look, many employees will base decisions on their gut feeling and integrity. By introducing a compliance bot, we have been able to provide easy access answers to compliance questions.

With GDPR, one of our use cases has been Article 30 records (required for documenting data processing activities), which are burdensome to write and rarely updated, but are nevertheless a fundamental GDPR compliance requirement. Through a conversation with an AI agent, employees without any privacy experience can document Article 30 records by answering questions in a structured walkthrough. This has proven to be a strong foundation for delegating GDPR compliance work into the business, thus freeing up time for the in-house team to focus on more strategic matters.

Another concern may be the same as above: that the AI provides a wrong Article 30 or provides an incorrect answer related to the code of conduct. Again, our point is that an overall increase in required documentation may be a benefit compared to no documentation. The same can be said about a compliance bot – it will increase engagement with the corpus of compliance policies in the organization, thereby strengthening the overall compliance awareness. However, as a legal leader, it is crucial to weigh the risks and opportunities of introducing AI. A guiding principle for Falck has been to focus on areas where the risk to people is minimal. This has also allowed us to understand the capabilities and limitations of the technology, allowing us to further improve on the adoption.

A natural evolutionary step for the implementation of genAI and automation of legal work is the introduction of self-service to the organization, which has several advantages. First, it will lessen the workload of the in-house team, which is particularly relevant with increasing demand and intake, and free up time to focus on high-value work. Furthermore, if set up correctly, it will allow for quicker turnaround time on matters, as it reduces or removes communication with the legal team altogether. While genAI-based self-service solutions may sound anxiety-inducing, it may be necessary to contemplate in any event, as our experience shows that internal stakeholders will consult genAI for legal advice on their own. Therefore, it becomes essential for risk management to provide such self-service solutions in a controlled environment. Additionally, self-service has the added benefit of driving the rest of the organization toward better contract compliance by using contract templates and self-service solutions designed by the in-house team.

Areas in which self-service works well is where there is an availability of templates that require little to no adjustments, which is why contracts with a high degree of standardization – such as NDAs, standardized sales contracts, and data processing agreements – are great candidates for self-service. In many organizations, contracts might be reviewed and signed without legal review. In some cases, this is per design (typically for low-value contracts); in others, it is not (due to oversight or a deliberate choice to bypass legal review). Such contracts can pose a risk, and self-service can mitigate this risk. Again, while an AI-based review may not be of optimal quality, it is often better than no legal review at all.

One caveat is that with significant self-service comes the risk of decreased communication between the in-house team and the rest of the organization. To counter this, it is paramount to ensure that the legal team maintains a good understanding of the business and can communicate the shift to higher-value work, leading to a seat at the table.

The reduction in external spending is another obvious cost saving. Solving work internally is likely to increase, as the introduction and use of genAI and automation will allow in-house teams to handle a larger intake and push non-legal colleagues to consult self-service solutions. This will in turn reduce external spending – for certain types of work, at least.

The question is, of course, how the legal leader ensures that the AI effort reduces relevant external spending and how the role of external advisors might change. What work would be insourced and what should be done externally highly depends on the strategic choices taken by the legal leader and the competencies of the legal team. The legal leader should consider which tasks and how much should be handled by external providers and who is on the external panel. It becomes a strategic consideration as to whether it makes sense to shift work from expensive external providers (typically law firms) to more budget-conscious alternative legal service providers (ALSP). This is not AI-specific, and is considered by in-house teams when planning a legal strategy. However, with more AI-based solutions, it is more likely that ALSPs will be able to compete with traditional law firms, delivering services that are at par and more cost-effective.[4]

Value increase

While not solely reserved for AI-powered solutions, AI might significantly improve the opportunity to identify customer contracts where prices of services or products delivered under a long-term contract might be adjusted or indexed. From experience, many contracts end up in the virtual drawer and are not managed for value. A supplier might be unaware of contractual opportunities to adjust prices to make the contract more profitable. This particular use case was our starting point in Falck when initially considering introducing a new contract lifecycle management setup. Our analysis revealed significant opportunities for adjusting prices in contracts that had not been sufficiently considered. The value capture from one business unit alone would justify acquiring the system.

It should be noted that the compound effect of a yearly price adjustment might significantly impact profitability throughout the lifetime of a contract.

AI can help identify service delivery against obligations and billing in customer relationships, to reduce the level of unbilled services. One of the ways to achieve this would be to compare invoices to contracts. If the AI is training on the contracts, there would be opportunities for refining the capabilities and identifying patterns that could suggest whether services are delivered but not invoiced, either through omission of invoicing in general or because a service that could have been invoiced separately was not invoiced.

Measuring value

Having a sense of capturing the value is not sufficient. As a legal leader, you must show the C-suite that the value is real and tangible. So, once you have established the definitions of value, the next step is to measure it.

When considering financial value, a natural starting point would be universally agreed fiat matrices such as "USD saved" or "EUR revenue uplift". However, it is not as simple when considering non-financial value. Non-financial value, although often overlooked, should not be underestimated. We believe that the long-term benefit of non-financial value could supersede the impact of direct financial value in the long term. This is also why we introduced this chapter with the concept of non-financial value.

However, no matter whether the value is financial or non-financial, caution should be adopted. The exact value of the capturing initiatives might be challenging to measure if there are no data and baselines against which to measure. In any case, it requires a good amount of faith.

Non-financial value

Non-financial value creation might have several causes, and the legal leader might introduce various initiatives; therefore, it is not always easy to gain full transparency into causal links between initiatives and added value. Often, the strategy of the in-house team will have several elements which all contribute to the same goals, such as improved collaboration, customer satisfaction, shift to high-value work, and better engagement score and retention of team members.

For overworked teams, there are opportunities with genAI to create a more meaningful professional life and potentially improve work–life balance. The legal leader could measure this through scrutiny of working hours to ensure the right work–life balance, in turn directly measured by the Employee Engagement Score or other similar metrics used to assess employee satisfaction. A breakdown of the work performed will serve as guidance on whether the time of the in-house team and the individual lawyers is spent productively. Through such oversight, the legal leader will have the opportunity to guide the legal team's work and have crucial conversations with internal customers on time spent.

A key differentiator between good and great in-house teams in the form of retention measured by churn: higher employee satisfaction means lower churn. Reducing churn will not only increase the average employee's insight into the business and the relationships between colleagues, but it will also have a positive financial effect. As a rule of thumb, the longer a person's period of employment with a particular organization is, the better understanding of commercial and operational aspects of the business that an in-house counsel serves. This is one of the reasons why in-house teams with long tenure tend to deliver superior service. Therefore, employee retention should be a major concern for the legal leader.

Furthermore, top legal talent might be difficult to attract and retain. In a market where many legal teams will be looking for the same talent with certain insight and experience, upskilling the existing legal team might be the most viable way of ensuring the skillset of tomorrow. The challenges and opportunities with upskilling are further explored below. Additionally, for larger corporations, brand value will be a significant parameter when attracting talent.

Contract lifecycle management holds several AI use cases. While enhanced contract management may be evaluated from a financial perspective, such as the opportunity to index or adjust pricing or to discontinue supply agreements that would otherwise auto-renew, it is also important to consider relevant non-financial metrics, such as customer satisfaction scores or customer retention rates, which might not necessarily have a financial value by themselves. Still, it will be a primer for future earnings.

The legal intake from the business might be another relevant matrix to look at – both in terms of quality and quantity. A close look at the legal intake and workload will reveal whether AI has shifted the advisory and support of the in-house team to higher value and more strategic work, allowing for a more productive team. At Falck, we have had a strong focus on and worked actively with prioritization as a way to measure this. We have grouped tasks into categories and ranked them in terms of their value and alignment with Falck's overall strategy. We can already see strong indications of a shift into strategic work, compared to low-value and operational work.

Internal customer satisfaction surveys are great tools to assess whether the in-house team understands issues from more than just a legal perspective and are perceived to be adding value to the business in a more holistic way. We suggest conducting a customer satisfaction survey with internal clients requesting legal services to gain insights that enable the in-house team to better understand the perspectives of its stakeholders and clearly grasp the organization's expectations and requests. Furthermore, it will serve as a benchmark for the AI journey. What the survey should include depends on the nature of the organization and the role of the in-house team. However, a good general offset could be the general satisfaction with the quality and speed of the work delivered.

Furthermore, we recommend setting up interviews with business leaders to get their deeper perspectives on legal services and understand how the in-house team can work with them strategically. Questions should also focus on the value of using AI in the organization. The conversation would naturally move to the introduction of self-service solutions, how to get colleagues to embrace and use them, and how to communicate them.

Such interviews form a great basis for understanding perceived value and concepts of quality and speed among stakeholders, allowing the in-house team to walk in their customers' shoes. The legal leader should not miss the opportunity to utilize these interviews as excellent communication channels and as an opportunity to explain to internal customers how the team works, what the focus is, and what both parties could do to improve the situation. In this aspect, a conversation on AI is critical.

The quality of the partnerships might be measured on external customer retention rates, customer satisfaction surveys, or internally as a view of disputes measured in absolute numbers and the financial value of conflicts with other suppliers or customers. For the in-house team, an appropriate metric would be how early the team is involved in relevant matters.

Finally, as discussed above, reputational value is essential when attracting talent. As a legal leader, you want to hire people who positively choose your organization. While the general economy and the job market will have a significant impact, it could be relevant to look at the number of relevant applications being received for the same level of positions, to determine whether the organizational attractiveness increases. The more significant the influx of appropriate candidates, the higher the likelihood of hiring top talent for the company and team. Additionally, for companies that track candidate experience, this would be relevant to consider.

Financial value

Financial value might have more objective measure tools than non-financial value. Financial value can be measured as either a cost saving or increased revenue to a specific value in the currency the company uses. However, in practice, it can be challenging to measure.

There is often no tradition for calculating value in in-house teams, and the economic impact is frequently solely measured by FTE costs and external spending. With such a narrow view, savings can be quantified by comparing the pre- and post-AI implementation FTE costs and external spending. The other issue is that many organizations lack data, impeding the measurement of the financial impact of AI. However, it makes sense to consider it more as a business opportunity and thereby assess the perceived value in the organization. Similarly to what we consider when trying to assess non-financial value, we take the stance of implementing AI because we believe in it, not because we fully measure it.

Contracts are a good case for understanding how financial value can be measured. Cost savings and revenue generation contribute to the bottom line, but they do so in different ways and have disparate implications for the business, and not every euro or dollar is "worth" the same. It matters where the value is found in the profit and loss statement (P&L). In the instance in which the use of AI reduces the time spent on a contract because of a quicker drafting or review – which is, in reality, an operational efficiency – such a reduction should lead to a decrease in the selling, general, and administrative expenses (SG&A) cost allocated to the contract or the portfolio of contracts of a certain type, and a lower spend across the contract portfolio or the business in question in general. However, only a minority of organizations distribute costs on a single-contract level. However, where the savings come from an opportunity to improve prices for components to products (or reduce unneeded goods or services), such a saving would reduce the cost of goods sold (COGS).

As discussed above, risk and disputes can have significant financial implications. With better oversight hereof through AI, the in-house team will successfully manage costs and risks, thereby contributing to cost savings. This can be measured by tracking the reduction in legal disputes and the corresponding savings in legal fees and settlements.

Indexation, price adjustments, and invoicing services that have not been invoiced will impact the revenue directly (and improve the bottom line if everything else remains the same). This will be measured by tracking the additional revenue generated from price adjustments and indexations. Do not forget the compound value. AI can also help identify unbilled services by comparing service delivery against contractual obligations and billing. The legal team can capture additional revenue by ensuring that all services delivered are invoiced correctly. This can be measured by tracking the increase in billed services and the corresponding revenue. However, a baseline is needed.

Another way of measuring financial value is by assessing how cash flow is impacted. This might be highly relevant for companies that are low on cash or might have limited resources allocated to investments in AI. Depending on the payment terms, cost savings typically result in immediate improvements in cash flow by reducing expenditures, while revenue generation may have a more gradual impact as additional revenue is realized over time. The in-house team can track the changes in cash flow before and after adopting AI solutions to measure the impact. This can be done by comparing the cash flow statements for the relevant periods and identifying the specific contributions of cost savings and revenue generation to the overall cash flow improvement. However, it should be noted that a myriad of things can impact the cash flow, and such analysis requires substantial data.

Another way to measure the attractiveness of the investment in AI is by calculating the return on investment (ROI), where the profitability of an investment is measured relative to its cost. This is done by quantifying the total investment in AI solutions for the legal team and the company, such as the costs related to licensing the software in question, purchasing necessary hardware, conducting training, and other associated fees. Next, the net benefits should be calculated by totaling the cost savings and additional revenue generated by the AI solutions. The ROI can then be calculated by dividing the net benefits by the total investment. A positive ROI indicates that the investment in AI has been profitable, while a negative ROI suggests that the costs have outweighed the benefits. This will help the legal leader assess the effectiveness of its AI investments and make informed decisions about future investments.

Setting the team

We will now explore how the strategic shift for in-house teams can best be driven by legal leaders by considering how to set the in-house team. We consider which new skills will be necessary in the future, and we discuss the benefits of upskilling rather than rehiring.

Future skills for lawyers

The legal profession has faced technological changes in the past: the emergence of word processing, e-mails, and so on. These technological shifts were very similar to the way lawyers were already working (an e-mail is fundamentally the same as a letter). The difference with genAI is the speed, availability, and capability to create and process information autonomously.

LLMs are languages, and law is language. GenAI is, therefore, a good match for the legal profession, as lawyers are naturally trained in language and writing. A key to the successful adoption of genAI is to leverage a skillset that we already have as lawyers. This is one of the main reasons why upskilling the existing team will bring great results, fast.

Prompting is currently at the heart of engagement with genAI. While prompting relies on natural language, it is also a specific way of communicating that will require some adjustment. It is easy to get the first steps right; practice then makes perfect. With the increasing sophistication of the models and their growing ability to understand linguistic inconsistencies and context, prompting moves closer to actual natural language. Some have argued that prompting is dead. We will not expand further on that; however, in our experience at Falck, we have learned that the technology does indeed evolve rapidly, and in-house leaders will need to embrace the speed of change and foster a continued experimental mindset. The general counsel can become a change agent. As we mentioned in the introduction to this chapter, the Falck in-house team has become a frontrunner in genAI adoption, allowing us to lead internally by example, with the team perceived as an innovative part of the organization.

Legal leaders should not see the change in the in-house team towards genAI as a traditional implementation project. It is a gradual adoption of new technology and a change in the typical way of working; therefore, these changes have the potential to profoundly transform the way we work. GenAI is readily available; with very little effort, lawyers can start engaging with the technology, allowing for an experimental approach that engrains the technology in the way the in-house team works.

Many in-house teams are currently considering which capabilities and resources should be hired to support an AI journey and possibly establish a dedicated legal operations team. While a gap analysis may reveal a need for competencies not already within the team, and while it may be relevant to recruit for certain roles, our recommendation is to begin with the existing team and focus on upskilling rather than hiring – particularly if there are budget constraints. As discussed above, genAI will form an important part of the strategy for in-house legal teams in the future. The legal leader must work to create an environment that fosters creativity and experimentation and be tenacious in this. GenAI will not initially give great results and require continued experimentation. It is key that the team shares insights and mistakes, thereby learning and growing together.

With a shift of legal work to genAI, there is a risk that we will no longer have the naturally occurring training of younger lawyers, as much of the time-consuming and repetitive work – through which lawyers hone their skills – disappears. How do we successfully train future generations of lawyers? Law schools have a momentous job here, but we, as employers on the intake side, must also consider how to implement this in our onboarding and in the continued training of younger lawyers. As leaders, we can make the conscious choice to have some work produced without the use of genAI and further increase our focus on coaching. Automating tasks may free up time for the senior lawyers in the team to do exactly that.

Complex problem-solving and critical thinking is paramount on this journey, and it will become increasingly important. AI will – whether we resist this change or embrace it – become a critical part of legal methodology and strategy and allow us to handle larger, complicated matters. Critical thinking will also mitigate the risks of genAI.

Next to technical legal skills, the primary skills of in-house teams are a strong understanding of the commercial, operational, and financial aspects of the business. When upskilling the in-house team, focusing on the core legal skills and business understanding is a path to value-adding AI adoption.

Upskilling

New and different skills will be needed for future lawyers. It may, therefore, be tempting for the legal leader to consider rehiring part of the in-house team. However, our recommendation is to begin with upskilling the existing team, rather than hiring new talent. Firstly, many teams are faced with budget constraints. Secondly, it may not be possible to attract legal talent with cutting-edge skills in an increasingly competitive market, in which in-house teams compete not only with each other but also with law firms. Thirdly – and we contend this is the most important reason – there are significant benefits to up- or reskilling the existing team. We will explore this third point further in the following.

In Falck, our strategy has been to train and upskill our existing in-house team. This has largely been based on a high degree of experimentation and open sharing of experiences and use cases – good or bad – within the team. We have seen clear benefits in the retention of organizational knowledge and business understanding in the team. Most importantly, as a legal or in-house leader, it is critical to upskill yourself. You are likely to benefit personally from this, and you must also lead by example!

A key driver to success has been buy-in from the executive team and proactive leadership to ensure a "safe space" for experimentation with the technology. We have constantly promoted the message that we, as a team, invest in technology and that we, as leaders, allow sufficient time for upskilling and transformation.

With new technology comes a need to understand it. GenAI is – to some extent – different from existing legal tech, as it allows for a very fast initial adoption; everyone can access one of the freely available chatbots and start experimenting (taking due consideration of confidentiality). This is in contrast with previous generations of legal tech, where many obstacles, such as technically difficult implementation, poor data quality, and lack of standardized workflows and processes, have prevented value gains. The key to working with genAI is being open and flexible. The very accessibility of AI means that AI literacy – the understanding of capabilities, limitations, and risks – has become a crucial skill. While the technology allows for initial experimentation and "fast starts", it will be necessary to approach adoption with more careful planning, to ensure and measure value.

It is commonly thought that younger generations are faster to adopt new technology. Younger generations of lawyers are digital natives, having grown up with the internet and digital technologies; for them, the use of tech should be second nature. However, in our experience, there is a curious generational effect. Experienced lawyers who are used to training and instructing younger colleagues can utilize that skillset when engaging with AI: by using a similar approach as the one they would adopt with a less experienced colleague. This generates extraordinarily strong results. Arguably, the lawyers best suited to benefit from the advantages of AI are those in the midpoint of their career, who can balance experience with the ability to adapt to technological changes.

When considering AI adoption, legal leaders will sometimes gravitate towards legal operations (legal ops), which may be an important factor in successful AI transformation; however, it is not a deciding factor. Legal ops drive cross-functional collaboration between the core or classic legal team and other corporate functions, such as tech, finance, sales, and operations. This function is, however, cost-heavy and typically reserved for larger legal teams. Smaller teams will not be able to invest in a dedicated legal ops function. In our experience, significant transformation can be achieved by developing the existing team's capabilities in some of the skills found in legal ops (e.g., process optimization and standardization of workflows, as well as basic technical skills). Value from legal ops can be achieved through work with genAI.

It may be necessary to assess skill gaps and deficiencies in the in-house team. Here, we also argue for an organic approach that allows for gradual and individual upskilling. Younger team members may intuitively adapt to the technology, while more experienced team members may drive more sophisticated value at a quicker pace. A The size of the in-house team plays a part in the approach taken. A large in-house team with different talent pools may greatly benefit from a more structured approach, while smaller teams will likely benefit solely from more experienced colleagues leading by example and setting the pace. This may also include allowing younger team members to spearhead some of the initial forays into AI. No matter the size of the team, we believe that experimentation is a key driver to success in genAI adoption.

There are many free online resources available, including on prompting, which are great places to start. In some instances, formal training and certifications may be valuable. Such upskilling efforts may also allow advancements in risk management, governance, and compliance. Leveraging external legal advisors as training providers is also effective. In our experience, an internal organic approach – whereby lawyers can gradually develop genAI competencies – has been very successful. Another highly effective way of adopting the technology and building a basic understanding of the possibilities and practical application (including some of the pitfalls) is to engage with other in-house teams in various ways, such as informal meetings, knowledge-sharing sessions, and so on. This has been one of the contributing factors to the success of the genAI adoption in Falck, as we have often had the pleasure of sharing our experiences with other in-house teams.

Measuring to what extent lawyers learn AI skills is important for successful upskilling. Here, we point primarily to the discussion above on measuring value. We recommend simple and flexible ways to track results. We caution against the reliance on fixed skillsets, given the fast-paced nature of the technology. Experimentation and an explorative mindset are key at this juncture.

A common obstacle in the adoption of new technology is an inherent and very human resistance to change. Lawyers are typically conservative and risk-averse. In-house teams will face a change management task when adopting AI. Here, the general counsel must step up and lead with boldness and empathy.

Conclusion

AI can provide a significant value generator for in-house teams and the organizations they serve. What will be the optimal use cases with the most value depends on the organization, its mission and strategy, organizational maturity, and not least the in-house team itself. No two organizations or legal teams are the same.

While it is easy to focus on the financial value, we encourage a more holistic view of value and suggest starting with an internal assessment of the in-house team when considering AI. AI is an area that evolves swiftly, and we encourage legal leaders to be open-minded, inquisitive about possibilities, and mindful about how to design the in-house team. There are good reasons as to why it makes sense to invest in the upskilling of the existing in-house function. The main reason is that upskilling will retain talent already in the team, leveraging one of the key competencies that separates the great in-house team from the good – namely, deep business understanding.

Furthermore, the demand for legal professionals with a deep understanding of AI continues to grow, and accessing the right talent may not be as straightforward as hiring managers might hope. Given the fast pace of technological development, it may also be difficult to assess the actual skills needed for the in-house team of the future.

One thing remains clear: for legal leaders, this is a time to embrace change and demonstrate flexibility and resourcefulness during transformative periods – not only to their own in-house teams, but to the legal profession.

References

1 Brunt, T., "How Generative AI is changing legal department functions", Deloitte, 6 September 2024. See: https://www.deloitte.com/global/en/services/legal/perspectives/how-generative-ai-is-changing-legal-department-functions.html.

2 For further information about grounding, see: Berger, E., "*Grounding LLMs*", Microsoft Tech Community, 9 June 2023. See: https://techcommunity.microsoft.com/t5/fasttrack-for-azure/grounding-llms/bap/ or Maher, M.L., Ventura, D., Magerko. B. et. al, "The grounding problem: an approach to the integration of cognitive and generative models", *Proceedings of the AAAI Symposium Series*, 2023, volume 2, issue 1, pp. 320–325. https://doi.org/10.1609/aaaiss.v2i1.27695.

3 CorpGov, , "What In-House Counsel Needs to Know About Generative AI", Vinson & Elkins, 2 December 2024. See: https://www.velaw.com/insights/what-in-house-counsel-needs-to-know-about-generative-ai/.

4 Martin, L., Whitehouse, N., Yiu, S. et al, "Better Call GPT, Comparing Large Language Models Against Lawyers", *arXiv*, 24 January 2024. See: https://arxiv.org/abs/2401.16212.

Chapter 11: Building AI-ready legal teams: strategies for hiring and integrating external talent

By Matthew Dunne, senior innovation and data science manager, Katten Muchin Rosenman LLP

The guiding theme of this chapter is how law firms can strategically build teams equipped to manage and leverage AI. This is a complicated question that requires examination of our assumptions and engagement with several interrelated concepts to come to a coherent, practical answer.

What follows is a progression through those concepts. We will first discuss what AI strategy means for law firms and how it can be a departure from traditional practice, before considering what skills will be necessary for that strategy and how to acquire and evaluate them. Finally, we will describe the current state of things in the market.

This chapter will hopefully serve as a starting point for you as you engage with AI in the legal field. Much of what is discussed below stems from the author's personal experience, as well as interactions with innovation and AI professionals at other law firms.

Strategy

Strategy defined

Strategy is a much-misused term. We will use the definition provided by Roger Martin, former dean of the Rotman School of Management at the University of Toronto, who characterizes strategy as an integrated set of choices that compels desired customer action.[1] This more precise definition will inform the rest of this chapter – let us unpack it.

First, it distinguishes between goals and the actions designed to achieve those goals. Law firms, like a lot of businesses, do not necessarily make this distinction. This can be doubly true in the context of AI where there is pressure to "just do something".

Second, our definition is customer-centric. The point is to emphasize the difference between the outcomes you cannot control and the inputs you can.

A law firm can grow and strengthen client relationships; it can make the client's choice compelling by creating certain conditions through its actions. However, it cannot make the choice for the client.

Third, it means strategy is about more than cutting costs. Firms can certainly have that goal, as their business model requires them to constantly find ways to increase profitability. AI can obviously be used in that effort, but these operational applications are something that firms can control and so do not fall under the scope of strategy as we have defined it.

AI within law firm strategy

How can AI be implemented in ways that compels clients to take action? The joke is that clients only switch firms when someone makes a big mistake or someone retires, but the reality is more complicated than that. As in all walks of life, people do different things in different contexts, sometimes through a cold cost-benefit analysis and sometimes from a gut feeling.

Law firms are in the business of providing high-quality legal services. Their focus should be on using generative AI (genAI) so that the firm's experts can continue to deliver a premium service. However, it must be remembered that all genAI does is process unstructured information to produce new content that previously required human intervention. In the legal space, this unstructured information is usually text, as opposed to video or audio. The question then becomes: what new content is valuable (or made valuable) by having a computer produce it, rather than a person? There are several ways this can manifest.

Efficiency

Lawyers charge (mostly) by the hour. Fewer hours to produce the same output means lower cost for clients. Not all work is like this; however, when it is, AI serves the firm's strategy by lowering costs for clients.

Effectiveness

Clients pay for expertise and additional levels of risk management. Saving thousands of dollars is not as compelling when millions or billions of dollars are on the line. Here, AI influences client behavior to the extent it can increase the probability of a favorable outcome. This might mean connecting the dots within some fact pattern in a high-stakes litigation, or being able to turn a deal around quicker in an industry where time is money.

Predictability
Clients must allocate financial resources between various needs. Most companies really would prefer to use money budgeted for legal expenses on something else. Knowing that they can use that money elsewhere is quite valuable. Indeed, there are circumstances where this certainty is more important than any savings from efficiency. Flat fees and other alternative fee arrangements are the usual vehicle for providing this certainty. To the extent law firms can use genAI to enable this (e.g., by controlling costs in predictable ways), clients may be more likely to steer business to those firms.

New types of work
There are certain types of work that law firms do not perform, because it is not economical to do so. The analysis is straightforward, but the scale of the task is cost-prohibitive when performed manually. genAI can dramatically lower the cost, thus making the effort worthwhile. This will lead to new insights that were previously not achievable given the manpower required. Not every firm will have the personnel, infrastructure, or imagination to leverage the technology. Those that do can distinguish themselves with clients.

User experience
Sometimes, clients are not moved by a dispassionate calculation of dollars and cents, but by how they feel when interacting with their outside counsel. It can be hard to judge the quality of the legal services in any event, and so clients rely on what heuristics they have. If deals seem to run smoother with a particular law firm, or if you can call a partner who knows the status of every part of the workflow, clients will then tend to hire that law firm, all else being equal. To the extent that genAI removes the friction in legal processes and enhances the user experience, it can serve this end.

The situations outlined above do not really tell law firms how they should position themselves or in which domains they want to compete (another way of defining strategy). The answer to those questions will vary from firm to firm, and there is no one-size-fits-all solution. They do, however, serve as a useful framework for law firms when judging whether AI provides an articulable benefit for clients.

Service as a software
Law firms are a service business. They license software to make that business

run more smoothly, but they do not create their own. They buy it from a vendor who creates one version of a tool, manages and supports that tool, and then sells it to as many people as possible. This is normally referred to as the "software as a service" model.

This works where a vendor can sell the same tool to multiple companies because those customers have the same underlying needs and processes. It does not work – or, at least, not very well –when the software needs to be highly customized. In such a situation, the vendors are not selling a product so much as providing a software customization service.

One of the promises of genAI is that it can perform the work that normally requires human intervention – even complex analysis requiring domain expertise. In other words, the software performs the service. In theory, one could create an application or agent that does everything a particular attorney does. In practice, this is unlikely. Legal work involves many different activities. Some of these are more appropriate to automate than others, either for technical or economic reasons.

Still, there are a few aspects of lawyers' services can be replicated through genAI. This is what makes the technology so significant. The term for this is "service as a software", meaning the software can replicate and, in effect, perform work that heretofore required human experts. The industry, and the clients it serves, are no longer limited by how many people it can throw at the problem; if you lower the cost of something, people will use more of it. Put another way, if an attorney can use genAI to analyze 1,000 documents in the time it takes to review one document manually, the scale and scope of services for clients changes dramatically.

Whither attorneys

Now that we have discussed AI in terms of clients, strategy, and how law firms traditionally think about software, let us reflect on what this means in terms of personnel. AI will not be of uniform utility across the various types of work that lawyers perform. The question is whether the advent of AI represents more of an opportunity than a crisis.

Hiring for AI-ready legal teams

Who we are hiring

AI is not a mature function in the legal industry, especially not genAI. There is no manual, and one cannot rely on years of accumulated wisdom built from success and failure. It is, therefore, better to think of AI as something you implement and iterate upon, rather than something to be managed. It also means that the personnel responsible for implementing the tech will likely have to be hired from the outside.

This chapter will focus on this outside hiring process. The right course of action in this regard will depend on the situation (i.e., the firm's strategy, who it has already hired, etc.), but we will attempt to provide generally applicable advice.

What we are hiring for

The core proposition of this chapter is as follows:

Law firms that benefit the most from genAI will be able to effectuate improved client service through some definable strategy. To do that, they will have to break down their complex analyses into manageable parts and map those parts onto the various tools and techniques that combine into specific genAI applications.

Firms that deliver on this core proposition can turn their service into a product or provide a better service. Each is attractive to clients and provides an advantage relative to other law firms, albeit in different ways. The effects of this will be most profound when creating new software, rather than licensing applications from vendors (the buy vs. build dichotomy), but it is still useful in the latter case, because it will help firms choose between different vendors. This is especially true where, as here, the technology is quickly changing, and investment decisions can be years-long commitments.

All hiring decisions should be made around this organizing principle of matching the tech to the workflows. The next section will provide some thought as to what type of skills and people will serve this end.

Hard skills are software; soft skills are hardware

Some definitions that will be helpful to the discussion:

- Hard skills are specific, technical abilities that relate to a domain of knowledge;
- Soft skills are personal qualities that enable you to interact and collaborate with other people;
- Hardware is the physical components of a computer (e.g., the CPU); and
- Software is the instructions for computers to perform tasks.

Why do I bring these up, and how do they relate?

Hard skills can be taught, and computers can be instructed. Humans are not empty vessels that one can just fill with knowledge, but most people can learn most skills, just as one can write software to instruct computers to perform pretty much any task of which they are capable. Assessing both is straightforward: either something works, or it does not; either a person knows, or they do not. The same is true for acquiring these skills. A person gets a formal (or informal) education in a subject; software has known uses that can be recombined depending on the use case. This may take effort, but the path is known.

Soft skills can be taught, but only up to a point. Personality traits are what they are; at a certain point, someone might just be in the wrong line of work. For example, I took an improv comedy class at The Second City several years ago. It was fun, and I would recommend it for almost anyone, but you will never see me on the main stage – it is just not me. This is much like computer hardware, which is always advancing but is still subject to the physical limits of computation – at least until quantum computing comes along.

Remember the core principle of this chapter: knowledge of the tech mapped onto the knowledge of the workflow. The hard skills are the two component knowledge bases (tech and legal), while the soft skills are the mapping function of one onto the other. Put another way, you can think of it as a mathematical operation: A × B = C (A times B equals C), in which:

- C = outcome you want from the employee;
- A = technical knowledge around genAI;
- B = familiarity with legal concepts and processes; and
- × (multiplication sign) = interaction, combination, etc. of A and B.

It should be noted that this is merely a conceptual way of expressing something mathematically and should not be interpreted too literally. Still, the use of multiplication in the above example is deliberate, because it underlines the importance of having something for both A and B. 3 + 3 = 6; 3 + 0 is still 3; but 0 × 3 is 0, just as knowledge of genAI is essentially useless without knowledge of what an attorney needs to do. The two disciplines are multiplicative, rather than additive.

Hard skills: importance and evaluation

For this chapter, we will discuss how law firms acquire these hard skills through hiring, rather than training. As to legal knowledge, it is rather unambiguous. The person needs to have gone to law school. There are exceptions: paralegals can do a lot within a law firm, as can librarians, and their knowledge may be more useful for a particular workflow. Likewise, you might need the additional knowledge of a specialist or someone with several years of experience in a particular area. Still, if someone has gone to law school, one can reasonably assume they will be able to figure out the legal side, because they know what questions to ask.

On the technical side, it is less straightforward, although there are reliable indicators. There are numerous degree programs in data science and machine learning, both at the undergraduate and graduate level. In fact, data science is now the most popular major at UC Berkeley.[2]

GenAI has not always been part of the curriculum of such programs. Indeed, my education had no such component. However, once you have a foundation in machine learning in general, and neural networks in particular, you can fill in the technical gaps. For example, DeepLearning.ai offers numerous courses to upskill the average data scientist on best practice for prompting, chaining, and retrieval – i.e., the building blocks of genAI applications.[3]

Unlike the legal side, autodidacts are perfectly welcome on the technical side. No one cares where you went to school, or even if you went to school. You can either deliver or you cannot. The difficulty is ensuring whether the person possesses the particular technical background for what the firm needs. Some job titles are more geared toward building applications, while others favor actionable insights for a business purpose. The questions to ask are:

- How much technical knowledge is enough?
- How does a law firm match what skills a candidate has to its larger goals?

An example from my own experience may help. I graduated with a Master's in Applied Data Science in 2019. That program covered natural language processing, big data, machine learning, and neural networks. Those are all useful to know when working with genAI, as they form many of the foundational aspects, but they are more necessary than sufficient.

More knowledge specific to genAI is needed. The most valuable skills – at least in legal – are downstream from training and fine-tuning the foundational models themselves. Let us look at some examples:

- *Chaining:* I define this here as using a large language model (LLM) in a series of separate but interrelated steps to complete a more complicated task than a standard chatbot. At each step, the LLM takes an input (normally a piece of text), processes it using a set of instructions, and produces an output. That processing can take many forms, such as summarization, extraction, and modification. The steps can be a predefined sequence or change based on a set of logical conditions.[4]

- *Retrieval optimization:* LLMs use vectors, which are a numerical representation of text or other data. Sometimes you want to search those vectors, and so you set up a vector database (this goes beyond basic retrieval augmented generation). There can be so much information in this database that advanced techniques are required to find what you are looking for (sentence window retrieval,[5] measures of relevance[6]) or make sure the search process is not unreasonably long (HNSW algorithm).[7]
- *Tools:* All LLMs do is predict the next word (technically, the next token). They cannot, for example, do math or run an internet search. For that, they need some method of interacting with the rest of the world. In the field, these are called "tools".[8]
- *Metadata:* Metadata is data that describes other data. An example would be when a particular file was last saved and by whom (i.e., information about the text contained in the file). LLMs can use metadata as input to improve performance. In the legal context, it would be useful to know where statutory language lies within a hierarchy of section and subsection, whether text from an opinion is from a dissenting judge, or what page something is on, so you can source it later.[9]

It is probably not necessary for the person leading a firm's AI effort to write the code that utilizes these techniques and optimize it to run at scale. Firms will hire specialists for that. What is important is knowing that these techniques exist and can be combined and applied to particular use cases. If a person can understand what the lawyer is trying to do and can figure out a general framework for how to make the software do that, the most difficult part of the problem is then solved.

Soft skills: importance and evaluation

Soft skills can be even more difficult to judge than hard skills, and their utility tends to be latent, indirect, and only discernible in combination with other, hard skills. Law firms do not traditionally recruit for these, at least not beyond general interpersonal skills or the ability to work well with others. However, implementing AI in the legal industry requires working across disciplines and synthesizing expertise to create something that is more than the sum of its parts. It is the soft skills that enable and accelerate these efforts.

In some cases, it is more about personality traits than a learned competency. The important thing to understand is that it departs from what law schools teach and much of what law firms value (in new hires, at least). A "lawyer's lawyer" type may not be predisposed toward success in this area. Instead, firms will need different, more idiosyncratic personas.

Law school and the law firm hiring process reward certain things. It is perhaps an oversimplification – but broadly correct – to say that the process favors those with the predisposition to persuade others to their own view in discussions involving abstract concepts. Implementing genAI requires this mindset to change in two fundamental ways.

First, it necessitates getting comfortable with "good enough" instead of "perfect". There is a reason that attorneys are the way they are. In school, you are tasked with being able to spot all the issues in hypothetical scenarios; the more you spot and the more cogent your analysis of those issues, the more points you get; the more points you get, the better your grades and the better your job prospects. Once in practice, it is not about who can complete a task that is sufficient in most cases at a reasonable cost. It is about delivering the best for that client in that situation. It does not scale, but it is not meant to.

Any junior attorney who misses an important issue or fact does so at their peril. Software is very different. The attitude is perhaps best summed up by Reid Hoffman, co-founder of LinkedIn, who has said, "If you are not embarrassed by the first version of your product, you've launched too late."

Second, building genAI software requires cooperation with individuals from different disciplines, rather than competition against peers. If you are a product manager at a tech company, you are effectively the CEO of a product. This means interacting with various teams, including marketing, sales, strategy, and software development, to bring that product to market. Each group has a valid viewpoint. No one is wholly right or wrong.

Lawyers do not really think this way. Their job is to convince others (a judge, jury, or counterparty) that they are right, and the other person is wrong. They might have to familiarize themselves with a given domain, especially in litigation, but legal analysis predominates over anything else at the end of the day.

Shifting one's mindset away from that of a lawyer is a challenge, although a surmountable one. You can change people's behavior if you change their incentives. It is much harder, if not impossible, to change their personalities.

Certain types of people go to law school, and there are numerous studies testing personality traits and where lawyers score relative to average. For purposes of this chapter, two such characteristics are relevant: namely, that lawyers are above average in skepticism and below average in resilience. Perhaps people can learn to be more resilient or more optimistic, but that is difficult to do. It may be much the same for lawyers trying to work with genAI. They need to be comfortable with some level of failure and identify possibilities, rather than focus on the dangers – no small task.

There are soft skills that become more important with this shift in mindset. These include time management, conflict resolution, and creativity. Communication is always important, but it must be remembered that it is a two-way skill. It is one thing to advocate for your own point of view, but quite another to understand someone else's.

This endeavor requires someone who can synthesize mental frameworks across different disciplines to deliver an end product. In the tech world, you might call a person with this set of soft skills a product manager, which we discussed earlier. This is a person who has sufficient technical knowledge, but who can also understand problems in terms of user experience, business need, strategy, and data. I would also add that the ability to be a systems thinker –meaning the ability to look at a complex system and consider its interconnectedness and interdependencies, not just its isolated components – is critical. Here, that complex system is a law firm, its practice groups, its business departments, its clients, and all their attendant motivations and interests.

Testing and evaluating these soft skills can be difficult. Interviews usually do a pretty good job establishing whether someone has some baseline level of skill, especially in communication. The trick is assessing whether their skills combine to achieve escape velocity.

One way to do this is to establish how a particular candidate is different from others. After several years in legal tech, you will find common ideas on roughly the same kind of subjects. Originality or genuine insight is relatively rare. Try to ask questions that bring this out of candidates.

Sometimes, one or two questions will tell you pretty much all you need to know. During World War II, the Royal Air Force needed fighter pilots in a hurry. The story goes that they asked applicants two questions to see if they had the right temperament for the job, which were: have you ever owned a motorcycle, and do you still own one? The RAF wanted to hear "yes" to the first question and "no" to the second, with the idea being that you wanted someone adventurous enough to ride a motorcycle, but sensible enough to know it was not a good idea in the long term.[10]

Some equivalent questions in the AI legal field might include:

- "Tell me why lawyers should care about the definition of 'agents', and tell me why software developers should not."
- "What have you heard about applying AI in the legal industry that sounds stupid but is not? What sounds smart that is not?"

The goal here is to see if the candidate has a deeper level of understanding, can go beyond the component parts of a problem and synthesize information, or otherwise provide novel insights. The point is not to be right, of course. It is about being able to perform the exercise in the first place.

Where to recruit

We have covered what to look for and how to conduct the process of doing so. Now, we will examine where to look. It is all well and good to be able to discern and choose wisely from a list of candidates, but you first need to assemble that list and populate it with high-quality talent.

It is widely accepted that law firms, even the largest ones, cannot compete for talent against Silicon Valley. The thought is tech companies can offer stock-based compensation that law firms simply cannot match, and so they get all the best people. There is much to this, but it misses some important nuances. First, there is plenty of talent out there that can work with genAI and are willing to do so in the professional services industry. Second, law firms do have the money to offer competitive salaries and a collection of interesting problems to work on, which can be very attractive to candidates.

Drawing from the well of legal education presents different challenges. Law schools are only beginning to include AI in their curriculum. They are hampered by the fact that law firms are not sure what skills their employees should have in the domain, and the industry standard technology is not available to students in the same way as the traditional tools, such as Westlaw or LexisNexis.

Furthermore, the traditional curriculum is not geared toward inculcating the soft and hard skills discussed above, and the usual sorting mechanisms do not incorporate them. At this stage of the cycle, it may be more practical for law firms to train new hires in AI rather than try to outsource it to law schools. Ironically, law firms may start hiring from the vendors themselves, as those vendors employ a number of former Big Law attorneys who help with the design, evaluation, and marketing of the technology.

What's next?

In this section, we will briefly cover other factors that influence the success of AI implementation. We will also survey what trends I have seen in the market as a practitioner. These go beyond strategy and hiring and are meant to give the reader an orientation on where we stand at present.

At the time of writing, it has been approximately 2–3 years since the introduction of ChatGPT. Before that point, lawyers' interest in AI was mostly theoretical. After its debut, interest was high, but use cases and implementation were lacking. Now, we are at an inflection point, with real applications and real software to license. Law firms have had time to think about where to use LLMs and where to devote resources. Fear of missing out is fading, while cautious optimism is growing.

Pump the brakes

Clients are unsure what they want their law firms to do with AI. However, they know what they do not want: inadvertent disclosure of confidential or privileged information; their data being used to train someone else's model; and overreliance on the tech, leading to bad outcomes. The effect of this is that their instructions to firms, as codified in their Outside Counsel Guidelines, can be unclear in their application. For example, a blanket ban on AI would technically include spam filters, autocomplete, and many features of the research tools that have become standard in the industry.

This can lead firms to institute a restriction on using AI on client documents or data, even when not explicitly required to do so. It makes sense if you are far more worried about a significant downside (which you absolutely want to avoid at almost any cost) than an undefined upside. It is not, however, particularly conducive to AI adoption.

There is a conversation to be had with clients about which uses are acceptable and which are not. It may be an uncomfortable conversation to have, and lawyers usually avoid those. However, the discomfort is not from contrary interests causing antagonism; it is from lack of familiarity, which can be addressed.

There is no single best way to have this conversation, but I have seen my fair share of misunderstandings. My suggestion would be to identify a scenario that is clearly a misuse of AI, articulate what the problem is, and then iterate on the fact pattern to find where people are comfortable. This process may not identify clear lines in the sand, but it will provide a framework for the discussion and may identify safe uses.

Another underappreciated constraint is the difficulty in going from the proof-of-concept stage to implementation at an enterprise level. Pilots tend to be cheap, and so management does not mind doing them. It is quite different, however, when asking for significant resources for an actual project or tool. In pilots, you can have one or two people in charge and assemble a list of opportunities over the course of six months or a year. However, when you need to scale up for your ten most promising use cases, this will require a larger commitment of resources. Leadership may hesitate.

Remember who you are

This chapter has focused on the application of AI in the practice of law. There is much buzz around the topic – for obvious reasons. However, we must not lose sight of the fact that the core business of law firms is to provide legal advice. Their clients will need as much guidance in the law of AI as the use of AI in law.

Happily, these two concepts are complementary, rather than unrelated. Firms that use AI, and especially those that build custom tools, are better placed to understand the idiosyncrasies and nuances that will inevitably become significant in regulating the technology. It is perhaps too much to say that AI law has not been written yet, but regulations and case law are only in their formative stage.

The market

AI in legal practice is early in its development, but we are close to the end of the first act. We might make some guesses on how the rest of this drama will unfold.

Until recently, law firms have tended to look for one person to be the face of the AI, the thought being that leadership has one person to look to, who must stay on top of everything. Job descriptions for this initial person have been very broad, with multiple functions falling under their jurisdiction that would be distributed among several different people in a more mature organization. Normally, the same person is not in charge of articulating the strategic vision, data infrastructure, governance, business intelligence, vendor management, and evangelizing use cases. Groups are now staffing up beyond this initial hire, looking for those knowledgeable about the disciplines that fall under the AI umbrella.[11]

Another noticeable trend is that the AI specialists at law firms are increasingly coming from outside the legal industry.[12] It has been expedient to treat AI – even genAI – as an extension of existing job descriptions, such as Knowledge Management or Innovation. There are merits to this approach, depending on what you plan to do with the tech, but firms are starting to realize that AI is its own domain, which requires specialists.

This is especially true for firms building applications internally. These include tools that lawyers will use, as well as agents that perform some of the back-office operational tasks that firms need. Deciding what to build is one thing; actually building it is quite another, and law firms have not generally employed many software developers until now.

Conclusion

A real AI strategy for a law firm is something designed to truly respond to client needs. Clients will find many things appealing about AI beyond just efficiency and cost savings. The difficulty for firms is that they will have to think and act in ways they are not accustomed to, even to the point of having software perform a significant portion of the services they have traditionally provided.

There is no framework or best practices in assembling the right mix of personnel, although some lessons can be learned from the tech world. The core task is to map legal workflows onto a new and constantly developing technology. This will require a mix of hard and soft skills that can be difficult to evaluate. It will also require firms to look for different types of people than they have traditionally hired, both in terms of technical competency and temperament.

The hype cycle (or the adoption cycle, if you prefer) has reached an inflection point, and the next two years will see far more progress than the last. However, firms still need to navigate pitfalls around security and establish the scope of their clients' comfort with the technology. Firms also need to keep in mind that AI affects their clients' businesses too, and they will need guidance on a host of complex legal issues.

No one really believes that the introduction of AI is the beginning of the end for lawyers. However, we have probably reached the end of the beginning of AI's introduction into the legal market. Strategies are being honed; teams are being hired; and lessons are being learned. What does the future hold? The only way to know is to create it.

References

1 Martin, R.L., "Strategy", 2025. See: https://rogerlmartin.com/thought-pillars/strategy.
2 Rothman, B., "Data science is now UC Berkeley's largest major", *The Daily Californian*, 14 March 2025. See: https://www.dailycal.org/news/campus/data-science-is-now-uc-berkeley-s-largest-major/article_a60c9faa-00ac-11f0-9789-2b1ff75395ce.html.
3 DeepLearning.AI, "All Courses: Grow your AI career with foundational specializations and skill-specific short courses taught by leaders in the field", 2025. See: https://www.deeplearning.ai/courses/.
4 Talamadupula, K., "A Guide to Comparing Different LLM Chaining Frameworks", symbl.ai., 2 September 2024. See: https://symbl.ai/developers/blog/a-guide-to-comparing-different-llm-chaining-frameworks/.
5 Krampah, P., "Advance Retrieval Techniques In RAG | Part 03 | Sentence Window Retrieval", Medium, 2 January 2024. See: https://ai.gopubby.com/advance-retrieval-techniques-in-rag-part-03-sentence-window-retrieval-9f246cffa07b.
6 Kanagaraj, A., "Understanding LLM Evaluation Metrics for Better RAG Performance", Protecto.ai, 1 February 2025. See: https://www.protecto.ai/blog/understanding-llm-evaluation-metrics-for-better-rag-performance#elementor-toc__heading-anchor-4.
7 Kumar, S., "Introduction to HNSW: Hierarchical Navigable Small World", Analytics Vidhya, 13 December 2023. https://www.analyticsvidhya.com/blog/2023/10/introduction-to-hnsw-hierarchical-navigable-small-world/.
8 LangChain, "Tools", 2025. See: https://python.langchain.com/v0.1/docs/modules/tools/.
9 https://solutionsreview.com/data-management/the-secret-to-more-accurate-intelligent-llms-metadata/.
10 Jayanthi, S., "The secret to more accurate, intelligent LLMs: metadata", *Solutions Review*, 1 August 2024. https://greenbackd.com/2013/05/20/why-a-complex-world-needs-simpler-rules-and-absolute-metrics-have-you-ever-owned-a-motorcycle/.
11 Lambert, G., "Cleary Gottlieb + Springbok AI: BigLaw Finally Gets It?", 3 Geeks and A Law Blog, 18 March 2025. See: https://www.geeklawblog.com/2025/03/cleary-gottlieb-springbok-ai-biglaw-finally-gets-it.html.
12 CDO Bureau, "Jane Rheem joins Sidley Austin as Chief Data and AI Officer", *Chief Data Officer Magazine*, 7 February 2025. See: https://www.cdomagazine.tech/leadership-moves/jane-rheem-joins-sidley-austin-as-chief-data-and-ai-officer.

Chapter 12:

Tech and law: how research prototyping drives genAI adoption in legal practice

Dr Megan Ma, founding executive director, Legal Innovation through Frontier Technology Lab (liftlab), Stanford Law School

When we consider the traditional roles of academia and industry, we would very rarely see much overlap, particularly in the legal domain. In fact, overlap was historically viewed as potentially threatening to the freedom of academic scholars to publish at their own will, especially in the instance of some form of industry intervention. However, as rising adoption of frontier technology – specifically, generative AI – continues to permeate across the legal sector, it would arguably be remiss for the academic community to not assert a more dominant role in not only the research, but also the direct development, of the technology.

Traditional legal academia has often dwelled in theoretical spaces, including analytical and critical frameworks for the interpretation and understanding of legal knowledge. Similarly, academic research in computer science and engineering has largely focused on general design, modelling, and application, rather than precise vertical integration. On the other hand, the legal profession was occupied with execution of the craft, whereas technology companies translated computational models into products digestible to their target consumers. Interestingly, at the intersection of these parties, legal technology vendors were tasked to develop tools that would support the profession.

The respective roles of research and industry were, therefore, well-defined. However, the integration of generative AI into legal practice represents a critical inflection point to these longstanding silos, demanding innovative research approaches that bridge theoretical possibilities with practical applications. This chapter proposes a framework for "research prototyping" – a methodology that accelerates understanding of how emerging technologies can transform legal processes while addressing ethical and practical constraints.

Unlike traditional legal research, which often remains theoretical, or technology implementations that prioritize commercial viability, this approach centers on lightweight, functional prototypes designed specifically to test research hypotheses about the future of human–machine collaboration, and technology's impact on legal reasoning and procedural efficiency. These prototypes serve as tangible artifacts that enable researchers, practitioners, and affected communities to engage with potential futures before large-scale implementation.

Through compression of the research–implementation cycle, this prototyping paradigm not only accelerates knowledge creation, but democratizes the evolution of legal technology, ensuring innovations are guided by empirical evidence of their effects on legal institutions, professional roles, and justice outcomes, rather than technological determinism.

The framework encompasses four key components:

1. Hypothesis-driven design focused on specific legal challenges;
2. Minimal viable functionality that isolates variables of interest;
3. Participatory evaluation, involving diverse stakeholders; and
4. iterative refinement based on empirical observations.

This methodology creates a feedback loop between technological capability and legal needs assessment that has been notably absent in traditional approaches.

Prior to diving into the specifics of the framework, I will walk through examples drawn from our existing collaborations with industry partners, to illustrate how co-creation of research and development across academia and industry enables more sustainable adoption of technology into legal practice.

Setting the stage

With the advent of state-of-the-art large language models (LLMs) in early 2023, the initial fascination and exploration of use cases encouraged applications that were well-established in the legal technology space. For example, legal research and document analysis became a focal point of the market.[1] Nevertheless, it became clear that the technology was unlike any the legal industry had previously experienced: not only in its technical capability to be infinitely malleable, but also in the attention it was receiving from the legal community itself. That is, for the first time, legal professionals were not only discussing how the technology should be regulated and governed but, rather, how it was directly impacting their own practice. Technology was, thus, not only an "IT" problem, but one that lawyers became broadly invested in.

Questions of how the technology would interface with legal workflows and improve various operational inefficiencies became a key area of interest. However, assessing productivity gains and enabling division of labor between machine and human require necessarily both quantifiable and qualitative metrics – empirical methods of evaluation, in other words. It also requires a deep understanding of how quality is determined in the legal domain. This simply is ill-defined, given that legal professional services are often sold as a credence good.[2] From the perspective of both historical development and the longstanding business model,[3] the modern law firm – nor legal practice at large – is built to explicitly articulate the art of their process.

However, as LLMs and other legal enterprise software became increasingly performant, the specific value-add of the legal lens rose in prominence. Law firm clients, as well as general consumers, now have the tools that offer the semblance of legal work product for a fraction of the price and time at their disposal. For legal professionals, internal processes (e.g., research, drafting, etc.) that used to require copious hours spent could now be performed with a few simple prompts. The glaring problem, of course, is that, without a proper articulation and/or definition of quality in legal work, existing gaps in the execution of legal processes not only persist, but become exponentially worse. One such example is the ability to train our attorneys. This was an observation garnered in the process of building the first-ever M&A negotiation simulator.

Prototyping with purpose: building fast and thinking slow

Following the release of OpenAI's GPT-4 model in March 2023, a number of academic papers were published that reflected on the ability of LLMs to collaborate and/or coordinate with one another. One fascinating paper reflected on and tested the ability of chat-based language models to cooperate with one another, while actively interpreting the intentions of the human user.[4] The researchers developed a novel communicative framework that supports and analyzes the behaviors of multiple agents as they interact and engage with one another. Similarly, another paper was released a few months later that described how LLMs may be capable of negotiating simple transactions.[5] In their findings, the researchers identified how language models were capable of reacting to feedback iteratively, while maintaining an understanding of the rules of the negotiation game. This triggered an interest in translating the outcomes of these papers and adapting their models to the more complex negotiations found in legal contexts.

In the summer of 2023, our research team began to experiment with how to leverage LLMs for larger-scale commercial transactions via contract negotiation. Interestingly, this experiment was rather short-lived, as an important element was missing – that is, we lacked the subject matter expertise available in practice. While legal academics could provide us with the context of what may be required in setting up the negotiation, the specific dynamics of the agents were markedly absent. It became evident that we needed a legal practitioner to support this experiment.

Fortunately, the founding partners of boutique M&A law firm, Flatiron Law Group, had made the bold decision to collaborate on this experiment. At first, the goal of the research endeavor was to answer a simple question: could LLMs act as negotiating agents in an M&A transaction? We arrived very quickly at the first astounding observation of the initial investigation: chat-based language model agents only inferred knowledge available from legal documents and, thereby, would hallucinate the processes surrounding the negotiation. In effect, LLMs were trained on legal products, rather than the practices that allow for the generation of the product. As a result, how senior lawyers are capable of assessing the leverage of the opposing counsel, the exogenous variables at play, and other confounding concerns are unknown to LLMs. In other words, LLMs are not trained on experiential knowledge and, therefore, cannot usefully provide insight into how legal practitioners consider the available options in a given M&A deal.

So, how does one train LLMs on the implicit knowledge of a senior lawyer? What became the foundation of the research project was the exercise of prototyping a simulation of an M&A negotiation. We refined the initial goal of the research task: from determining whether LLMs could negotiate to how the LLMs should negotiate. We broke down the specific components of a given M&A deal into modules, as well as the objectives of the buyer and seller of the transaction. We also narrowed the simulation to the initial phase of transaction: pre-signing of the letter of intent (LOI). We intentionally chose this phase for two primary reasons: (1) following the signing of the LOI, the seller significantly loses their leverage, as they become locked into the deal for an average of 45–60 days; and (2) this typically is a highly strategic moment that requires deep understanding of several skillsets, including initial due diligence and acute awareness of client expectations.

We began with the simpler task of negotiating the representations and warranties. We chose this specific area as it was the most well-defined for both the buyer and seller; we also developed a basic fact pattern for the negotiation. Undoubtedly, the most intricate element was the actual development of the language model "lawyer agent" which would negotiate with the human lawyer. To build this agent, our research team needed to solicit the expertise of computer scientists familiar with modelling agentic behavior. Further collaboration then began with the researchers that had released the aforementioned communicative agent's framework. These researchers shared their knowledge of a particular type of agentic modelling that dates back to the late 1980s, known as the Belief–Desire–Intention (BDI) agent.[6] The Belief represents the underlying knowledge of the language model and what it should hold to be true; the Desire represents the relevant goals and what it anticipates achieving; and the Intention represents that short-term and immediate actions it will take in light of information received, balanced against its Belief and Desire. In short, this architecture structures the operational motives of the agent, providing a method of developing its thought process.

Leveraging this modelling, we began to unpack the senior partners' experiences of negotiating the representations and warranties in an M&A deal, organizing them as sets of BDI. This was not a simple task and required significant iteration over the course of several months in order to translate the "alchemy" and/or intuition of strategic tactics into concrete, actionable steps. The result of this training process was a language model agent capable of reacting in real-time to dynamic questioning and introduction of previously unknown facts – not unlike a real M&A transaction.

Fundamentally, this effort in prototyping an LLM-based negotiation simulator became the first foray into multiple paths of both research and industry application. We made the findings of this project, as well as the initial code, openly accessible to the public.[7] Recently, we released an updated and more sophisticated platform of the negotiation simulator, known as DealMentor, transforming the tool into a customizable multi-agent system capable of accounting for multivariate circumstances, as well as integrations with external databases. Importantly, this simulation shed light on significant opportunities for the technology that extended beyond the purview of existing use cases. Namely, LLMs were excellent at role-playing and, therefore, could be useful in training law students and young attorneys and/or strategic game-playing of different types of legal workflows. Ultimately, these two use cases further advanced our research team's interest in understanding the role of specific persona-based training on LLMs. Put differently, what is the relative impact of training our LLMs to behave like certain specific stakeholders (e.g., clients, senior partners, specialty counsel) in comparison to training LLMs on the collective knowledge of a given area of law?

Testing and evaluating prototypes

This became the impetus for a parallel area of investigation: evaluation. As LLMs became increasingly adopted in legal research and drafting, headline news erupted regarding hallucinations and problems with both the safety and reliability of these tools. Research papers demonstrated the inability of LLMs to accurately retrieve information on case precedent, as well as incorrectly and falsely cite cases.[8] At the same time, legal technology startups began to break through the market on services to evaluate LLMs on legal performance.[9] As a result, a broader call for increased transparency and trustworthiness on the use of LLMs for legal research became a core topic of significant examination.

The underlying problem, as discussed, is a lack of a baseline understanding of how human lawyers would perform in the execution of comparable tasks. Importantly, there are no clear criteria defining quality in legal work. Anecdotally, and in a recent empirical study, one senior partner's preferences and definition of valuable work product may differ dramatically from another.[10] This could simply stem from differences in their subjective experiences of their practice.

Consequently, due to the state-of-the-art techniques available[11] and the subjective nature of the industry, evaluation is monumentally complicated relative to other industries with known, explicit, and objective metrics. Nevertheless, herein lies another clear opportunity for cross-sectoral collaboration between academia and industry. Our research team had the privilege of working with a Tier-1 law firm in this regard. Together, we had co-designed an exercise that aimed to better clarify the underlying preference ratings of senior lawyers when asked to assess a given set of subtasks within a specific legal workflow. In this case, we selected a litigation workflow with four interrelated subtasks. Mid-level associates from this firm, in addition to general purpose LLMs (e.g., GPT-4.0, Claude 3.5-Sonnet, etc.) and legal enterprise software (e.g., CoCounsel, Lexis+, etc.), were tasked to complete the workflow. The outputs from both machine and human were then anonymized and coded as "Exhibits".

Senior litigation partners of this firm were given three random exhibits (one from each respective group: human, general purpose, legal enterprise software) and asked to provide their preference rating from most to least preferred. While the full results of the study will soon be made publicly available, this research endeavor revealed a convergence on certain criteria when it came to evaluating human versus machine performance. Moreover, despite heterogeneity of their respective practices, there was indeed an underlying standard that was implicitly understood and internalized by senior lawyers when it came to assessing how well a specified task was done. Perhaps one of the most significant observations is that the existing criteria of evaluation for LLMs in executing legal work did not reflect those that senior lawyers were concerned about. That is, rather than a fixation on accuracy, completeness, and/or comprehensiveness, senior lawyers scrutinized the argument structure and intention behind the advocacy. These preferences better elucidated where machines have seemingly outperformed human counterparts, and the relative value add of enterprise rather than general purpose tools.

What may be understood is that academic rigor alone is insufficient to yield meaningful observations, such as those from the aforementioned study. Accordingly, collaborations across academia and industry not only help bring to light where in the workflow LLMs may be usefully integrated into practice; they also allow technology vendors to assess how to best optimize the performance of these tools. This encourages clarity around division of labor between humans and machines, grounding the next generation of legal service provision.

Future directions

Furthermore, this empirical study sparked numerous efforts in future-facing developments and evaluation of generative AI for legal purposes. For example, with the increasing interest in AI agents,[12] we are beginning to evaluate questions of user experience for the legal professional. Prior to the advent of generative AI, the tools made available to lawyers hardly ever accounted for their specific thought processes. Put differently, legal professionals were asked to wrangle with the peculiarities of the software, encouraging relatively steep learning curves for seemingly trivial undertakings (i.e., formatting). This resulted in the sunk cost fallacy, contributing to problems of change management.

In effect, one of the known complexities of the industry and for current legal technology vendors is to overcome existing paradigms of legacy software. This has hindered meaningful developments of new forms of engagement with frontier technology. Our research team is currently tackling this hard problem with various prototyping efforts to test and iterate on how legal professionals should be interacting with highly performant LLM-based AI agents. Namely, what does it mean to collaborate in an era of mixed competences? Working in tandem with law firm partners and other legal experts, we are first taking stock of how knowledge is cultivated and curated both via existing infrastructure and in the experiences of the personnel. That is, if we were capable of simulating how a law firm operates, what observations might we be able to glean?

Drawing from our existing research in building the negotiation simulator, we are in the works of developing a multi-agent simulation of a law firm, empirically testing how various interactions between associates and partners, as well as other related stakeholders, have an impact on the tactical approaches and business value of the practice. Our first prototype has focused on the use case of drafting and filing patent claims. Through in-depth interviews with in-house counsel from a large Big Tech company and a few of their outside counsel firms, we have been mapping the interactions between in-house counsel and the relevant associates and partners. We have also been noting the specific technical processes and responsibilities that each individual stakeholder (e.g., senior associate) is tasked with.

Together, the goal is to apply findings from prior scholarly research in the use of generative agents for social simulation (see, for example, generative agents[13] and the Agent Hospital[14]) to not only verify that firm practices are consistent with the expected value of the company, but to also identify any additional potential areas of strategic opportunity. To reiterate, these new methods of evaluation are made possible because of a marriage across technological advancement and the cross-pollination between academia and industry through partnered research activities.

Concluding remarks

The use cases examined throughout this paper effectively illustrate and extrapolate to a broader methodological framework characterized by four distinct yet interconnected components:

- Hypothesis-driven design targeting specific legal challenges;
- Minimal viable functionality to isolate key variables;
- Participatory evaluation, engaging diverse stakeholder perspectives; and
- Iterative refinement grounded in empirical insights.

Crucially, the viability and effectiveness of this approach hinge upon robust collaborations across academia and industry, leveraging complementary expertise, resources, and perspectives to bridge gaps between theoretical insights and practical implementation. By adopting this collaborative and iterative methodology, researchers can establish a dynamic feedback loop, aligning technological capabilities with nuanced legal needs – a critical dimension traditionally overlooked in conventional legal scholarship. Consequently, embedding research prototyping as an essential pillar of legal academic research, supported by interdisciplinary and cross-sectoral collaborations, will not only enhance theoretical rigor, but will also foster practical innovation, contributing in fundamental ways to more responsive and impactful solutions across the legal domain.

References

1 Ma, M., Sinha, A., Tandon, A., and Richards, J., "A View into the Generative AI Legal Landscape 2024", Stanford Law School, 7 March 2024. See: https://law.stanford.edu/2024/03/07/a-view-into-the-generative-ai-legal-landscape-2024/.

2 Kerschbamer, R. and Sutter, M., "The economics of credence goods – a survey of recent lab and field experiments", *CESifo Economic Studies*, 2017, volume 63, issue 1, pp. 1–23. https://doi.org/10.1093/cesifo/ifx001.

3 Garg, A. and Ma, M., "Opportunities and Challenges in Legal AI", Stanford Law School, 6 January 2025. See: https://law.stanford.edu/publications/opportunities-and-challenges-in-legal-ai/.

4 Li, G., Al Kader Hammoud, H.A., Itani, H., et al, "CAMEL: Communicative Agents for "Mind" Exploration of Large Language Model Society", arXiv, 2 November 2023. https://doi.org/10.48550/arXiv.2303.17760.

5 Fu, Y., Peng, H., Khot, T., and Lapata, M., "Improving Language Model Negotiation with Self-Play and In-Context Learning from AI Feedback", arXiv, 17 May 2023. https://doi.org/10.48550/arXiv.2305.10142.

6 Rao, A.S. and Georgeff, M.P., "BDI Agents: From Theory to Practice", Australian Artificial Intelligence Institute, 1995.

7 Ma, M., El Kader Hammoud, H.A., Itani, H., Nuara, L., and Everhard, C., "M&A Negotiation Simulator: Open-Source Release of Alpha Prototype", Stanford Law School, 1 August 2024. See: https://law.stanford.edu/2024/08/01/ma-negotiation-simulator-open-source-release-of-alpha-prototype/.

8 Dahl, M., Magesh, M., Suzgun, M., and Ho, D.E., "Hallucinating Law: Legal Mistakes with Large Language Models are Pervasive", Stanford University: Human-Centered Artificial Intelligence, 11 January 2024. See: https://hai.stanford.edu/news/hallucinating-law-legal-mistakes-large-language-models-are-pervasive.

9 Vals.ai, "Public Enterprise LLM Benchmarks", 22 April 2025. See: https://www.vals.ai/home.

10 Ma, M., Waldon, B., and Nyarko, J., "Conceptual questions in developing expert-annotated data", *Proceedings of the Nineteenth International Conference on Artificial Intelligence and Law* (ICAIL '23), 2023, pp. 427–431. https://doi.org/10.1145/3594536.3595139.
11 Guha, N., Nyarko, J., Ho, D.E. et al, "LegalBench: A Collaboratively Built Benchmark for Measuring Legal Reasoning in Large Language Models", arXiv, 20 August 2023. https://doi.org/10.48550/arXiv.2308.11462.
12 GitHub, "What are AI agents?", 6 February 2025. See: https://github.com/resources/articles/ai/what-are-ai-agents.
13 Park, J.S., O'Brien, J.C., Cai, C.J., et al, "Generative Agents: Interactive Simulacra of Human Behavior", arXiv, 6 August 2023. https://doi.org/10.48550/arXiv.2304.03442.
14 Li, J., Lai, Y., Li, W. et al, "Agent Hospital: A Simulacrum of Hospital with Evolvable Medical Agents", arXiv, 17 January 2025. https://doi.org/10.48550/arXiv.2405.02957.

About Globe Law and Business

Globe Law and Business was established in 2005. From the very beginning, we set out to create legal books that are sufficiently high level to be of real use to the experienced professional, yet still accessible and easy to navigate. Most of our authors are drawn from Magic Circle and other top commercial firms, both in the United Kingdom and internationally.

Our titles are carefully produced, with the utmost attention paid to editorial, design and production processes. We hope this results in high-quality publications that are easy to read and a pleasure to own.

In 2021, we were very pleased to announce the start of a new chapter for Globe Law and Business following the acquisition of law books under the imprint Ark Publishing. Our law firm management list is now significantly expanded with many well-known and loved Ark Publishing titles.

We are also pleased to announce the launch of our online content platform, Globe Law Online, which allows for easy access across firms. Details of all titles included can be found at www.globelawonline.com. Email glo@globelawandbusiness.com for further details and to arrange a free trial for you or your firm.

We'd very much like to hear from you with your thoughts and ideas for improving what we offer. Please do feel free to email me on sian@globelawandbusiness.com. Happy reading and thank you for your time.

Sian O'Neill
Managing director
Globe Law and Business
www.globelawandbusiness.com

www.ingramcontent.com/pod-product-compliance
Ingram Content Group UK Ltd.
Pitfield, Milton Keynes, MK11 3LW, UK
UKHW020146200625
459882UK00004B/42

9 781837 230884